Reflections Upon a Sinking Ship

GORE VIDAL

LITTLE, BROWN AND COMPANY · BOSTON · TORONTO

LIBRARY OF CONGRESS CATALOG CARD NO. 68-30880

FIRST EDITION

Most of the essays in this volume were originally published in
periodicals, and grateful acknowledgment is made to *Book Week*,
Book World, *Encounter*, *Esquire*, *New Statesman*, *New York Review of Books*, *The New York Times Book Review*, *Partisan
Review*, *The Reporter*, and *The Times Literary Supplement*
(London). "The City and the Pillar After Twenty Years" is re-
printed from *The City and the Pillar Revised* by Gore Vidal by
permission of the publishers, E.P. Dutton & Co., Inc. and William
Heinemann Ltd. Copyright 1948, © 1965 by Gore Vidal.

For Barbara and Jason Epstein

Preface

SEVEN years ago when I first put together a book of essays, I titled it, somewhat vaingloriously, *Rocking the Boat*. Since then the boat has begun to ship water (no thanks to me), and I am again drawn to a nautical image. With no melodramatic intent I have selected a title which seems to me altogether apt this bright savage spring with Martin Luther King dead and now Robert Kennedy. The fact that these deaths occurred at a time when the American empire was sustaining a richly deserved defeat in Asia simply makes for added poignancy, if not tragedy. But it is not only the American ship which is foundering. Nearly half the human beings ever born are now alive, breeding like bacteria under optimum conditions. As a result, the planet's air, water, and earth are being poisoned and used up, and there are those who believe it is already too late to save this ark of fools. Nevertheless, to take the positive view, if war and famine do not soon reduce population (and it is quite likely that the two in tandem will at least make a beginning: famine is now with us and the smell of blood's already upon the air), a world authority must be established in order to limit births, while attempting, simultaneously, the restoration in our favor of the planet's ecological balance. Needless to say, this new world order will create a society more repressive than any man has so far endured, and what little is of value in our civilization is certain to be spoiled by the managers. There is something about a bureaucrat that does not like a poem. Yet

Is there another word in the English language quite so useful, so hopeful, so truly pregnant as "yet"? I have just looked up "yet" in the OED and find with some pleasure that it is — like us — of "obscure origin"; among its adverbial meanings is "the possibility of subsequent change, while there is still time." Optimists are great "yet" users; the rest of us are encouraged simply knowing the word exists. Therefore (to invoke the spirit of yet), although it has been our experience that managers given the power to restrict human action in one area seldom confine themselves to that area — finding irresistible the total ordering of the lives of others — it is still possible that individual freedom might be maintained, even increased once the pressures due to overpopulation are removed. In any case, the alternative to a planned society is no society, a grim knowledge which tends to shadow one's works and days.

All but two of the pieces in this collection were written as book reviews, a parasitic craft of some value at a time when unread books are thought by many to contain valuable information that ought somehow to be made available, preferably through the reports of professional readers. I am aware that my reports have the reputation of being harsh. Yet reading through these essays I believe that I have been unkind only in one instance, and that was to John Hersey (who wished, I am told, to sue me). If I was too hard on him, it was as much the result of a sudden (and mercifully short-lived) duodenal ulcer as of reading *Hiroshima*. Elsewhere, it seems to me, I am blunt about issues but not about people, which perhaps makes for a degree of uniqueness among American commentators since it is a national characteristic to take everything personally. In fact, Mr. James Reston, referring to "The Holy Family" (a study of some recent books about the Kennedys) accused me of having written a "vicious polemic." I suspect that Mr. Reston was so overcome by *Esquire's* minatory cover with its series of presidential Kennedys extending far into the future that he did not actually read what I wrote. If he had, he would have realized that my subject was not really the Kennedys but a political system which makes it so easy for the wealthy to rise and so difficult for the poor to be noticed. But I doubt if those who read what I actually wrote will find much — even now — that is not apposite. Money is everything in politics and families like the Kennedys and Rockefellers will dominate the scene for some time to come.

I have written a good deal about the novel in this volume. It is the literary form I like best, and its decline as a popular art tells us a good deal about the way we are. In writing about individual novels, I start from the premise that the creator is "right." I try to inhabit his work, to enjoy it, to be — very simply — had by the artist. Only later does one attempt to answer the question: to what extent has the maker of the work accomplished what he set out to do? This is obviously the most difficult part of criticism since it is quite easy to misread the text . . . and it is the text which is the subject under scrutiny, not its author, contrary to the current journalistic practice of repeating gossip about the author with a view to establishing whether or not he is a nice man. But then moralizing in a vacuum is as much a vice of the United Statesman as murder, and as difficult to discourage.

I find the general tone of these pieces a good deal less hopeful than that of *Rocking the Boat*, possibly because in youth one thinks that all the changes which ought to be made will be made in one's lifetime, while in middle age (where I am now irritably lodged), it becomes quite plain that very little one hoped would happen will happen. I can imagine a posthumous volume of essays called *Submarine*. But there is still "yet." Some bad things do change for the better. A liberalization of American sexual mores is taking place even though to date no American state legislature has recognized that under our Constitution and Bill of Rights private morals are not the law's affair. On the other hand, some things grow worse. For instance, the American attitude toward drugs is absurd. There is no doubt in my mind that marijuana is less dangerous to the user than alcohol, and should be made legal. In fact, all drugs should be made available (with due warning as to their effect), and those who want to kill themselves should be allowed to do so; the rest will soon get the point and not take them . . . there cannot be many secret iodine drinkers in the land. Of course the question still remains: is it a good thing deliberately to numb and derange the senses? I suspect not. But since most lives are bitterly boring, men crave the anodyne, and it is no business of the state to deny anyone his dreams or even death.

Politically, the second law of thermodynamics appears to obtain: the American political system is running down. The New Left have declared it hopeless (though they propose no alternative), while the average citizen grows more and more cynical, realizing that politics today is all a matter of money, polls and computerized issues. Even so, there are still changes that could be made. Free television time should be made available to a wide range of candidates. National campaigns should be restricted to four weeks, in the British manner, while some other means of selecting presidential candidates must be found since the present system is inequitous and corrupt, and everyone knows it. Whether or not there is time left us to make these changes depends largely upon the race war in the United States . . . not to mention what is, in effect, a race war in Asia where the United States has been for some years trying to contain Dean Rusk's Yellow Peril, blithely unaware that we are a weak minority whose ultimate survival will depend upon the sufferance of "colored" billions. The national luck appears to be running out all at once. There is, however, a somber satisfaction in knowing that the race as a whole is in quite as much trouble as the American empire.

All times have seemed bad to those living in them; and all societies are sick. But some societies are sicker than others and some times are, potentially, more dangerous than others. We can blow up the earth. That is new. We can breed ourselves out of existence. That is new. To ponder these matters is to know despair which is why I personally find myself vacillating between living in Rome and raging in New York, between silence and exhortation, between human despair and animal hope. Stendhal wrote that politics in a work of art is like a pistol shot at a concert. But that was another century. Today the pistol shots are the concert while the work of art is the discordant interruption. To interrupt catastrophe is the artist's highest goal at a time when, like it or not, pure novelist and worldly polemicist are both in the same boat (to revert to my original metaphor), each bailing water since it is not (yet) man's nature to drown without a struggle.

Rome
June 6, 1968

Contents

Reflections Upon a Sinking Ship

Writers and the World

RECENTLY *Variety*, an American paper devoted to the performing arts, reviewed a television program about life inside the Harlem ghetto. The discussion was conducted "by literary oriented . . . Norman Podhoretz, editor of *Commentary* magazine [*sic*], who initially tried to guide the colloquy along bookish lines. . . ." And apparently failed. "Podhoretz, who described himself as a 'cold, detached intellectual,' is given to verbosity and for about half the program was annoyingly the obtrusive interviewer, more eager to talk than to probe his subject. He receded in the second half, however, and overall was a good foil. . . ."

For several years, *Variety* has been reviewing television's talking writers in precisely the same terms that they review comedians and singers. Mary McCarthy, James Baldwin, Dwight Macdonald are now familiar actors in the world of *Variety*. Yet until this decade, no more than half a dozen writers were known to the mass audience at any given moment. It took a generation of constant performing for someone like Carl Sandburg to become a national figure. Today fame is the work of a night. As a result, any number of contemporary novelists, poets, and critics are known to the innocent millions, who value them not only as entertainers but seem to take them seriously as public moralists. As resonant chorus to the Republic's drama, the writers have replaced the clergy. It is to Norman Mailer, not to Norman Vincent Peale, that the television producer turns when he wants a discussion of "America's Moral Decline" or "The Meaning of Violence."

This dramatic change in literature's estate is not due to any sudden passion for books among the people. Americans have never liked reading. According to the ubiquitous Dr. Gallup, fifty per cent of the adult population never reads a book once school is done. Nor was the writers' condition altered by the brief re-creation of Camelot beside the Potomac. It was reassuring to the intellectual community to know that the thirty-fifth President knew the difference between Saul Bellow and Irwin Shaw, but it was also true that he preferred Shaw to Bellow and Ian Fleming to either. What he did respect was success in the arts, which is not quite the same thing as excellence, though more easily identified. Finally, it was neither the public nor the New Frontier which glorified the writers. It was around-the-clock television and its horror of "dead air." Producers discovered that one way of inexpensively enlivening the air is to invite people to talk to one another while the camera records. There are now literally thousands of talk shows, national and local, ranging from the "Today Show," which commands the attention of most of the country's "opinion makers," to late-night educational symposia where literary men deal with such knotty questions as "Has There Been a *Really* Important American Novel Since *A Passage to India*?" The thought of people sitting at home watching other people talk is profoundly sad. But that is the way we live now, electronic villagers tuned in to the machine if not to the pundits.

In the search for talkers, it was soon discovered that movie stars need a script and that politicians are not only evasive but apt to run afoul of the "equal time for the opposition" statute. Of the well known, only the writers were entirely suitable and perfectly available. From poets (Auden haggling

with Professor Trilling over who was older) to journalists
(Walter Lippmann benignly instructing his countrymen in the
ways of history), the writers responded to the Zeitgeist's call
with suspicious alacrity. From the commercialite peddling his
latest book-club choice to the serious critic getting in a good
word for *Partisan Review*, the writers are now public in a
way that they have never been before, and this has created
all sorts of problems for them and their admirers, many of
whom believe that it is degrading for a distinguished man of
letters to allow himself to be questioned by an entertainer in
front of an audience of forty million people who have not a
clue as to who he is other than the vague knowledge that he
has written a book.

To this charge, the highbrow writer usually replies that any
sort of exhibitionism is good for selling books. After all, no
one would criticize him for giving a paid reading at a university. The middlebrow murmurs something about educating the
masses. The lowbrow echoes the highbrow: "exposure" is good
for trade. Yet in actual fact, there is no evidence that television appearances sell books. Most people who watch television regularly do not read books or much of anything else.
Yet this does not deter the talking writers. There are other
pleasures and duties than trade. For one thing, those who
have strong views of a political or moral nature are free to
express them (aesthetic judgments are not encouraged by
compères for obvious reasons). Finally if the writer talks
often enough, he will acquire a movie-star persona which
ought eventually to increase the audience for his books if,
meanwhile, he has found the time to write them. Yet even if
the writer who talks well continues to write well, there are
those who believe that publicness of any kind must somehow
be corrupting, like Hollywood. Americans prefer their serious
writers obscure, poor, and, if possible, doomed by drink or
gaudy vice. It is no accident that those contemporary writers

most admired within the academy are the ones whose lives were disorderly and disastrous, in vivid contrast to their explicators, quietly desperate upon Midwestern campuses.

From the beginning, the American civilization has been simultaneously romantic and puritan. The World is corrupt. If the virtuous artist does not avoid its pomps and pleasures, he will crack up like Scott Fitzgerald or shoot his brains out like Ernest Hemingway, whose sad last days have assured him a place in the national pantheon which his novels alone would not have done. Of living writers, only Norman Mailer seems willing to live a life that is bound to attract lengthy comment of a cautionary sort. America's literary critics and custodians are essentially moralists who find literature interesting only to the extent that it reveals the moral consciousness of the middle class. The limitations of this kind of criticism were re-marked upon more than twenty years ago by John Crowe Ransom, who thought there was a place for at least one ontological critic in the American literary hierarchy. The place of course is still there; still vacant.

"I stayed home and wrote," Flaubert used to say, quoting Horace, and to the serious-minded this priestlike dedication is still the correct way for the good writer to live, even though it means that his biography will be disappointingly slim. Re-mote from public affairs, the unworldly American artist ought not to be concerned with aesthetic matters either. Whenever literary questions were put to William Faulkner, he would say, "I'm just a farmer," neglecting to add that for thirty years most of his farming was of a seasonal nature in Holly-wood, writing films. Yet he was always given credit for having turned his back upon the World, like J. D. Salinger, who is regarded with a certain awe because he lives entirely with-drawn from everyone. Never photographed, never interviewed, perfectly silent (except when the *New Yorker* is attacked), Mr. Salinger turns out fictions which, for a time, were taken to be more serious than they are because of the entirely admirable way their author lives.

Except for a brief time during the thirties, the notion of the writer as citizen has not been popular. In fact, during the forties, the intellectual catchword was "alienation." The writers simply ignored the Republic, their full attention reserved for those dramas of the interior where Greek myths are eternally re-enacted in vague places beyond time, and Alcestis wears seersucker and majors in Comp. Lit. at Princeton. The fifties were the time of the Great Golfer, and there was a death in the land to which the only response was the Beats. They were not even alienated. They just went. And felt. Then as swiftly as they appeared, they vanished; nothing but a whiff of marijuana upon the air to mark their exuberant passage. The sixties began with a flourish. The young President detested all rhetoric except his own, in which he resembled most of the writers. An intellectual, he knew how to flatter even the most irritable man of letters. A master of publicity, he realized the value of having well-known people support him. If James Baldwin was an effective and admired television performer, then it was only common sense to try to win his support.

In 1960 politics and literature officially joined forces. The politician had literary longings; the writer saw himself as President, leading the polity to the good life by means of lysergic acid or the more copious orgasm or whatever bee buzzed loudest in his bonnet. More to the point, through television, the talking writer was able to command an audience in a way few politicians can. Not only is the writer a celebrity, he is also a free agent who does not have to be re-elected or even to be responsible. And so, not unnaturally, writers have been drawn more and more to actual as opposed to symbolic politics. Many worked for the elections of both Kennedy and Johnson. Saul Bellow contemplated writing a biography of

Hubert Humphrey. Norman Mailer took credit for Kennedy's election because at a crucial moment in the campaign he gave the candidate the moment's accolade; called him "hipster." After Kennedy's election, writers were regularly invited to the White House. It was a heady thousand days.

But since Johnson's accession, the links between poetry and power have snapped. Literary people annoy and confuse the President. The precise nature of Saul Bellow's achievement does not seem to weigh heavily upon him. Nevertheless, like his predecessor, he knows the propaganda value of artists and he has somewhat wistfully tried to win them over. It has not been easy. Despite the good things he has done at home, the President's Asian adventures alarm the talking writers and they talk against him. In retaliation, he has refused to bestow Freedom Medals, Kennedy's order of merit for excellence in science and art. But this state of siege is hardly permanent. For better or worse, the writers are very much in the real world, and the politicians know it.

Simultaneously with their new-found celebrity, the writers have become the beneficiaries of a peculiar crisis in American publishing. Fifteen years ago the mass magazines lost much of their advertising revenue to television. To survive, they were forced to make radical changes. At the prodding of young editors, they began to raid the literary quarterlies. Overnight the work of writers like Bellow, McCarthy, Baldwin, and Paul Goodman replaced those cheerful fictions and bland commentaries that had made the popular magazines the despair of the intellectuals for half a century. All sorts of miracles began to occur: James Baldwin was allowed to deliver a sermon in the *New Yorker*, while Dr. Leslie Fiedler, having deserted raft, Huck, and Jim, became *Playboy's* "writer of the year." Curiously enough, the readers who had for so long been soothed by Clarence Budington Kelland seemed not to mind the abrasiveness of the new writers. More to the point, young people found them interesting, a matter of some importance to publishers, since the age of the average American is now twenty-seven and growing younger. In fact, those in college form the largest single subculture in the United States, far more numerous, say, than the organized-labor movement or nature's noblemen, the farmers. As a result, courses in contemporary literature have made a generation of young people aware of writers who ordinarily might have gone on to the end in honorable obscurity. This new audience has at last been reflected in the publishing of books, both hard- and soft-cover.

For the first time since New England's brief Indian summer, good writers with some regularity outsell commercial ones in hard cover. In recent years Mary McCarthy has outsold Daphne du Maurier; Bellow has outsold Uris; Auchincloss has outsold O'Hara. Financially, inflation has set in. The paperback publishers are pursuing the new best sellers with advances that go as high as half a million dollars. No one knows whether or not the publishers will ever earn back these huge advances, but meanwhile they gain valuable newsstand space, and in the wake of a famous book they can display their less showy wares, which include, often as not, the best books. As a result, a serious and well-reviewed novel which has sold twenty-five hundred copies in hard cover can, in paperback, reach an audience of many thousands of readers, mostly young. This is the first sign that the novel, which has steadily declined as a popular art form in this century, may be able at last to hold its own not only with films and television but also with that high journalism which has so distracted the intellectuals since the Second War.

Affluence, publicity, power, can these things be said to "corrupt" the artist? In themselves, no. Or as Ernest Hemingway nicely put it: "Every whore finds his vocation." Certainly it is romantic melodrama to believe that publicity in itself destroys the artist. Too many writers of the first rank have been devoted self-publicists (Frost, Pound, Yeats), perfectly able to do their work quite unaffected by a machine they have learned how to run. Toughness is all. Neither Hollywood nor the World destroyed Scott Fitzgerald. He would have made the same hash of things had he taught at a university, published unnoticed novels, and lived in decorous obscurity. The spoiling of a man occurs long before his first encounter with the World. But the romantic-puritan stereotype dies hard. The misbehavior of the artist thrills the romantic; his subsequent suffering and punishment satisfy the puritan. Yet today new situations exist, and the old archetypes, never true, seem less relevant than ever. To be outside the World is not necessarily a virtue. To be in the World does not necessarily mean a loss of craft, a fall from grace, a fatness of soul. William Faulkner's thirty years as a movie writer affected his novels not at all. He could do both. Finally, it is truly impertinent to speculate as to whether or not the effect of this or of that on a writer's character is good or bad. What is pertinent is the work he does. Mary McCarthy is no less intelligent a literary critic because she plays games on television. But even if her work should show a sudden falling off, only the simplest moralist would be able to find a causal link between her appearances as a talking writer and her work as a writing writer.

It has been observed that American men do not read novels because they feel guilty when they read books which do not have facts in them. Made-up stories are for women and children; facts are for men. There is something in this. It is certainly true that this century's romantic estrangement of writer from the World has considerably reduced the number of facts in the American novel. And facts, both literal and symbolic, are the stuff of art as well as of life. In *Moby Dick* Melville saw to it that the reader would end by knowing as much about whaling as he did. But today there are few facts in the American novel, if only because the writers do not know much about anything except their own immediate experience, which is apt to be narrow. It is no accident that the best of

American writing since the war has been small, private, interior. But now that the writers have begun to dabble in the World, even the most solipsistic of them has begun to suspect that there are a good many things that other people know that he does not. Though Senators tend to be banal in public statements, none is ever quite so wide of the mark as an impassioned novelist giving his views on public affairs, particularly if he accepts the traditional romantic view that passion is all, facts tedious, reflection a sign of coldness, even impotence, and the howl more eloquent than words. Fortunately, as writers come up against the actual World they are bound to absorb new facts, and this ought to be useful to them in their work. As for the World, only good can come of the writers' engagement in public affairs. Particularly in the United States, a nation governed entirely by lawyers, those professional "maintainers of quarrels" which the sympathetic Henry IV Plantagenet sensibly barred from sitting in Parliament. At last other voices are being heard, if only late at night on television.

The obvious danger for the writer is the matter of time. "A talent is formed in stillness," wrote Goethe, "a character in the stream of the world." Goethe, as usual, managed to achieve both. But it is not easy, and many writers who choose to be active in the World lose not virtue but time, and that stillness without which literature cannot be made. This is sad. Until one recalls how many bad books the World may yet be spared because of the busyness of writers turned Worldly. The romantic-puritans can find consolation in that, and take pleasure in realizing that there is a rude justice, finally, even in the best of worlds.

[*Times Literary Supplement,* November 25, 1965]

French Letters: Theories of the New Novel

TO say that no one now much likes novels is to exaggerate very little. The large public which used to find pleasure in prose fictions prefers movies, television, journalism, and books of "fact." But then, Americans have never been enthusiastic readers. According to Dr. Gallup, only five per cent of our population can be regarded as habitual readers. This five per cent is probably a constant minority from generation to generation, despite the fact that at the end of the nineteenth century there were as many bookstores in the United States as there are today. It is true that novels in paperback often reach a very large audience. But that public is hardly serious, if one is to believe a recent New York *Times* symposium on paperback publishing. Apparently novels sell not according to who wrote them but according to how they are presented, which means that *Boys and Girls Together* will outsell *Pale Fire*, something it did not do in hard cover. Except for a handful of entertainers like the late Ian Fleming, the mass audience knows nothing of authors. They buy titles, and most of those titles are not of novels but of nonfiction: books about the Kennedys, doctors, and vivid murders are preferred to the work of anyone's imagination no matter how agreeably debased.

In this, if nothing else, the large public resembles the clerks, one of whom, Norman Podhoretz, observed nine years ago that "A feeling of dissatisfaction and impatience, irritation and boredom with contemporary serious fiction is very widespread," and he made the point that the magazine article is preferred to the novel because the article is useful, specific, relevant — something that most novels are not. This liking for fact may explain why some of our best-known novelists are read with attention only when they comment on literary or social matters. In the highest intellectual circles, a new novel by Mary McCarthy or William Styron or Norman Mailer — to name at random three celebrated novelists — is apt to be regarded with a certain embarrassment, hostage to a fortune often too crudely gained, and bearing little relation to its author's distinguished commentaries.

An even odder situation exists in the academy. At a time when the works of living writers are used promiscuously as classroom texts, the students themselves do little voluntary reading. "I hate to read," said a Harvard senior to a New York *Times* reporter, "and I never buy any paperbacks." The undergraduates' dislike of reading novels is partly due to the laborious way in which novels are taught: the slow killing of the work through a close textual analysis. Between the work and the reader falls the explication, and the explicator is prone to regard the object of analysis as being somehow inferior to the analysis itself.

In fact, according to Saul Bellow, "Critics and professors have declared themselves the true heirs and successors of the modern classic authors." And so, in order to maintain their usurped dignity, they are given "to redescribing everything downward, blackening the present age and denying creative scope to their contemporaries." Although Mr. Bellow overstates the case, the fact remains that the novel as currently practiced does not appeal to the intellectuals any more than it does to the large public, and it may well be that the form will become extinct now that we have entered the age which Professor Marshall McLuhan has termed post-Gutenberg. Whether or not the Professor's engaging generalities are true (that linear type, for centuries a shaper of our thought, has been superseded by electronic devices), it is a fact that the generation now in college is the first to be brought up entirely within the tradition of television and differs significantly from its predecessors. Quick to learn through sight and sound, today's student often experiences difficulty in reading and writing. Linear type's warm glow, so comforting to Gutenberg man, makes his successors uncomfortably hot. Needless to say, that bright minority which continues the literary culture exists as always, but it is no secret that even they prefer watching movies to reading novels. John Barth ought to interest them more than Antonioni, but he doesn't.

For the serious novelist, however, the loss of the audience should not be disturbing. "I write," declared one of them serenely. "Let the reader learn to read." And contrary to Whitman, great audiences are not necessary for the creation of a high literature. The last fifty years have been a particularly good time for poetry in English, but even that public which can read intelligently knows very little of what has been done. Ideally, the writer needs no audience other than the few who understand. It is immodest and greedy to want more. Unhappily, the novelist, by the very nature of his coarse art, is greedy and immodest; unless he is read by everyone, he cannot delight, instruct, reform, destroy a world he wants, at the least, to be different for his having lived in it. Writers as various as Dickens and Joyce, as George Eliot and Proust, have suffered from this madness. It is the nature of the beast. But now the beast is caged, confined by old forms that have ceased to attract. And so the question is: can those forms be changed, and the beast set free?

Since the Second World War, Alain Robbe-Grillet, Nathalie Sarraute, Michel Butor, Claude Simon, and Robert Pinget, among others, have attempted to change not only the form of the novel but the relationship between book and reader, and though their experiments are taken most seriously on the Continent, they are still too little known and thought about in those countries General de Gaulle believes to be largely populated by Anglo-Saxons. Among American commentators, only Susan Sontag in *Against Interpretation, and Other Essays*, published in 1966, has made a sustained effort to understand what the French are doing, and her occasional essays on their work are well worth reading, not only as reflections of an interesting and interested mind but also because she shares with the New Novelists (as they loosely describe themselves) a desire for the novel to become "what it is not in England and America, with rare and unrelated exceptions: a form of art which people with serious and sophisticated [sic] taste in the other arts can take seriously." Certainly Miss Sontag finds nothing adventurous or serious in "the work of the American writers most admired today: for example, Saul Bellow, Norman Mailer, James Baldwin, William Styron, Philip Roth, Bernard Malamud." They are "essentially unconcerned with the problems of the novel as an art form. Their main concern is with their 'subjects.'" And because of this, she finds them "essentially unserious and unambitious." By this criterion, to be serious and ambitious in the novel, the writer must create works of prose comparable to those experiments in painting which have brought us to Pop and Op art and in music to the strategic silences of John Cage. Whether or not these experiments succeed or fail is irrelevant. It is enough, if the artist is serious, to attempt new forms; certainly he must not repeat old ones.

The two chief theorists of the New Novel are Alain Robbe-Grillet and Nathalie Sarraute. As novelists, their works do not much resemble one another or, for that matter, conform to each other's strictures. But it is as theorists not as novelists that they shall concern us here. Of the two, Alain Robbe-Grillet has done the most to explain what he thinks the New Novel is and is not, in *Snapshots* and *For a New Novel*, translated by Richard Howard (1965). To begin with, he believes that any attempt at controlling the world by assigning it a meaning (the accepted task of the traditional novelist) is no longer possible. At best, meaning was

> an illusory simplification; and far from becoming clearer and clearer because of it, the world has only, little by little, lost all its life. Since it is chiefly in its presence that the world's reality resides, our task is now to create a literature which takes that presence into account.

He then attacks the idea of psychological "depth" as a myth. From the Comtesse de La Fayette to Gide, the novelist's role was to burrow "deeper and deeper to reach some ever more intimate strata." Since then, however, "something" has been "changing totally, definitively in our relations with the universe." Though he does not define that ominous "something," its principal effect is that "we no longer consider the world as our own, our private property, designed according to our needs and readily domesticated." Consequently:

> the novel of characters belongs entirely to the past; it describes a period: and that which marked the apogee of the individual. Perhaps this is not an advance, but it is evident that the present period is rather one of administrative numbers. The world's destiny has ceased, for us, to be identified with the rise or fall of certain men, of certain families.

Nathalie Sarraute is also concerned with the idea of man the administrative number in *Tropisms* and in *The Age of Suspicion*, translated by Maria Jolas (1964). She quotes Claude-Edmonde Magny: "Modern man, overwhelmed by mechanical civilization, is reduced to the triple determinism of hunger, sexuality and social status: Freud, Marx and Pavlov." (Surely in the wrong order.) She, too, rejects the idea of human depth: "The deep uncovered by Proust's analyses had already proved to be nothing but a surface."

Like Robbe-Grillet, she sees the modern novel as an evolution from Dostoevsky-Flaubert to Proust-Kafka; and each agrees (in essays written by her in 1947 and by him in 1958) that one of its principal touchstones is Camus' *The Stranger,* a work which she feels "came at the appointed time," when the old psychological novel was bankrupt because, paradoxically, psychology itself, having gone deeper than ever before, "inspired doubts as to the ultimate value of all methods of research." *Homo absurdus,* therefore, was Noah's dove, the messenger of deliverance. Camus' stranger is shown entirely from the inside, "all sentiment or thought whatsoever appears to have been completely abolished." He has been created without psychology or memory; he exists in a perpetual present. Robbe-Grillet goes even further in his analysis:

> It is no exaggeration to claim that it is things quite specifically which ultimately lead this man to crime: the sun, the sea, the brilliant sand, the gleaming knife, the spring among the rocks, the revolver . . . as, of course, among these things, the leading role is taken by Nature.

Only the absolute presence of things can be recorded; certainly the depiction of human character is no longer possible. In fact, Miss Sarraute believes that for both author and reader, character is "the converging point of their mutual distrust," and she makes of Stendhal's "The genius of suspicion has appeared on the scene" a leitmotiv for an age in which "the reader has grown wary of practically everything. The reason being that for some time now he has been learning too many things and he is unable to forget entirely all he has learned." Perhaps the most vivid thing he has learned (or at least it was vivid when she was writing in 1947) is the fact of genocide in the concentration camps:

> Beyond these furthermost limits to which Kafka did not follow them but to where he had the superhuman courage to pre-

cede them, all feeling disappears, even contempt and hatred; there remains only vast, empty stupefaction, definitive total, don't understand.

To remain at the point where he left off or to attempt to go on from there are equally impossible. Those who live in a world of human beings can only retrace their steps.

The proof that human life can be as perfectly meaningless in the scale of a human society as it is in eternity stunned a generation, and the shock of this knowledge, more than anything else (certainly more than the discoveries of the mental therapists or the new techniques of industrial automation), caused a dislocation of human values which in turn made something like the New Novel inevitable.

Although Nathalie Sarraute and Alain Robbe-Grillet are formidable theorists, neither is entirely free of those rhetorical plangencies the French so often revert to when their best aperçus are about to slip the net of logic. Each is very much a part of that French intellectual tradition so wickedly described in *Tristes Tropiques* by Lévi-Strauss (1964, translated by John Russell):

> First you establish the traditional "two views" of the question. You then put forward a common-sensical justification of the one, only to refute it by the other. Finally, you send them both packing by the use of a third interpretation, in which both the others are shown to be equally unsatisfactory. Certain verbal maneuvers enable you, that is, to line up the traditional "antitheses" as complementary aspects of a single reality: form and substance, content and container, appearance and reality, essence and existence, continuity and discontinuity, and so on. Before long the exercise becomes the merest verbalizing, reflection gives place to a kind of superior punning, and the "accomplished philosopher" may be recognized by the ingenuity with which he makes ever-bolder play with assonance, ambiguity, and the use of those words which sound alike and yet bear quite different meanings.

Miss Sarraute is not above this sort of juggling, particularly when she redefines literary categories, maintaining that the traditional novelists are formalists, while the New Novelists, by eschewing old forms, are the true realists because

> their works, which seek to break away from all that is pre-scribed, conventional and dead, to turn towards what is free, sincere and alive, will necessarily, sooner or later, become fer-ments of emancipation and progress.

This fine demagogy does not obscure the fact that she is obsessed with form in a way that the traditional writer seldom is. It is she, not he, who dreams

> of a technique that might succeed in plunging the reader into the stream of those subterranean dreams of which Proust only had time to obtain a rapid aerial view, and concerning which he observed and reproduced nothing but the broad motionless lines. This technique would give the reader the illusion of repeating these actions himself, in a more clearly aware, more orderly, distinct and forceful manner than he can do in life, without their losing that element of indetermination, of opacity and mystery, that one's own actions always have for the one who lives them.

This is perilously close to fine lady-writing (Sarraute is addicted to the triad, particularly of adjectives), but despite all protestations, she is totally absorbed with form; and though she dislikes being called a formalist, she can hardly hope to avoid the label, since she has set herself the superb task of continuing consciously those prose experiments that made the early part of the twentieth century one of the great ages of the novel.

In regard to the modern masters, both Robbe-Grillet and Miss Sarraute remark with a certain wonder that there have been no true heirs to Proust, Joyce, and Kafka; the main line of the realistic novel simply resumed as though they had never existed. Yet, as Robbe-Grillet remarks:

Flaubert wrote the new novel of 1860, Proust the new novel of 1910. The writer must proudly consent to bear his own date, knowing that there are no masterpieces in eternity, but only works in history, and that they have survived only to the degree that they have left the past behind them and heralded the future.

Here, as so often in Robbe-Grillet's theorizing, one is offered a sensible statement, followed by a dubious observation about survival (many conventional, even reactionary works have survived nicely), ending with a look-to-the-dawn-of-a-new-age chord, played fortissimo. Yet the desire to continue the modern tradition is perfectly valid. And even if the New Novelists do not succeed (in science most experiments fail), they are at least "really serious," as Miss Sontag would say.

There is, however, something very odd about a literary movement so radical in its pronouncements yet so traditional in its references. Both Miss Sarraute and Robbe-Grillet continually relate themselves to great predecessors, giving rise to the suspicion that, like Saul Bellow's literary usurpers, they are assuming for themselves the accomplishments of Dostoevsky, Flaubert, Proust, Joyce, and Beckett. In this, at least, they are significantly more modest than their heroes. One cannot imagine the Joyce of *Finnegans Wake* acknowledging a literary debt to anyone or Flaubert admitting — as Robbe-Grillet does — that his work is "merely pursuing a constant evolution of a genre." Curiously enough, the writers whom Robbe-Grillet and Miss Sarraute most resemble wrote books which were described by Arthur Symons for the *Encyclopaedia Britannica* as being

> made up of an infinite number of details, set side by side, every detail equally prominent. . . . [the authors] do not search further than "the physical basis of life," and they find everything that can be known of that unknown force written visibly upon the sudden faces of little incidents, little expressive moments. . . . It is their distinction — the finest of their

inventions — that, in order to render new sensations, a new vision of things, they invented a new language.

They, of course, are the presently unfashionable brothers Edmond and Jules de Goncourt, whose collaboration ended in 1870.

In attacking the traditional novel, both Robbe-Grillet and Miss Sarraute are on safe ground. Miss Sarraute is particularly effective when she observes that even the least aware of the traditionalists seems "unable to escape a certain feeling of uneasiness as regards dialogue." She remarks upon the self-conscious way in which contemporary writers sprinkle their pages with "he saids" and "she replieds," and she makes gentle fun of Henry Green's hopeful comment that perhaps the novel of the future will be largely composed in dialogue since, as she quotes him, people don't write letters any more: they use the telephone.

But the dialogue novel does not appeal to her, for it brings "the novel dangerously near the domain of the theater, where it is bound to be in a position of inferiority" — on the ground that the nuances of dialogue in the theater are supplied by actors while in the novel the writer himself must provide, somehow, the sub-conversation which is the true meaning. Opposed to the dialogue novel is the one of Proustian analysis. Miss Sarraute finds much fault with this method (no meaningful depths left to plumb in the wake of Freud), but concedes that "In spite of the rather serious charges that may be brought against analysis, it is difficult to turn from it today without turning one's back on progress."

"Progress," "*New* Novel," "permanent creation of tomorrow's world," "the discovery of reality will continue only if we abandon outward forms," "general evolution of the genre" . . . again and again one is reminded in reading the manifestos of these two explorers that we are living (one might even say that we are trapped) in the age of science. Miss Sarraute particularly delights in using quasi-scientific references. She refers to her first collection of pieces as "Tropisms." (According to authority, a tropism is "the turning of an organism, or part of one, in a particular direction in response to some special external stimulus.") She is also addicted to words like "larval" and "magma," and her analogies are often clinical: "Suspicion, which is by way of destroying the character and the entire outmoded mechanism that guaranteed its force, is one of the morbid reactions by which an organism defends itself and seeks another equilibrium. . . ."

Yet she does not like to be called a "laboratory novelist" any more than she likes to be called a formalist. One wonders why. For it is obvious that both she and Robbe-Grillet see themselves in white smocks working out new formulas for a new fiction. Underlying all their theories is the assumption that if scientists can break the atom with an equation, a dedicated writer ought to be able to find a new form in which to redefine the "unchanging human heart," as Bouvard might have said to Pécuchet. Since the old formulas have lost their efficacy, the novel, if it is to survive, must become something new; and so, to create that something new, they believe that writers must resort to calculated invention and bold experiment.

It is an interesting comment on the age that both Miss Sarraute and Robbe-Grillet take for granted that the highest literature has always been made by self-conscious avant-gardists. Although this was certainly true of Flaubert, whose letters show him in the laboratory, agonizing over that double genitive which nearly soured the recipe for *Madame Bovary*, and of Joyce, who spent a third of his life making a language for the night, Dostoevsky, Conrad, and Tolstoi — to name three novelists quite as great — were not much concerned with laboratory experiments. Their interest was in what Miss Sontag calls "the subject"; and though it is true they did not leave the form of the novel as they found it, their art was not the product of calculated experiments with form so much as it was the result of their ability, by virtue of what they were, to transmute the familiar and make it rare. They were men of genius unobsessed by what Goethe once referred to as "an eccentric desire for originality." Or as Saul Bellow puts it: "Genius is always, without strain, avant-garde. Its departure from tradition is not the result of caprice or of policy but of an inner necessity."

Absorbed by his subject, the genius is a natural innovator — a fact which must be maddening to the ordinary writer, who, because he is merely ambitious, is forced to approach literature from the outside, hoping by the study of a master-piece's form and by an analysis of its content to reconstruct the principle of its composition in order that he may create either simulacra or, if he is furiously ambitious, by rearranging the component parts, something "new." This approach from the outside is of course the natural way of the critic, and it is significant that the New Novelists tend to blur the boundary between critic and novelist. "Critical preoccupation," writes Robbe-Grillet, "far from sterilizing creation, can on the contrary serve it as a driving force."

In the present age the methods of the scientist, who deals only in what can be measured, demonstrated and proved, are central. Consequently, anything as unverifiable as a novel is suspect. Or, as Miss Sarraute quotes Paul Tournier:

> There is nobody left who is willing to admit that he invents. The only thing that matters is the document, which must be precise, dated, proven, authentic. Works of the imagination are banned, because they are invented. . . . The public, in order to believe what it is told, must be convinced that it is not being "taken in." All that counts now is the "true fact."

This may explain why so many contemporary novelists feel they must apologize for effects which seem unduly extravagant or made up ("but that's the way it really happened!").

Nor is it to make a scandal to observe that most "serious" American novels are autobiographies, usually composed to pay off grudges. But then the novelist can hardly be held responsible for the society he reflects. After all, much of the world's reading consists of those weekly news magazines in which actual people are dealt with in fictional terms. It is the spirit of the age to believe that any fact, no matter how suspect, is superior to any imaginative exercise, no matter how true. The result of this attitude has been particularly harrowing in the universities, where English departments now do their best to pretend that they are every bit as fact-minded as the physical scientists (to whom the largest appropriations go). Doggedly, English teachers do research, publish learned findings, make breakthroughs in F. Scott Fitzgerald and, in their search for facts, behave as if no work of literature can be called complete until each character has been satisfactorily identified as someone who actually lived and had a history known to the author. It is no wonder that the ambitious writer is tempted to re-create the novel along what he believes to be scientific lines. With admiration, Miss Sontag quotes William Burroughs:

> I think there's going to be more and more merging of art and science. Scientists are already studying the creative process, and I think that the whole line between art and science will break down and that scientists, I hope, will become more creative and writers more scientific.

Recently in France the matter of science and the novel was much debated. In an essay called *Nouvelle Critique ou Nouvelle Imposture*, Raymond Picard attacked the new critic Roland Barthes, who promptly defended himself on the ground that a concern with form is only natural since structure precedes creation (an insight appropriated from anthropology, a discipline recently become fashionable). Picard then returned to the attack, mocking those writers who pretend to be scientists, pointing out that they

> improperly apply to the literary domain methods which have proved fruitful elsewhere but which here lose their efficiency and rigor. . . . These critical approaches have a scientific air to them, but the resemblance is pure caricature. The new critics use science roughly as someone ignorant of electricity might use electronics. What they're after is its prestige: in other respects they are at opposite poles to the scientific spirit. Their statements generally sound more like oracles than useful hypotheses: categorical, unverifiable, unilluminating.

Picard is perhaps too harsh, but no one can deny that Robbe-Grillet and Nathalie Sarraute often appropriate the language of science without understanding its spirit — for instance, one can verify the law of physics which states that there is no action without reaction, but how to prove the critical assertion that things in themselves are what caused Camus' creature to kill? Yet if to revive a moribund art form writers find it helpful to pretend to be physicists, then one ought not to tease them unduly for donning so solemnly mask and rubber gloves. After all, Count Tolstoi thought he was a philosopher. But whether pseudo scientists or original thinkers, neither Robbe-Grillet nor Miss Sarraute finds it easy to put theory into practice. As Robbe-Grillet says disarmingly: "It is easier to indicate a new form than to follow it without failure." And he must be said to fail a good deal of the time: is there anything more incantatory than the repetition of the word "lugubre" in Last Year at Marienbad? Or more visceral than the repetition of the killing of the centipede in Jealousy? While Miss Sarraute finds that her later essays are "far removed from the conception and composition of my first book" — which, nevertheless, she includes in the same volume as the essays, with the somewhat puzzling comment that "this first book contains *in nuce* all the raw material that I have continued to develop in my later works."

For Robbe-Grillet, the problem of the novel is — obviously — the problem of man in relation to his environment, a relationship which he believes has changed radically in the last fifty years. In the past, man attempted to personalize the universe. In prose, this is revealed by metaphor: "majestic peaks," "huddled villages," "pitiless sun." "These anthropomorphic analogies are repeated too insistently, too coherently, not to reveal an entire metaphysical system." And he attacks what he holds to be the humanistic view: "On the pretext that man can achieve only a subjective knowledge of the world, humanism decides to elect man the justification of everything." In fact, he believes that humanists will go so far as to maintain that "it is not enough to show man where he is: it must further be proclaimed that man is everywhere." Quite shrewdly he observes: "If I say 'the world is man,' I shall always gain absolution; while if I say things are things, and man is only man, I am immediately charged with a crime against humanity."

It is this desire to remove the falsely human from the nature of things that is at the basis of Robbe-Grillet's theory. He is arguing not so much against what Ruskin called "the pathetic fallacy," as against our race's tendency to console itself by making human what is plainly nonhuman. To those who accuse him of trying to dehumanize the novel, he replies that since any book is written by a man "animated by torments and passion," it cannot help but be human. Nevertheless, "suppose the eyes of this man rest on things without indulgence, insistently: he sees them but he refuses to appropriate them." Finally, "man looks at the world but the world does not look back at him, and so, if he rejects communion, he also rejects tragedy." Somewhat inconsistently, he later quotes with admiration Joé Bousquet's "We watch things pass by in order to forget that they are watching us die."

Do those things watch or not? At times Miss Sarraute writes as if she thought they did. Her *Tropisms* are full of things invested with human response ("The crouched houses standing watch all along the gray streets"), but then she is not so strict as Robbe-Grillet in her apprehension of reality. She will accept "those analogies which are limited to the instinctive irresistible nature of the movements . . . produced in us by the presence of others, or by objects from the outside world." For Robbe-Grillet, however, "All analogies are dangerous."

Man's consciousness has now been separated from his environment. He lives in a perpetual present. He possesses memory but it is not chronological. Therefore the best that the writer can hope to do is to impart a precise sense of man's being in the present. To achieve this immediacy, Miss Sarraute favors "some precise dramatic action shown in slow motion"; a world in which "time was no longer the time of real life but of a hugely amplified present." While Robbe-Grillet, in commenting upon his film *Last Year at Marienbad*, declares:

> The Universe in which the entire film occurs is, characteristically, in a perpetual present which makes all recourse to memory impossible. This is a world without a past, a world which is self-sufficient at every moment and which obliterates itself as it proceeds.

To him, the film is a ninety-minute fact without antecedents. "The only important 'character' is the spectator. In his mind unfolds the whole story which is precisely imagined by him." The verb "imagine" is of course incorrect, while the adverb means nothing. The spectator is *not* imagining the film; he is watching a creation which was made in a precise historic past by a writer, a director, actors, cameramen, etc. Yet to have the spectator or reader involve himself directly and temporally in the act of creation continues to be Robbe-

Grillet's goal. He wants "a present which constantly invents itself" with "the reader's creative assistance," participating "in a creation, to invent in his turn the work — and the world — and thus to learn to invent his own life." This is most ambitious. But the ingredients of the formula keep varying. For instance, in praising Raymond Roussel, Robbe-Grillet admires the author's "*investigation* which destroys, in the writing itself, its own object." Elsewhere: "The work must seem necessary but necessary for nothing; its architecture is without use; its strength is untried." And again: "The genuine writer has nothing to say. He has only a way of speaking. He must create a world but starting from nothing, from the dust. . . ." It would not seem to be possible, on the one hand, to invent a world that would cause the reader to "invent his own life" while, on the other hand, the world in question is being destroyed as it is being created. Perhaps he means for the reader to turn to dust, gradually, page by page: not the worst of solutions.

No doubt there are those who regard the contradictions in Robbe-Grillet's critical writing as the point to them — rather in the way that the boredom of certain plays or the incompetence of certain pictures are, we are assured, their achievement. Yet it is worrisome to be told that a man can create a world from nothing when that is the one thing he cannot begin to do, simply because, no matter how hard he tries, he cannot dispose of himself. Even if what he writes is no more than nouns and adjectives, who and what he is will subconsciously dictate order. Nothing human is random and it is nonsense to say:

> Art is based on no truth that exists before it; and one may say that it expresses nothing but itself. It creates its own equilibrium and its own meaning. It stands all by itself . . . or else it falls.

Which reminds us of Professor Herzog's plaintive response to the philosophic proposition that modern man at a given moment fell into the quotidian: so where was he standing before the fall? In any case, how can something unique, in Robbe-Grillet's sense, rise or fall or be anything except itself? As for reflecting "no truth that existed before it," this is not possible. The fact that the author is a man "filled with torments and passion" means that all sorts of "truths" are going to occur in the course of the writing. The act of composing prose is a demonstration not only of human will but of a desire to reflect truth — particularly if one's instinct is messianic, and Robbe-Grillet is very much in that tradition. Not only does he want man "to invent his own life" (by reading Robbe-Grillet), but he proposes that today's art is "a way of living in the present world, and of participating in the permanent creation of tomorrow's world." It also seems odd that a theory of the novel which demands total existence in a self-devouring present should be concerned at all with the idea of future time since man exists, demonstrably, only in the present — the future tense is a human conceit, on the order of "majestic peaks." As for the use of the adjective "permanent," one suspects that rhetoric, not thought, forced this unfortunate word from the author's unconscious mind.

The ideal work, according to Robbe-Grillet, is

> A text both "dense and irreducible"; so perfect that it does not seem "to have touched," an object so perfect that it would obliterate our tracks. . . . Do we not recognize here the highest ambition of every writer?

Further, the only meaning for the novel is the invention of the world. "In dreams, in memory, as in the sense of sight, our imagination is the organizing force of our life, of *our* world. Each man, in his turn, must reinvent the things around him." Yet, referring to things, he writes a few pages later,

They refer to no other world. They are the sign of nothing but themselves. And the only contact man can make with them is to imagine them.

But how is one to be loyal to the actual fact of things if they must be reinvented? Either they are *there* or they are not. In any case, by filtering them through the imagination (re-invention), true objectivity is lost, as he himself admits in a further snarling of his argument: "Objectivity in the ordinary sense of the word — total impersonality of observation — is all too obviously an illusion. But freedom of observation should be possible and yet it is not" — because a "continuous fringe of culture (psychology, ethics, metaphysics, etc.) is added to things, giving them a less alien aspect." But he believes that "humanizing" can be kept to a minimum, if we try "to construct a world both more solid and more immediate. Let it be first of all by their presence that objects and gestures establish themselves and let this presence continue to prevail over the subjective." Consequently, the task of the New Novel is nothing less than to seek

> new forms for the novel . . . forms capable of expressing (or of creating) new relations between man and the world, to all those who have determined to invent the novel, in other words, to invent man. Such writers know that the systematic repetition of the forms of the past is not only absurd and futile, but that it can even become harmful: blinding us to our real situation in the world today, it keeps us, ultimately, from constructing the world and man of tomorrow.

With the change of a noun or two, this could easily be the coda of an address on American foreign policy, delivered by Professor Arthur Schlesinger, Jr., to the ADA.

Like Robbe-Grillet, Nathalie Sarraute regards Camus' *The Stranger* as a point of departure. She sees the book's immediate predecessors as "the promising art of the cinema" and "the wholesome simplicity of the new American novel." Incidentally, she is quite amusing when she describes just what the

effect of these "wholesome" novels was upon the French during the years immediately after the war:

> By transporting the French reader into a foreign universe
> in which he had no foothold, [he] lulled his wariness, aroused
> in him the kind of credulous curiosity that travel books inspire,
> and gave him a delightful impression of escape into an un-
> known world.

It is reassuring to learn that these works were not regarded
with any great seriousness by the French and that Horace
McCoy was not finally the master they once hailed him. Apparently the American novel was simply a vigorous tonic for
an old literature gone stale. Miss Sarraute is, however, sincerely admiring of Faulkner's ability to involve the reader in
his own world. To her the most necessary thing of all is "to
dispossess the reader and entice him, at all costs, into the
author's territory. To achieve this the device that consists in
referring to the leading characters as 'I' constitutes a means."
The use of the first person seems to her to be the emblem of
modern art. ("Since Impressionism all pictures have been
painted in the first person.") And so, just as photography
drove painters away from representing nature (ending such
ancient arts as that of the miniaturist and the maker of portrait busts), the cinema "garners and perfects what is left of it
by the novel." The novel must now go where the camera may
not follow. In this new country the reader has been aided by
such modern writers as Proust and Joyce; they have so awakened his sensibilities that he is now able to respond to what is
beneath the interior monologue, that "immense profusion of
sensations, images, sentiments, memories, impulses, little larval actions that no inner language can convey." For her,
emphasis falls upon what she calls the sub-conversation, that
which is sensed and not said, the hidden counterpoint to the
stated theme (obviously a very difficult thing to suggest, much
less write, since "no inner language can convey it").

"Bosquet's universe — ours — is a universe of signs," writes Robbe-Grillet. "Everything in it is a sign; and not the sign of something else, something more perfect, situated out of reach, but a sign of itself, of that reality which asks only to be revealed." This answer to Baudelaire's *The Salon of 1859* is reasonable (although it is anthropomorphic to suggest that reality *asks* to be revealed). Robbe-Grillet is equally reasonable in his desire for things to be shown, as much as possible, as they are.

> In the future universe of the novel, gestures and objects will be there before being *something*; and they will still be there afterwards, hard, unalterably, eternally present, mocking their own "meaning," that meaning which vainly tries to reduce them to the role of precarious tools, etc.

One agrees with him that the integrity of the nonhuman world should be honored. But what does he mean (that proscribed verb!) when he says that the objects will be *there*, after meaning has attempted to rape them? Does he mean that they will still exist on the page, in some way inviolate in their thing-ness? If he does, surely he is mistaken. What exists on the page is ink; or, if one wishes to give the ink designs their agreed-upon human meaning, letters have been formed to make words in order to suggest things not present. What is on the page are not real things but their word-shadows. Yet even if the things were there, it is most unlikely that they would be so human as to "mock their own meaning." In an eerie way, Robbe-Grillet's highly rhetorical style has a tendency to destroy his arguments even as he makes them; critically, this technique complements ideally the self-obliterating anecdote.

On the question of how to establish the separateness, the autonomy of things, Robbe-Grillet and Miss Sarraute part company. In contemplating her method, she ceases altogether to be "scientific." Instead she alarmingly intones a hymn to words — all words — for they "possess the qualities needed to seize upon, protect and bring out into the open those subterranean movements that are at once impatient and afraid." (Are those subterranean movements really "impatient and afraid"?) For her, words possess suppleness, freedom, iridescent richness of shading, and by their nature they are protected "from suspicion and from minute examination." (In an age of suspicion, to let words off scot-free is an act of singular trust.) Consequently, once words have entered the other person, they swell, explode, and "by virtue of this game of actions and reactions . . . they constitute a most valuable tool for the novelist." Which, as the French say, goes without saying.

But of course words are not at all what she believes they are. All words lie. Or as Professor Frank Kermode put it in *Literary Fiction and Reality*: "Words, thoughts, patterns of word and thought, are enemies of truth, if you identify that with what may be had by phenomenological reductions." Nevertheless, Miss Sarraute likes to think that subterranean movements (tropisms) can be captured by words, which might explain why her attitude toward things is so much more conventional than that of Robbe-Grillet, who writes:

> Perhaps Kafka's staircases lead *elsewhere*, but they are *there*, and we look at them step by step following the details of the banisters and the risers.

This is untrue. First, we do not look at the staircases; we look at a number of words arranged upon a page by a conscious human intelligence which would like us to consider, among a thousand other things, the fact of those staircases. Since a primary concern of the human mind is cause and effect, the reader is bound to speculate upon why those staircases have been shown him; also, since staircases are usually built to connect one man-made level with another, the mind will naturally speculate as to what those two levels are like.

Only a far-gone schizophrenic (or an LSD tripper) would find entirely absorbing the description of a banister.

Perhaps the most naïve aspect of Robbe-Grillet's theory of fiction is his assumption that words can ever describe with absolute precision anything. At no point does he acknowledge that words are simply fiat for real things; by their nature, words are imprecise and layered with meanings — the signs of things, not the things themselves. Therefore, even if Robbe-Grillet's goal of achieving a total reality for the world of things was desirable, it would not be possible to do it with language, since the author (that man full of torments and passions) is bound to betray his attitude to the sequence of signs he offered us; he has an "interest" in the matter, or else he would not write. Certainly if he means to reinvent man, then he will want to find a way of defining man through human (yes, psychological) relations as well as through a catalogue of things observed and gestures coolly noted. Wanting to play God, ambition is bound to dictate the order of words, and so the subjective will prevail just as it does in the traditional novel. To follow Robbe-Grillet's theory to its logical terminus, the only sort of book which might be said to be *not* a collection of signs of absent things but the actual things themselves would be a collection of ink, paper, cardboard, glue, and typeface, to be assembled or not by the reader-spectator. If this be too heavy a joke, then the ambitious writer must devise a new language which might give the appearance of maintaining the autonomy of things, since the words, new-minted, will possess a minimum of associations of a subjective or anthropomorphic sort. No existing language will be of any use to him, unless it be that of the Trobriand Islanders: those happy people have no words for "why" or "because"; for them, things just happen. Needless to say, they do not write novels or speculate on the nature of things.

The philosophic origins of the New Novel can be found (like most things French) in Descartes, whose dualism was the reflection of a split between the subjective and the objective, between the irrational and the rational, between the physical and the metaphysical. In the last century Auguste Comte, accepting this dualism, conceived of a logical empiricism which would emphasize the "purely" objective at the expense of the subjective or metaphysical. An optimist who believed in human progress, Comte saw history as an evolution toward a better society. For him the age of religion and metaphysics ended with the French Revolution. Since that time the human race was living in what he termed "the age of science," and he was confident that the methods of the positive sciences would enrich and transform human life. At last things were coming into their own. But not until the twentieth century did the methods of science entirely overwhelm the arts of the traditional humanists. To the scientific-minded, all things, including human personality, must in time yield their secrets to orderly experiment. Meanwhile, only that which is verifiable is to be taken seriously; emotive meaning must yield to cognitive meaning. Since the opacity of human character has so far defeated all objective attempts at illumination, the New Novelists prefer, as much as possible, to replace the human with objects closely observed and simple gestures noted but not explained.

In many ways, the New Novel appears to be approaching the "pure" state of music. In fact, there are many like Miss Sontag who look forward to "a kind of total structuring" of the novel, analogous to music. This is an old dream of the novelist. Nearly half a century ago, Joyce wrote (in a letter to his brother), "Why should not a modern literature be as unsparing and as direct as song?" Why not indeed? And again, why? The answer to the second "why" is easy enough. In the age of science, the objective is preferred to the subjective. Since human behavior is notoriously irrational and mysterious, it can be demonstrated only in the most impressionistic and unscientific way; it yields few secrets to objective analysis. Mathematics, on the other hand, is rational and verifiable, and music is a form of mathematics. Therefore, if one were to eliminate as much as possible the human from the novel, one might, through "a kind of total structuring," come close to the state of mathematics or music — in short, achieve that perfect irreducible artifact Robbe-Grillet dreams of.

The dates of Miss Sarraute's essays range from 1947 to 1956, those of Robbe-Grillet from 1955 to 1963. To categorize in the French manner, it might be said that their views are particularly representative of the fifties, a period in which the traditional-minded (among whom they must be counted) still believed it possible to salvage the novel — or anything — by new techniques. With a certain grimness, they experimented. But though some of their books are good (even very good) and some are bad, they did not make a "new" novel, if only because art forms do not evolve — in literature at least — from the top down. Despite Robbe-Grillet's tendency to self-congratulation ("Although these descriptions — motionless arguments or fragments of scene — have acted on the readers in a satisfactory fashion, the judgment many specialists make of them remains pejorative"), there is not much in what he has so far written that will interest anyone except the specialist. It is, however, a convention of the avant-garde that to be in advance of the majority is to be "right." But the New Novelists are not in advance of anyone. Their works derive from what they believe to be a need for experiment and the imposition of certain of the methods of science upon the making of novels. Fair enough. Yet in this they resemble everyone, since to have a liking for the new is to be with the dull majority. In the arts, the obviously experimental is almost never denounced *because* it is new: if anything, our taste-makers tend to be altogether too permissive in the presence of what looks to be an experiment, as anyone who reads New York art criticism knows. There is not much likelihood that Robbe-

Grillet will be able to reinvent man as a result of his exercises in prose. Rather he himself is in the process of being reinvented (along with the rest of us) by the new world in which we are living.

At the moment, advance culture scouts are reporting with a certain awe that those men and women who were brought up as television watchers respond, predictably, to pictures that move and talk but not at all to prose fictions; and though fashion might dictate the presence of an occasional irreducible artifact in a room, no one is about to be reinvented by it. Yet the old avant-garde continues worriedly to putter with form.

Surveying the literary output for 1965, Miss Sontag found it "hard to think of any one book [in English] that exemplifies in a *central* way the possibilities for enlarging and complicating the forms of prose literature." This desire to "enlarge" and "complicate" the novel has an air of madness to it. Why not minimize and simplify? One suspects that out of desperation she is picking verbs at random. But then, like so many at present, she has a taste for the random. Referring to William Burroughs's resolutely random work *The Soft Machine*, she writes: "In the end, the voices come together and sound what is to my mind the most serious, urgent and original voice in American letters to be heard for many years." It is, however, the point to Mr. Burroughs's method that the voices *don't* come together: he is essentially a sport who is (blessedly) not serious, not urgent, and original only in the sense that no other American writer has been so relentlessly ill-humored in his send-up of the serious. He is the Grand Guy Grand of American letters. But whether or not Miss Sontag is right or wrong in her analyses of specific works and general trends, there is something old-fashioned and touching in her assumption (shared with the New Novelists) that if only we all try hard enough in a "really serious" way, we can come up with the better novel. This attitude reflects not so much the spirit of art as it does that of Detroit.

No one today can predict what games post-Gutenberg man will want to play. The only certainty is that his mind will work differently from ours; just as ours works differently from that of pre-Gutenberg man, as Miss Frances Yates demonstrated so dramatically in *The Art of Memory*. Perhaps there will be more Happenings in the future. Perhaps the random will take the place of the calculated. Perhaps the ephemeral will be preferred to the permanent: we stop in time, so why should works of art endure? Also, as the shadow of atomic catastrophe continues to fall across our merry games, the ephemeral will necessarily be valued to the extent it gives pleasure in the present and makes no pretense of having a future life. Since nothing will survive the firewind, the ashes of one thing will be very like those of another, and so what matters excellence?

One interesting result of today's passion for the immediate and the casual has been the decline, in all the arts, of the idea of technical virtuosity as being in any way desirable. The culture (*kitsch* as well as camp) enjoys singers who sing no better than the average listener, actors who do not act yet are, in Andy Warhol's happy term, "super-stars," painters whose effects are too easily achieved, writers whose swift flow of words across the page is not submitted to the rigors of grammar or shaped by conscious thought. There is a general Zen-ish sense of why bother? If a natural fall of pebbles can "say" as much as any shaping of paint on canvas or cutting of stone, why go to the trouble of recording what is there for all to see? In any case, if the world should become, as predicted, a village united by an electronic buzzing, our ideas of what is art will seem as curious to those gregarious villagers as the works of what we used to call the Dark Ages appear to us.

Regardless of what games men in the future will want to play, the matter of fiction seems to be closed. Reading skills —as the educationalists say—continue to decline with each new generation. Novel reading is not a pastime of the young now being educated, nor, for that matter, is it a preoccupation

of any but a very few of those who came of age in the last
warm years of linear type's hegemony. It is possible that
fashion may from time to time bring back a book or produce
a book which arouses something like general interest (Miss
Sontag darkly suspects that "the nineteenth-century novel has a
much better chance for a comeback than verse drama, the
sonnet, or landscape painting"). Yet it is literature itself
which seems on the verge of obsolescence, and not so much
because the new people will prefer watching to reading as
because the language in which books are written has become
corrupt from misuse.

In fact, George Steiner believes that there is a definite possibility that "The political inhumanity of the twentieth century
and certain elements in the technological mass-society which
has followed on the erosion of European bourgeois values
have done injury to language. . . ." He even goes so far as to
suggest that for now at least silence may be a virtue for the
writer — when

> language simply ceases, and the motion of spirit gives no
> further outward manifestation of its being. The poet enters
> into silence. Here the word borders not on radiance or music,
> but on night.

Although Mr. Steiner does not himself take this romantic
position ("I am not saying that writers should stop writing.
This would be fatuous"), he does propose silence as a proud
alternative for those who have lived at the time of Belsen
and of Vietnam, and have witnessed the perversion of so
many words by publicists and political clowns. The credibility
gap is now an abyss, separating even the most honorable
words from their ancient meanings. Fortunately, ways of communication are now changing, and though none of us under-
stands exactly what is happening, language is bound to be
affected.

But no matter what happens to language, the novel is not

apt to be revived by electronics. The portentous theorizings of the New Novelists are of no more use to us than the self-conscious avant-gardism of those who are forever trying to figure out what the next "really serious" thing will be when it is plain that there is not going to be a next serious thing in the novel. Our lovely vulgar and most human art is at an end, if not the end. Yet that is no reason not to want to practice it, or even to read it. In any case, rather like priests who have forgotten the meaning of the prayers they chant, we shall go on for quite a long time talking of books and writing books, pretending all the while not to notice that the church is empty and the parishioners have gone elsewhere to attend other gods, perhaps in silence or with new words.

[*Encounter*, December 1967]

Miss Sontag's Second New Novel

THE beginning of a novel tends to reveal the author's ambition. The implicit or explicit obeisance he pays to previous works of literature is his way of "classing" himself, thereby showing interest in the matter. But as he proceeds, for better or worse his true voice is bound to be heard, if only because it is not possible to maintain for the length of a novel a voice pitched at a false level. Needless to say, the best and the worst novels are told in much the same tone from beginning to end, but they need not concern us here.

In the early pages of *Death Kit*, Susan Sontag betrays great ambition. Her principal literary sources are Nathalie Sarraute, Robbe-Grillet, Sartre, and Kafka, and she uses these writers in such a way that they must be regarded not so much as influences upon her prose as collaborators in the act of creation. Contemplating Nathalie Sarraute's *Portrait of a Man Unknown*, Sartre made much of Sarraute's "protoplasmic vision" of our interior universe: roll away the stone of the commonplace and we will find running discharges, slobberings, mucus; hesitant, amoeba-like movements. The Sarraute vocabulary is incomparably rich in suggesting the slow centrifugal creeping of these viscous, live solutions. "Like a sort of gluey slaver, their thought filtered into him, sticking to him, lining his insides." This is a fair description of Sarraute's manner, which Miss Sontag has entirely appropriated.

The first few pages of *Death Kit* are rich with Sarrautesque phrases: "inert, fragile, sticky fabric of things," "the soft interconnected tissuelike days," "surfaces of people deformed and bloated and leaden and crammed with vile juices" (but Miss Sarraute would not have written "leaden" because a bloated person does not suggest metal; more to the point, "leaden" is not a soft, visceral word), "his jellied porous boss" (but isn't the particular horror of the true jelly its consistency of texture? a porous jelly is an anomaly). Fortunately, once past the book's opening, Miss Sontag abandons the viscous vision except for a brief reprise in mid-passage when we encounter, in quick succession, "affable gelatinous Jim Allen," "chicken looks like boiled mucus," "oozing prattling woman," "sticky strip of words." But later we are reminded of Miss Sarraute's addiction to words taken from the physical sciences. In "The Age of Suspicion" (an essay admired by Miss Sontag in her own collection of essays *Against Interpretation*), Miss Sarraute wrote that the reader "is immersed and held under the surface until the end, in a substance as anonymous as blood, a magma without name or contours." Enchanted by the word "magma," Miss Sontag describes *her* characters as being "All part of the same magma of sensation, in which pleasure and pain are one." But Miss Sarraute used the word precisely, while Miss Sontag seems not to have looked it up in the dictionary, trusting to her ear to get the meaning right, and failing.

The plot of *Death Kit* is elaborate. Aboard the Privateer (yes), a train from Manhattan to Buffalo, Diddy (a divorced man in his thirties who inhabits a life he does not possess) observes a blind girl and an older woman. He wonders who they are; he also meditates on the other occupants of the compartment (as in Proust). Then the train stalls in a tunnel. The lights go out. After what seems a long time, Diddy gets off the train. He makes his way in the dark to the front of the train, where he finds a workman removing a barrier. When the man does not respond to his questions, Diddy grows alarmed. Finally the man does speak: he appears to threaten Diddy, who kills him with a crowbar, a murder which is almost gratuitous, almost Gide. Diddy returns to the compartment to find the older woman asleep. He talks to the blind girl, whose name is Hester (*The Scarlet Letter?*). Then the train starts and he takes Hester to the washroom, where, excited by his murder (Mailer's *An American Dream*), he makes love to her. Later Hester tells him that he did not leave the compartment and so could not have killed the workman. But of course she is blind, while the older woman, her aunt, was asleep and so cannot bear witness. In any case, hallucination has begun, and we are embarked upon another of those novels whose contemporary source is Kafka. Do I wake or dream?

Diddy dreams a very great deal and his dreams are repeated at length. When awake, he attends business meetings of his company, whose trademark is a gilded dome, whose management is conservative, whose business is worldwide, whose prospects are bad . . . too much undercutting from the East (what can Miss Sontag *mean?*). He broods about the "murder" and moons about Hester, who is in a local clinic waiting for an operation to restore her sight. Diddy visits her; he loves her. But he is still obsessed by the murder. In the press he reads that a workman named Angelo Incarnadona (incarnated angel) was killed in the tunnel by the Privateer, which had not, apparently, stalled in the tunnel. Diddy's quest begins. Did he kill the angel? He talks to the widow, who tells him that the body was cremated; he is safe, there can never be an investigation. Meanwhile Hester's operation is a failure. But Diddy has decided to marry her. They return to Manhattan. He quits his job. They withdraw from the world, seldom leaving his apartment. Slowly he begins to fade, grows thinner, vaguer. Finally he (apparently) takes Hester with him to the tunnel in an effort to make her *see* what it was that he did . . . or did he (Diddy)? In the tunnel they find a workman similar to the angel made flesh: again the man is at work removing a barrier. The scene more or less repeats the original, and once again Diddy separates the angel from its fleshly envelope with a crowbar. Then he makes love to Hester on the tunnel floor. But now we cease to see him from the outside. We enter his declining world, we become him as he walks naked through one subterranean room after another, among coffins and corpses heavy with dust, and in this last progress, simply written, Miss Sontag reveals herself as an artist with a most powerful ability to show us what it is she finally, truly sees.

The flash of talent at the book's end makes all the more annoying what precedes it. Miss Sontag is a didactic, naturalistic, Jewish-American writer who wants to be an entirely different sort of writer, not American but high European, not Jewish but ecumenical, not naturalistic in style but allusive, resonant, ambiguous. It is as an heiress to Joyce, Proust, and Kafka that she sees herself; her stand to be taken on foreign rather than on native ground. The tension between what she is and what she would like to be creates odd effects. She presents Diddy as a Gentile. But, to make a small point, middle-class American goyim do not address each other continually by name while, to make a larger point, Diddy's possession of a young brother who is a virtuoso musician seems better suited to a Clifford Odets drama than to one by Sherwood Anderson or William Faulkner. But Miss Sontag is nothing if not contemporary and perhaps she is reflecting the current fashion for Jewish writers to disguise Jewish characters as Gentiles, in much the same way that the homosexualists in our theater are supposed to write elaborate masquerades in which their own pathological relationships are depicted as heterosexual, thus traducing women and marriage. These playwrights have given us all many an anxious moment. Now the Jewish novelists are also indulging in travesty, with scandalous results.

As for style, Miss Sontag demonstrates a considerable gift for naturalistic prose, particularly in the later parts of the book when she abandons her sources and strikes out on her own. But she is not helped by the form in which she has cast her work. For no apparent reason, certain passages are indented on the page, while at maddeningly regular but seemingly random intervals she inserts the word "now" in parenthesis. If she intends these (now)s to create a sense of immediacy, of presentness, she fails. Also, though the story is told in the third person, on four occasions she shifts to the first person plural. It is a nice surprise, but one that we don't understand. Also, her well-known difficulties in writing English continue to make things hard for her. She is altogether too free with "sort ofs" and "kind ofs" and "reallys"; she often confuses number, and her ear, oddly enough, is better attuned to the cadences of the lower orders than to those of the educated. In the scenes between Diddy and the dead workman's widow, she writes not unlike Paddy Chayevsky at his best. She is, however, vulgar at moments when she means not to be, and on several occasions she refers to someone as "balding," betraying, if nothing else, her lovely goosey youth: those of us battered by decades of Timestyle refuse to use any word invented by that jocose and malicious publishing enterprise which has done so much to corrupt our Empire's taste, morals, and prose.

In a strange way, Miss Sontag has been undone as a novelist by the very thing that makes her unique and valuable among American writers: her vast reading in what English Departments refer to as comparative literature. As a literary broker, mediating between various contemporary literatures, she is awesome in her will to understand. This acquired culture sets her apart from the majority of American novelists (good and bad) who read almost nothing, if one is to admit as evidence the meager texture of their works and the idleness of their occasional commentaries. When American novelists do read, it is usually within the narrow limits of the American canon, a strange list of minor provincial writers grandiosely inflated into "world classics." Certainly few of our writers know anything of what is now being written in Europe, particularly in France. Yet for all the aridities and pretensions of the French "New Novelists," their work is the most interesting being done anywhere, and not to know what they are up to is not to know what the novel is currently capable of. As an essayist (and of course interpreter!) Miss Sontag has been, more than any other American, a link to European writing today. Not unnaturally, her reading has made her impatient with the unadventurous novels which our country's best-known (and often best) writers produce. She continues to yearn, as she recently wrote, for a novel "which people with serious and sophisticated [sic] taste in the other arts can take seriously," and she believes that such a work might be achieved "by a kind of total structuring" that is "analogous to music." This is all very vague, but at least she is radical in the right way; also her moral seriousness is considerably enhanced by a perfect absence of humor, that most devastating of gifts usually thrust at birth upon the writer in English. Unhindered by a sense of humor, she is able to travel fast in the highest country, unafraid of appearing absurd, and of course invulnerable to irony.

Unfortunately, Miss Sontag's intelligence is still greater than her talent. What she would do, she cannot do — or at least she has not done in *Death Kit*, a work not totally structured, not even kind of. Worse, the literary borrowings entirely obscure her own natural talent while the attitudes she strikes confuse and annoy, reminding one of Gide's weary complaint that there is nothing more unbearable than those writers who assume a tone and manner not their own. In the early part of *Death Kit*, Miss Sontag recklessly uses other writers in much the same way that certain tribes eat parts of their enemies in the hope that, magically, they may thus acquire the virtues and powers of the noble dead. No doubt the tribesmen do gain great psychological strength through their cannibalizing, but in literature only writers of the rank of Goethe and Eliot can feed promiscuously and brazenly upon the works of other men and gain strength. Yet the coda of Miss Sontag's novel suggests that once she has freed herself of literature, she will have the power to make it, and there are not many American writers one can say that of.

[*Book World,* September 10, 1967]

John O'Hara's Old Novels

IN 1938, writing to a friend, George Santayana described his first (and presumably last) encounter with the writing of Somerset Maugham. "I could read these [stories], enticed by the familiarity he shows with Spain, and with Spanish Americans, in whose moral complexion I feel a certain interest; but on the whole I felt . . . wonder at anybody wishing to write such stories. They are not pleasing, they are not pertinent to one's real interests, they are not true; they are simply graphic or plausible, like a bit of a dream that one might drop into in an afternoon nap. Why record it? I suppose it is to make money, because writing stories is a profession . . ." In just such a way, the Greek philosophers condemned the novels of the Milesian school. Unpleasing, impertinent, untruthful — what else can one say about these fictions except to speculate idly on why grown men see fit to write them. Money? There seems nothing more to be said.

Yet there is at least one good reason for a serious consideration of popular writing. "When you are criticizing the Philosophy of an epoch," wrote Alfred Whitehead in *Adventures Of Ideas*, "do not chiefly direct your attention to those intellectual positions which its exponents feel it necessary to defend. There will be some fundamental assumption which adherents of all the various systems within the epoch unconsciously presuppose." Writers of fiction, even more than systematic philosophers, tend to reveal unconscious presuppositions. One might even say that those writers who are the most popular are the ones who share the largest number of common assumptions with their audience, subliminally reflecting prejudices and aspirations so obvious that they are never stated and, never stated, never precisely understood or even recognized. John O'Hara is an excellent example of this kind of writer, and useful to any examination of what we are.

Over the last three decades, Mr. O'Hara has published close to thirty volumes of stories, plays, essays and novels. Since 1955 he has had a remarkable burst of activity: twelve books. His most recent novel, *Elizabeth Appleton,* was written in 1960 but kept off the market until 1963 in order that five other books might be published. His latest collection of short stories, *The Hat on the Bed,* is currently a best seller and apparently gives pleasure to the public. In many ways, Mr. O'Hara's writing is precisely the sort Santayana condemned: graphic and plausible, impertinent and untrue. But one must disagree with Santayana as to *why* this sort of work is done (an irrelevant speculation, in any case). Money is hardly the motive. No man who devotes a lifetime to writing can ever be entirely cynical, if only because no one could sustain for a lifetime the pose of being other than himself. Either the self changes or the writing changes. One cannot have it both ways. Mr. O'Hara uses himself quite as fully and obsessively as William Faulkner. The difference between them lies in capacity, and the specific use each makes of a common obsession to tell what it is like to be alive. But where Faulkner re-created his society through a gifted imagination, Mr. O'Hara merely re- flects that society, making him, of the two, rather the more interesting for our immediate purpose, which is to examine through certain popular works the way we live now.

Mr. O'Hara's work is in the naturalistic tradition. "I want to get it all down on paper while I can. The U. S. in this century, what I know, and it is my business to write about it to the best of my ability with the sometimes special knowledge that I have." He also wants "to record the way people talked and thought and felt, and to do it with complete honesty and variety." In this, he echoes Sinclair Lewis, Emile Zola, and (rather dangerously) the brothers Goncourt.

The Hat on the Bed is a collection of twenty-four short stories. They are much like Mr. O'Hara's other short stories, although admirers seem to prefer them to earlier collections. Right off, one is aware of a passionate interest in social distinctions. Invariably we are told not only what university a character attended but also what prep school. Clothes, houses, luggage (by Vuitton), prestigious restaurants are all carefully noted, as well as brand names. With the zest of an Internal Revenue man examining deductions for entertainment, the author investigates the subtle difference between the spending of old middle-class money and that of new middle-class money. Of course social distinctions have always been an important aspect of the traditional novel, but what disturbs one in reading Mr. O'Hara is that he does so little with these details once he has noted them. If a writer chooses to tell us that someone went to St. Paul's and to Yale and played squash, then surely there is something about St. Paul's and Yale and squash which would make him into a certain kind of person so that, given a few more details, the reader is then able to make up his mind as to just what that triad of experience means, and why it is different from Exeter-Harvard-lacrosse. But Mr. O'Hara is content merely to list schools and sports and the makes of cars and the labels on clothes. He fails to do his own job in his own terms, which is to show us *why* a character who went to Andover is not like one who went to Groton, and how the two schools, in some way, contributed to the difference. It would seem that Mr. O'Hara is excited by fashionable schools in much the same way that Balzac was by money, and perhaps for the same reason, a cruel deprivation. Ernest Hemingway (whose malice was always profound) once announced that he intended to take up a collection to send John O'Hara through Yale. In his own defense, Mr. O'Hara has said that his generation did care passionately about colleges. Granting him this, one must then note that the children and grandchildren of his contemporaries do not care in the *same* way, a fact he seems unaware of.

The technique of the short stories does not vary much. The prose is plain and rather garrulous; the dialogue tends to run on, and he writes most of his stories and novels in dialogue because not only is that the easiest kind of writing to read but the easiest to do. In a short story like "The Mayor" one sees his technique at its barest. Two characters meet after three pages of setting up the scene (describing a hangout for the town's politicians and setting up the personality of the mayor, who often drops in). Then two characters start to talk about a third character (the mayor) and his relationship with a fourth, and after some four pages of dialogue – and one small uninteresting revelation – the story is over. It has been, in Santayana's image, a daydream. One has learned nothing, felt nothing. Why record it?

Another short story, "How Can I Tell You?" is purest reverie. Once upon a time there was a car salesman who by all worldly standards is a success; he even gets on well with his wife. All things conspire to make him happy. But he suffers from accidie. The story begins *in medias res*. He is making an important sale. The woman buying the car talks to him at great length about this and that. Nothing particularly relevant to the story is said. The dialogue wanders aimlessly in imitation of actual speech as it sounds to Mr. O'Hara's ear, which is good but unselective, with a tendency to use arcane slang ("plenty of glue") and phonetic spellings ("wuddia"). Yet despite this long conversation, the two characters remain vague and undefined. Incidentally, Mr. O'Hara almost never gives a physical description of his characters, a startling continence for a naturalistic writer, and more to be admired than not.

The woman departs. The salesman goes to a bar, where the bartender immediately senses that "You got sumpn eatin' you, boy." The salesman then goes home. He looks at his sleeping wife, who wakes up and wants to know if something is wrong. "How the hell can I tell you when I don't know myself?" he says. She goes back to sleep. He takes down his gun. He seems about to kill himself when his wife joins him and says, "Don't. Please?" and he says, "I won't." And there the story ends. What has gone wrong is that one could not care less about this Richard Cory (at least we were told that the original was full of light and that people envied him), because Mr. O'Hara's creation has neither face nor history. What the author has shown us is not a character but an event, and though a certain kind of writing can be most successful dealing only with events, this particular story required character shown from the inside, not a situation described from the outside and through dialogue.

Elizabeth Appleton, O'Hara's latest novel, takes place in a Pennsylvania university town. Will the dean, Elizabeth's husband, be made president of the college? He is a popular choice, and in line for the post. Elizabeth has been a conscientious faculty wife, in spite of being "aristocratic" (her family used to go to Southampton in the summer). Elizabeth also has money, a fact which her patrician good taste insists she hide from her husband's world. But hidden or not, for those who know true quality Elizabeth is the real thing. She even inspires the reverence of a former New York policeman who happens to be sitting next to her during a plane trip. There has been bad weather. Danger. Each is brave. The danger passes. Then they talk of . . . what else do Mr. O'Hara's people talk of in a pinch? Schools. "You're a New York girl, even if you did get on at Pittsburgh." Elizabeth allows that this is so. Then with that uncanny shrewdness the lower orders often demonstrate when they are in the presence of their betters, the flatfoot asks, "Did you ever go to Miss Spence's Finishing School? I used to help them cross the street when I was in that precinct." No Franklin High School for him. "I went to Miss Chapin's," says Elizabeth quietly, as if declaring, very simply, that she is a Plantagenet. Needless to say, the fuzz knows all about Chapin, too. He is even more overcome when he learns her maiden name. He knows exactly who her father was. He even recalls her family house "on the north side of Fifty-Sixth between Madison and Park. Iron grillwork on the ground floor windows. . . . Those were the good days, Mrs. Appleton, no matter what they say," he declares in an ecstasy of social inferiority.

Like so many of O'Hara's novels, the book seems improvised. The situation is a simple one. Appleton is expected to become Spring Valley's next president. He wants the job, or nearly (readers of the late John P. Marquand will recognize with delight that hesitancy and melancholy which inevitably attend success in middle age. Is this all there is to it? Where are my dreams, my hopes, my love?). Elizabeth wants the promotion, partly for her husband's sake, partly because she is guilty because *she has had an affair*. It is over now, of course. Her lover has taken to drink. But with the aid of flashbacks we can savor the quality of their passion, which turns out to have been mostly talk. Sometimes they talked about schools, sometimes about games; occasionally they discussed the guilt each feels toward her husband, and the possibility of their own marriage one day. But aside from talk nothing happens. In fact, there is almost no action in Mr. O'Hara's recent work. Everything of consequence takes place offstage, to be reported later in conversation — perhaps his only resemblance to classical literature.

To be effective, naturalistic detail must be not only accurate but relevant. Each small fact must be fitted to the overall pattern as tightly as mosaic. This is a tiresomely obvious thing to say, but repetition does not seem to spoil the novelty of it as criticism. Unfortunately Mr. O'Hara does not relate things one to the other, he simply puts down the names of schools, resorts, restaurants, hotels for the simple pleasure of recording them (and perhaps, magically, possessing them in the act of naming). If he can come up with the name of an actual entertainer who performed in a real club of a known city in a particular year, he seems to feel that his work as recorder has been justified. This love of minutiae for their own sake can be as fatal to the serious novelist as it is necessary to the success of the popular writer . . . which brings us to the audience and its unconscious presuppositions.

Right off, one is struck by the collective narcissism of those whose tastes create the best-seller lists. Until our day, popular writers wrote of kings and queens, of exotic countries and extreme situations, of worlds totally unlike the common experience. No longer. Today's reader wants to look at himself, to find out who *he* is, with an occasional glimpse of his next-door neighbor. This self-absorption is also reflected in the ubiquitous national polls that fascinate newspaper readers and in those magazine articles that address themselves with such success to the second person singular. Certainly, fiction is, to a point, an extension of actual life, an alternative world in which a reader may find out things he did not know before and live in imagination a life he may not live in fact. But I suggest that never before has the alternative world been so close to the actual one as it is today in the novels of John O'Hara and his fellow commercialites. Journalism and popular fiction have merged, and the graphic and the plausible have become an end in themselves. The contemporary public plainly prefers mirrors to windows.

The second unconscious presupposition Mr. O'Hara reveals is the matter of boredom. Most of the people he describes are bored to death with their lives and one another. Yet they never question this boredom, nor does their author show any great awareness of it. He just puts it all down. Like his peers, he reflects the *taedium vitae* without seeming to notice it. Yet it lurks continually beneath the surface, much the way a fear of syphilis haunted popular writing in the nineteenth century. One can read O'Hara by the yard without encountering a single character capable of taking pleasure in anything. His creatures are joyless. Neither art nor mind ever impinges on their garrulous self-absorption. If they read books, the books are by writers like Mr. O'Hara, locked with them in a terrible self-regard. Strangely enough, they show little true curiosity about other people, which is odd since the convention of each story is almost always someone telling someone else about so-and-so. They want to hear gossip but only in a desultory, time-passing way.

Finally, there is the matter of death. A recent survey among young people showed that since almost none believed in the continuation of personality after death, each felt, quite logically, that if this life is all there is, to lose it is the worst that can happen to anyone. Consequently, none was able to think of a single "idea," political or moral, whose defense might justify no longer existing. To me this is the central underlying assumption of our society and one which makes us different from our predecessors. As a result, much of the popular writers' glumness reflects the unease of a first generation set free from an attitude toward death which was as comforting as it was constraining. Curiously enough, this awareness is responsible for one of Mr. O'Hara's few entirely successful works, the short story "The Trip," from *Assembly.*

An elderly New York clubman is looking forward to a boat trip to England, the scene of many pleasures in his youth (the Kit Kat Club with the Prince of Wales at the drums, etc.). He discusses the trip with his bridge partners, a contented foursome of old men, their pleasant lives shadowed only by the knowledge of death. An original member of the foursome died some years earlier, and there had been some criticism of him because he had collapsed "and died while playing a hand. The criticism was mild enough, but it was voiced, one player to another; it was simply that Charley had been told by his doctor not to play bridge, but he had insisted on playing, with the inevitable, extremely disturbing result." But there were those who said how much better it was that Charley was able to die among friends rather than in public, with "policemen going through his pockets to find some identification. Taxi drivers pointing to him. Look, a dead man." Skillfully O'Hara weaves his nightmare. Shortly before the ship is to sail for England, one of the foursome misses the afternoon game. Then it is learned that he has died in a taxicab. Once again the "inevitable, extremely disturbing" thing has happened. The trip is called off because "I'd be such a damn nuisance if I checked out in a London cab." This particular story is beautifully made, and completely effective. Yet Boccaccio would have found it unfathomable: isn't death everywhere? and shouldn't we crowd all the pleasure that we can into the moment and hope for grace? But in Mr. O'Hara's contemporary mirror, there is neither grace nor God nor — one suspects — much pleasure in living.

Why our proud Affluency is the way it is does not concern us here. Enough to say that Mr. O'Hara, for all his faults, is a reliable witness to our self-regard, boredom, and terror of not being. Nor is he without literary virtues. For one thing, he possesses that rare thing, the narrative gift. For another, he has complete integrity. What he says he sees, he sees. Though his concern with sex used to trouble many of the Good Gray Geese of the press, it is a legitimate concern. Also, his treatment of sexual matters is seldom irrelevant, though touchingly old-fashioned by today's standards, proving once again how dangerous it is for a writer to rely too heavily on contemporary sexual mores for his effects. When those mores change, the moments of high drama become absurd. "Would you marry me if I weren't a virgin?" asks a girl in one of the early books. "I don't know. I honestly don't know," is the man's agonized response, neither suspecting that even as they suffer, in literature's womb Genet and Nabokov, William Burroughs and Mary McCarthy are stirring to be born. But despite Mr. O'Hara's passionate desire to show things as they are, he is necessarily limited by the things he must look at. Lacking a moral imagination and not interested in the exercise of mind or in the exploration of what really goes on beneath that Harris tweed suit from J. Press, he is doomed to go on being a writer of gossip who is read with the same mechanical attention any newspaper column of familiar or near-familiar names and places is apt to evoke. His work, finally, cannot be taken seriously as literature, but as an unconscious record of the superstitions and assumptions of his time, his writing is "pertinent" in Santayana's sense, and even "true."

[*New York Review of Books*, April 16, 1964]

The Revelation of John Horne Burns

IN 1947 *The Gallery* by John Horne Burns was published, to great acclaim: the best book of the Second War. That same year Burns and I met several times, each a war novelist and each properly wary of the other. Burns was then thirty-one with a receding hairline above a face striking in its asymmetry, one ear flat against the head, the other stuck out. He was a difficult man who drank too much, loved music, detested all other writers, and wanted to be great (he had written a number of novels before the war, but none was published). He was also certain that to be a good writer it was necessary to be homosexual. When I disagreed, he named a half dozen celebrated contemporaries, "A Pleiad," he roared delightedly, "of pederasts!" But what about Faulkner, I asked, and Hemingway. He was disdainful. Who said *they* were any good? And besides, hadn't I heard how Hemingway once . . .

I never saw Burns after 1947. But we exchanged several letters. He was going to write a successful play and become rich. He was also going to give up teaching in a prep school and go live in Europe. He did achieve Europe, but the occasion of the return was not happy. His second novel, *Lucifer with a Book* (1949), was perhaps the most savagely and unjustly attacked book of its day. Outraged, and with good reason, Burns exchanged America for Italy. But things had started to go wrong for him, and Italy did not help. The next novel, *A*

Cry of Children (1952), was bad. He seemed to have lost some inner sense of self, gained in the war, lost in peace. He disintegrated. Night after night, he would stand at the Excelsior Hotel bar in Florence, drinking brandy, eating hard candy (he had a theory that eating sugar prevents hangovers . . . it does not), insulting imagined enemies and imagined friends, and all the while complaining of what had been done to him by book reviewers. In those years one tried not to think of Burns: it was too bitter. The best of us all had taken the worst way. In 1958 when I read that he was dead, I felt no shock. It seemed right. One only wondered how he had achieved extinction. Sunstroke was the medical report. But it being Burns, there were rumors of suicide, even of murder; however, those who knew him at the last say that his going was natural and inevitable. He was thirty-seven years old.

Twenty-one years ago the U. S. Army occupied Naples and John Horne Burns, a young soldier from Boston — Irish, puritan, unawakened — was brought to life by the human swarm he encountered in the Galleria Umberto, "a spacious arcade opening off Via Roma. . . . It was like walking into a city within a city." From this confrontation Burns never recovered. As he put it, "I thought I could keep a wall between me and the people. But the monkeys in the cage reach out and grab the spectator who offers them a banana." It was the time when cigarettes, chocolate, and nylons were exchanged for an easy sex that could become, for a man like Burns, unexpected love. He was startled to find that Italians could sell themselves with no sense of personal loss and, unlike their puritan conquerors, they could even take pleasure in giving pleasure; their delight in the fact of life persisted, no matter how deep the wound. Unlike "the Irish who stayed hurt all their lives, the Italians had a bounce-back in them."

The Gallery is a collection of "Portraits" and "Promenades"; a study of men and women brought together in one way or another by the fact of the Galleria and war. The characters, some shadowy, some startlingly brilliant, have sex, make love, lose themselves, find themselves. A young soldier retreats into visions of himself as Christ; a major in censorship builds himself a bureaucratic empire; a Catholic chaplain quibbles with a Protestant chaplain; a soldier grimly endures the VD ward and wonders how he could ever have loved the girl who put him there; and Momma, a genial Italian lady, presides over the Galleria's queer bar, finding her charges mysteriously *simpatico*, quite unlike the other conquerors. Finally, it is not so much what these characters do as the effect that Naples has on them. One discovers "the difference between love and Having Sex." To another: "It seemed that in our lethargic and compassionate caresses we were trying to console each other for every hurt the world had ever inflicted." To the demented visionary: "These people are all in search of love. The love of God, or death, or of another human being. They're all lost. That's why they walk so aimlessly. They all feel here that the world isn't big enough to hold them — and look at the design of this place. Like a huge cross laid on the ground, after the corpus is taken off the nails."

In the classic tradition of northern visitors to the South, Burns is overwhelmed by the spontaneity of the Italians. Even their rapacity and cruelty strike him as being closer to some ideal of the human than the moral numbness of the American. He contrasts Italian delicacy in human matters with the harshness of our own soldiers and their pathological loathing for the "inferior" races that war forced them to deal with. For the thousandth time in history, gross northern warriors were loose among the ancient civilization at the edge of the southern sea, and for Burns it was a revelation to realize that he belonged not to an army of civilized liberators but to a barbarian horde humanly inferior to the conquered.

Burns's style is energetic, very much that of the forties, with distracting attempts at phonetic spelling ("furren" for "foreign") and made-up verbs ("he shrilled"). Burns's ear for dialogue was not always true; his dislike of those speaking often came between him and accuracy. He was also sometimes operatic in his effects (penicillin hurled at the Galleria: symbolic revenge). But when he is good, the style has a compelling drive that displays the national manner at its best. "Their faces complemented one another as a spoon shapes what it holds," thinks a character who has "contracted a bad case of irrelevance."

Of the well-known books of the Second War, I have always thought that only Burns's record was authentic and felt. To me the others are redolent of ambition and literature. But for Burns the war was authentic revelation. In Naples he fell in love with the idea of life. And having obtained a sense of his own identity, he saw what life might be. That the vision was a simple one makes no difference. It was his. "There'll be Neapolitans alive in 1960. I say, more power to them. They deserve to live out the end of their days because they caught on sooner than we how simple human life can be, uncomplicated by advertising and Puritanism and those loathsome values of a civilization in which everything is measured in terms of commercial success." His indictment is now a cliché, but it struck a nerve twenty years ago. Also I suspect he never understood his own people very well; nor do I think he would have been so entirely pleased by the Neapolitans of 1960 who, in their relative affluence, have begun to resemble us. But the spirit of his revelation remains true. "For I got lost in the war in Naples in August 1944. Often from what I saw I lost the power of speech. It seemed to me that everything happening there could be happening to me. A kind of madness, I suppose. But in the twenty-eighth year of my life I learned that I too must die. Until that time the only thing evil that could be done to me would be to hurry me out of the world before my time. Or to thwart my natural capacities. If this truth held for me, it must be valid for everybody else in the world."

Burns hurried himself out of the world before his time. But he had had his moment. And now that the war we lived through is history, we are able to recognize that the novel he wrote about it is literature. Burns was a gifted man who wrote a book far in excess of his gift, making a masterpiece that will endure in a way he himself could not. Extreme circumstances made him write a book which was better than his talent, an unbearable fate for an ambitious artist who wants to go on, but cannot — all later work shadowed by the splendid accident of a moment's genius. I suspect that once Burns realized his situation, he chose not to go on, and between Italian brandy and Italian sun contrived to stop.

As for the man, Burns had the luck to know, if only briefly, what it was to be alive with all senses responsive to all things; able to comprehend another person and to share that truth which is "valid for everybody else." Describing a soldier much like himself, even to the first name, Burns shows us a man discovering himself for the first time in the act of love on a hot August night. But then, love made, he is too keyed up to fall asleep, too restless with discovery; and so he is soothed and comforted in the dark, and the whispered Italian of his companion strikes the note of epitaph: "Buona notte e sogni d'oro. . . . Dormi, John."

[*New York Times Book Review*, May 30, 1965]

John Hersey's *Here to Stay?*

JOHN HERSEY has brought together a number of pieces in a volume called *Here to Stay*, and a baffling collection it is. To give Mr. Hersey his due — and who is so hard as not to give it to him? — he is good-hearted, right-minded, and, as they used to say of newspaper reporters, "tireless." Unfortunately he is almost always dull, and this dullness is not easily accounted for, since he deals with interesting subjects: Connecticut floods, concentration-camp survivors, returning war veterans, battle-fatigue cases, and the famous study of Hiroshima. He is fascinated by death, holocaust, and man's monotonous inhumanity to man. He can describe a disaster chastely and attentively. He has an eye for minutiae (here begins his failure, for he has not much gift for selection). He is willing to take on great themes, yet despite all efforts, his creations are stillborn. Why?

In a preface, Mr. Hersey expresses the hope "that this volume will give its readers a draught of adrenalin, that bitter elixir, sufficient sips of which may help put us on our guard against blunderers, tyrants, madmen and ourselves. . . . Drink deeply, therefore, dear reader, of the adrenal wine." Aside from the fact that adrenalin is a stimulant, not a "bitter elixir," and taken by injection, not by cup, Mr. Hersey does not really invite us dear readers to do more than watch passively his newsreels of horror. He certainly does not stimulate us to right action, and there I suggest is the flaw in his method.

The Hersey technique is, simply, to collect an immense amount of data, and then use most of it. For instance, in one ten-line paragraph, Mr. Hersey tells us that the town of Winsted has 11,000 people, that the Mad River, swollen by water from Highland Lake, has several times washed out bridges and houses, that in '36 and '38 Main Street was flooded, and that after a flash flood on New Year's Eve ('47–'48), P. Francis Hicks, the mayor, got the Army to dredge the river at the cost of $250,000. Then we are told what happened at 6:10 and 7:48. Mr. Hersey has a passion for the right time and in almost every piece the time of day is given at least once, often oftener. Again, why? To what end does Mr. Hersey in his level, fact-choked style insist that we attend these various disasters human and natural? Admittedly the simple declarative sentences are excellent at conveying action, but they are less good at suggesting atmosphere and they are hopeless at expressing a moral point of view even by indirection. It is possible that some private theory of "style" may inhibit Mr. Hersey from intruding himself upon us — and in an age of self-serving first-person journalists this is a decent continence. But no matter what the motive, he does little but feed us facts in the worst tradition of those often useful but invariably overwritten profiles of the obscure with which the *New Yorker* has for years burdened our era's social archives — works in which the writer supplies the facts, the reader the interpretation. It is too cruel.

Mr. Hersey in his prefatory note does try to provide a certain moral basis for his journalism when he writes, "Love can be a mortal enemy of death, especially of living death. . . ." But is this true? Maybe. Does he prove it? In context, no. Yet once in a while the simple — even simple-minded — style pays off. Referring to certain Hungarian youths at the time of the 1956 uprising: "A political system is nothing more, in the end, than a system of human relationships, and what these boys understood of politics was simply that they—and all the Hungarians they knew—were being treated badly as individuals by other individuals who had taken charge of things, and they had come to believe that freedom is the sense of being treated well and that life without that sense is not worth living." False-naïve, perhaps, but good stuff, suitable for any high-school book on civics and blessedly lacking the sententiousness of his usual prose.

It is in Mr. Hersey's celebrated *Hiroshima* that all his virtues and faults are most revealed. He employs a familiar device of popular fiction: a number of characters are carefully described just before, during, and after a disaster, in this case the atomic bomb the Americans dropped on a Japanese city. The material is certainly interesting, but it should be fascinating. The simple clear descriptive sentences march and march, taking the myriad facts along the way like an obstacle course. Just as one is close to pity and awe, there is a sudden injection of details (the italics are mine): ". . . and *ten* nurses came in from the city of Yamaguchi with extra bandages and antiseptic, and the *third* day though another physician and a *dozen* more nurses arrived from Matuseyet, there were still only *eight* doctors for *ten thousand* patients. In the afternoon of the *third* day . . ." At crucial moments this numbers game is infuriating.

Of course Mr. Hersey is to be praised for avoiding emotional journalism and overt editorializing (though a week of reading Zola might do him good). Yet despite his properly nervous preface, he does not seem to realize that the only point to writing serious journalism is to awaken in the reader not only the sense of *how* something was, but the apprehension of *why* it was, and to what moral end the writer recording the event is leading us, protesting or not. But Mr. Hersey does not take us into his confidence. True, he finds war hell and human suffering terrible, but that is nowhere near enough. At no point in his deadpan chronicle of Hiroshima is there any sense of what the Bomb meant and means. He does not even touch on the public debate as to whether or not there was any need to use such a weapon when Japan was already making overtures of surrender. To Mr. Hersey it just fell, that's all, and it was terrible, and he would like to tell us about it. If he has any attitude about the moral position of the United States before and after this extraordinary human happening, he keeps it safely hidden beneath all those little sentences and small facts.

To use Mr. Hersey's own unhappy image, in reading him one does not drink the bitter elixir of adrenalin, one merely sips a familiar cup of something anodyne, something not stimulating but barbiturate, and the moral sense sleeps on.

[*New York Review of Books*, February 27, 1963]

The Wit and Wisdom of J. K. Galbraith

IS there no end to the variety of Professor J. K. Galbraith? A superb diplomatist, a masterful popularizer of economics, a pundit who has walked with pandits yet kept his uncommon touch, Professor Galbraith now allows us a glimpse of yet another aspect of his protean genius. In the spirit of Voltaire's proposition that "true comedy is the speaking picture of the follies and foibles of a nation," the Professor, mysteriously disguised as "Mark Epernay," has just published *The Mc-Landress Dimension*, a "book" consisting of seven magazine articles, each based on a single joke. For instance, the McLandress Coefficient "is the arithmetic mean or average of the intervals of time during which a subject's thoughts remain centered on some substantive phenomenon other than his own personality." That's all there is to it. We learn that Elizabeth Taylor can think about something other than herself for three minutes (theater people have low coefficients). Politicans also tend to be low. At twenty-nine minutes, President Kennedy's coefficient is relatively high. Senator Javits at four minutes is about par. Richard Nixon's three seconds is unusually low. Professor Galbraith clocks himself in at one minute fifteen seconds, which seems fair. But then what is one to make of: "both Mr. Arthur Miller and Mr. Tennessee Williams have a rating of thirty-five minutes. Mr. Gore Vidal, by contrast, has a rating of twelve and a half minutes"? I find this . . . one finds this odd.

The game amuses for a page or two. Then it palls because to make this sort of thing work one must either have considerable powers of invention or a style so perfectly aphoristic that each judgment sounds like the Earl of Rochester on a good day. Unfortunately, Professor Galbraith's prose, although lucid, lacks the bite of the true satirist. One wearies of the jokes even more rapidly than one did of those made by his two immediate predecessors, Stephen Potter and the author of Parkinson's Law. The Professor rings no unexpected changes. He continually forces his wit and wit, forced, is a poor thing. Only occasionally does he hit the right note. When he does, the result is remarkably satisfying, particularly when he explains why the people at a court (like that of the Kennedys) tend to have low ratings because "association with the great leads, evidently, to reflection less on the great associate than on the association. So thought returns to self." This is first-rate.

The second piece describes "The McLandress Solution," a system whereby national leaders can be given safe answers to great questions. He also demonstrates how the conventional wisdom tends to be internally contradictory. "The United States has a highly dynamic economy. However, the rate of growth is not satisfactory." Or: "In dealing with the Berlin problem we always stand ready to negotiate. However, we must recognize that any concessions will be taken by the Soviets as a sign of weakness." The true statesman will sidestep not only the contradiction but the issue in favor of some responsible if tangential goal. We are given a fine example of this in a report made by the Rockefeller Brothers' Fund: "Industry and labor should continue to seek out new production and construction methods to reduce costs and increase production as a positive approach against inflation."

"The American Sociometric Peerage" concerns who's

really who in the United States and how celebrity is achieved. "The Fully Automated Foreign Policy" is just that: a machine takes over the State Department. Since our foreign policy is entirely predictable, a machine can easily do the work of the thousands who now grind out "policy." In the course of a somewhat laborious piece, Professor Galbraith observes shrewdly that "the truly sophisticated man argues not for the wisdom or even the prudence of a foreign policy but for its continuity. Few things more clearly mark the amateur in diplomacy than his inability to see that even the change from the wrong policy to the right policy involves the admission of previous error and hence is damaging to national prestige." Reading this, one wishes that our former Ambassador to India would cut the clowning and tell us of his own adventure as diplomat, in precisely this sharp vein.

"The Confidence Machine" (ways of reassuring businessmen about government) is dull. "Allston Wheat's Crusade" is a good little joke. A right-winger sets out to prove that team sports are a tool of the Communist conspiracy since they tend to diminish the individual while glorifying the group. At one point the author nicely parodies the Bircher prose style: "America is a country of team sports. We must see these sports for what they are. They are brainwashing stations for individualism. They are training schools for collectivism, socialism, authoritarianism and totalitarianism." "The Takeover" concerns the end of capitalism when one man takes over the economic life of the United States. This piece seems to have been written in great haste.

With this mild oat sown, it is to be hoped that Professor Galbraith will now bury Mark Epernay and become himself again. In his curious way, he is a national asset. As economic apostle to the middlebrows, he has no equal (and almost no competition). He writes a graceful prose. He has a sharp eye for the folly of others. He would make a splendid memoirist, for he betrays that edgy self-love which adds true passion to those diaries that best illuminate the political scene. A journalist in the purest sense, Professor Galbraith could easily become another Harold Ickes if not Saint Simon, earning for himself, in the sinister Mark Epernay's phrase, a lasting "Maximum Prestige Horizon."

[*New York Review of Books*, February 12, 1963]

E. Nesbit's Use of Magic

AFTER Lewis Carroll, E. Nesbit is the best of the English fabulists who wrote about children (neither wrote *for* children), and like Carroll she was able to create a world of magic and inverted logic that was entirely her own. Yet Nesbit's books are relatively unknown in the United States. Publishers attribute her failure in these parts to a witty and intelligent prose style (something of a demerit in the land of the dull and the home of the literal) and to the fact that a good many of her books deal with magic, a taboo subject nowadays. Apparently, the librarians who dominate the "juvenile market" tend to the brisk tweedy ladies whose interests are mechanical rather than imaginative. Never so happy as when changing a fan belt, they quite naturally want to communicate their joy in practical matters to the young. The result has been a depressing literature of how-to-do things while works of invention are sternly rejected as not "practical" or "useful." Even the Oz books which had such a powerful influence on three generations of Americans are put to one side in certain libraries, and children are discouraged from reading them because none of the things described in those books could ever have happened. Even so, despite such odds, attempts are being made by gallant publishers to penetrate the tweed curtain, and a number of Nesbit's books are currently

available in the United States, while in England she continues
to be widely read.

Born in 1858, Edith Nesbit was the daughter of the head
of a British agricultural college. In 1880 she married Hubert
Bland, a journalist. But though they had a good deal in common — both were socialists, active in the Fabian Society —
the marriage was unhappy. Bland was a philanderer; worse, he
had no gift for making a living. As a result, simply to support
her five children, Nesbit began to write books about children.
In a recent biography, *Magic and the Magician*, Noel Streat-
feild remarks that E. Nesbit did not particularly like children,
which may explain why those she created in her books are so
entirely human. They are intelligent, vain, aggressive, humor-
ous, witty, cruel, compassionate . . . in fact, they are like adults,
except for one difference. In a well-ordered and stable society
(England in the time of the gross Edward), children are as
clearly defined a minority group as Jews or Negroes in other
times and places. Physically small and weak, economically
dependent upon others, they cannot control their environment.
As a result, they are forced to develop a sense of communal-
ity; and though it does not necessarily make them any nicer
to one another, at least it helps them to see each other with
perfect clarity. Nesbit's genius is to see them as clearly and
unsentimentally as they see themselves, thus making for that
sense of life upon the page without which no literature.

Nesbit's usual device is to take a family of children ranging
in age from a baby to a child of ten or eleven and then involve
them in adventures, either magical or realistic (never both at
the same time). *The Story of the Treasure Seekers*, *The
Wouldbegoods*, and *The New Treasure Seekers* are realistic
books about the Bastable children. They are told by Oswald
Bastable, whose style owes a great deal to that of Julius
Caesar. Like the conqueror, Oswald is able through a cunning
use of the third person to establish his marked superiority to
others. Wondering if his younger brother H. O. is mentally

retarded, he writes, "H. O. is eight years old, but he cannot tell the clock yet. Oswald could tell the clock when he was six." Oswald is a delightful narrator and the stories he tells are among Nesbit's best. For the most part they deal with scrapes the children get into while searching for treasure in familiar surroundings, and the strategies they employ in coping as sensibly as possible with the contrary world of grown-ups. In a Nesbit book there is always some sort of domestic trouble. One parent is usually missing, and there is never enough money — although to the twentieth-century reader, her "impoverished" middle-class households, each with its three servants and large house, suggest an entirely golden aristocratic age. Yet many of the children's adventures have to do with attempts to improve the family's finances.

To my mind, it is in the "magic books" that Nesbit is at her best, particularly the trilogy which involves the Five Children. In the first volume, *Five Children and It*, they encounter a Psammead, a small bad-tempered, odd-looking creature from pre-history. The Psammead is able to grant wishes by first filling itself with air and then exhaling. ("If only you knew how I hate to blow myself out with other people's wishes, and how frightened I am always that I shall strain a muscle or something. And then to wake up every morning and know that you've got to do it. . . .")

But the children use the Psammead relentlessly for their wishes, and something almost always goes wrong. They wish "to be more beautiful than the day," and find that people detest them, thinking they look like Gypsies or worse. Without moralizing, Nesbit demonstrates, literally, the folly of human wishes, and amuses at the same time. In *The Phoenix and the Carpet*, they become involved with the millennial phoenix, a bird of awesome vanity ("I've often been told that mine is a valuable life"). With the use of a magic carpet, the phoenix and the children make a number of expeditions about the world. Yet even with such an ordinary device as a magic carpet, Nesbit's powers of invention are never settled easily. The carpet has been repaired, and the rewoven section is not magic; whoever sits on that part travels neither here nor there. Since most intelligent children are passionate logicians, the sense of logic is a necessary gift in a writer of fantasy. Though a child will gladly accept a fantastic premise, he will insist that the working out of it be entirely consistent with the premise. Careless invention is immediately noticed; contradiction and inconsistencies irritate, and illusion is destroyed. Happily, Nesbit is seldom careless and she anticipates most questions which might occur to a child. Not that she can always answer him satisfactorily. A condition of the Psammead's wishes is that they last only for a day. Yet the effects of certain wishes in the distant past did linger. Why was this? asked one of the children. "*Autres temps,*" replied the Psammead coolly, "*autres mœurs.*"

In *The Story of the Amulet,* Nesbit's powers of invention are at their best. It is a time-machine story, only the device is not a machine but an Egyptian amulet whose other half is lost in the past. By saying certain powerful words, the amulet becomes a gate through which the children are able to visit the past or future. Pharaonic Egypt, Babylon (whose dotty queen comes back to London with them and tries to get her personal possessions out of the British Museum), Caesar's Britain — they visit them all in search of the missing part of the amulet. Nesbit's history is good. And there is even a look at a Utopian future, which turns out to be everything a good Fabian might have hoped for. Ultimately, the amulet's other half is found, and a story of considerable beauty is concluded in a most unexpected way.

There are those who consider *The Enchanted Castle* Nesbit's best book. J. B. Priestley has made a good case for it, and there *is* something strange about the book that sets it off from the bright world of the early stories. Four children encounter magic in the gardens of a great deserted house. The mood is midnight. Statues of dinosaurs come alive in the moonlight, the gods of Olympus hold a revel, Pan's song is heard. Then things go inexplicably wrong. The children decide to give a play. Wanting an audience, they create a number of creatures out of old clothes, pillows, brooms, umbrellas. To their horror, as the curtain falls, there is a ghastly applause. The creatures have come alive, and they prove to be most disagreeable. They want to find hotels to stay at. Thwarted, they turn ugly. Finally, they are locked in a back room, but not without a scuffle. It is the sort of nightmare that might have occurred to a high-strung child, perhaps to Nesbit herself. And one must remember that a nightmare was a serious matter for a child who had no electric light to switch on when a bad dream awakened him; he was forced to continue in darkness, the menacing shadows undispelled.

My own favorites among Nesbit's work are *The House of Arden* and *Harding's Luck*, two books that comprise a sort of diptych, one telling much the same story as the second, yet from a different point of view. The mood is somewhere between that of *The Enchanted Castle* and of the *Five Children*, not midnight yet hardly morning. Richard Harding, a crippled boy, accompanies an old tramp about England. The Dickensian note is struck but without the master's sentimentality. Through magic, Harding is able to go into the past where he is Sir Richard Harding in the age of Henry VIII, and not lame. But loyalty to the tramp makes him return to the present. Finally he elects to remain in the past. Meanwhile in *The House of Arden* a contemporary boy, Edred, must be tested before he can become Lord Arden and restore the family fortunes. He meets the Mouldiwarp (a mole who appears on the family coat of arms). This magic creature can be summoned only by poetry, freshly composed in its honor—a considerable strain on Edred and his sister Elfrida, who have not the gift. There are adventures in the past and the present, and the story of Richard Harding crosses their own. The magic comes and goes in a most interesting way.

As a woman, E. Nesbit was not to everyone's taste. H. G. Wells described her and Hubert Bland as "fundamentally intricate," adding that whenever the Blands attended meetings of the Fabian Society "anonymous letters flitted about like bats at twilight" (the Nesbit mood if not style is contagious). Yet there is no doubt that she was extraordinary. Wanting to be a serious poet, she became of necessity a writer of children's books. But though she disdained her true gift, she was peculiarly suited by nature to be what in fact she was. As an adult writing of her own childhood, she noted, "When I was a little child I used to pray fervently, fearfully, that when I should be grown up I might never forget what I thought and felt and suffered then." With extraordinary perceptiveness, she realized that each grown-up must kill the child he was before he himself can live. Nesbit's vow to survive somehow in the enemy's consciousness became, finally, her art — when this you see remember me — and the child continued to the end of the adult's life.

E. Nesbit's failure in the United States is not entirely mysterious. We have always preferred how-to-do to let's-imagine-that. As a result, in the last fifty years we have contributed relatively little in the way of new ideas of any sort. From radar to rocketry, we have had to rely on other societies for theory and invention. Our great contribution has been, characteristically, the assembly line.

I do not think it is putting the case too strongly to say that much of the poverty of our society's intellectual life is directly due to the sort of books children are encouraged to read. Practical books with facts in them may be necessary, but they are not everything. They do not serve the imagination in the same way that high invention does when it allows the mind to investigate *every* possibility, to set itself free from the ordinary, to enter a world where paradox reigns and nothing is what it seems. Properly engaged, the intelligent child begins to question all presuppositions, and thinks on his own. In fact, the moment he says, "Wouldn't it be interesting if . . .?" he is on his way and his own imagination has begun to work at a level considerably more interesting than the usual speculation on what it will be like to own a car and make money. As it is, the absence of imagination is cruelly noticeable at every level of the American society, and though a reading of E. Nesbit is hardly going to change the pattern of a nation, there is some evidence that the child who reads her will never be quite the same again, and that is probably a good thing.

[*New York Review of Books*, December 3, 1964]

The Waking Dream: Tarzan Revisited

THERE are so many things the people who take polls never get around to asking. Fascinated as we all are to know what our countrymen think of great issues (approving, disapproving, don't-knowing, with that native shrewdness which made a primeval wilderness bloom with Howard Johnson signs), the pollsters never get around to asking the sort of interesting personal questions our new Romans might be able to answer knowledgeably. For instance, how many adults have an adventure serial running in their heads? How many consciously daydream, turning on a story in which the dreamer ceases to be an employee of IBM and becomes a handsome demigod moving through splendid palaces, saving maidens from monsters (or monsters from maidens: this is a jaded time). Most children tell themselves stories in which they figure as powerful figures, enjoying the pleasures not only of the adult world as they conceive it but of a world of wonders unlike dull reality. Although this sort of Mittyesque daydreaming is supposed to cease in maturity, I suggest that more adults than we suspect are bemusedly wandering about with a full Technicolor extravaganza going on in their heads. Clad in tights, rapier in hand, the daydreamers drive their Jaguars at fantastic speeds through a glittering world of adoring love objects, mingling anachronistic historic worlds with science fiction. "Captain, the time-warp's been closed! We are now trapped in a parallel world, inhabited entirely by women with three breasts!" Though from what we can gather about these imaginary worlds, they tend to be more Adlerian than Freudian: the motor drive is the desire not for sex (other briefer fantasies take care of that) but for power, for the ability to dominate one's environment through physical strength, best demonstrated in the works of Edgar Rice Burroughs, whose books are enjoying a huge revival.

When I was growing up, I read all twenty-three Tarzan books, as well as the ten Mars books. My own inner story-telling mechanism was vivid. At any one time, I had at least three serials going as well as a number of tried and true re-runs. I mined Burroughs largely for source material. When he went to the center of the earth à la Jules Verne (much too fancy a writer for one's taste), I immediately worked up a thirteen-part series, with myself as lead and various friends as guest stars. Sometimes I used the master's material, but more often I adapted it freely to suit myself. One's daydreams tended to be Tarzanish pre-puberty (physical strength and freedom) and Martian post-puberty (exotic worlds and subtle *combinazione* to be worked out). After adolescence, if one's life is sufficiently interesting, the desire to tell oneself stories diminishes. My last serial ran into sponsor trouble when I was in the Second World War, and it was never renewed.

Until recently I assumed that most people were like my-self: daydreaming ceases when the real world becomes inter-esting and reasonably manageable. Now I am not so certain. Pondering the life and success of Burroughs leads one to be-lieve that a good many people find their lives so unsatisfactory that they go right on year after year telling themselves stories in which they are able to dominate their environment in a way that is not possible in the overorganized society.

According to Edgar Rice Burroughs, "Most of the stories I wrote were the stories I told myself just before I went to sleep." He is a fascinating figure to contemplate, an archetypal

American dreamer. Born in 1875 in Chicago, he was a drifter until he was thirty-six. He served briefly in the U.S. Cavalry; then he was a gold miner in Oregon, a cowboy in Idaho, a railroad policeman in Salt Lake City; he attempted several businesses that failed. He was perfectly in the old- American grain: the man who could take on almost any job, who liked to keep moving, who tried to get rich quick but could never pull it off. And while he was drifting through the unsatisfactory real world, he consoled himself with an inner world where he was strong and handsome, adored by beautiful women and worshiped by exotic races. His principal source of fantasy was Rider Haggard. But even that rich field was limited, and so, searching for new veins to tap, he took to reading the pulp magazines, only to find that none of the stories could compare for excitement with his own imaginings. Since the magazine writers could not please him, he had no choice but to please himself, and the public. He composed a serial about Mars and sold it to *Munsey's*. The rest was easy, for his fellow daydreamers recognized at once a master dreamer.

In 1914 Burroughs published *Tarzan of the Apes* (Rousseau's noble savage reborn in Africa), and history was made. To date the Tarzan books have sold over twenty-five million copies in fifty-six languages. There is hardly an American male of my generation who has not at one time or another tried to master the victory cry of the great ape as it issued from the androgynous chest of Johnny Weissmuller, to the accompaniment of thousands of arms and legs snapping during attempts to swing from tree to tree in the backyards of the Republic. Between 1914 and his death in 1950, the squire of Tarzana, California (a prophet more than honored in his own land), produced over sixty books, while enjoying the unique status of being the first American writer to be a corporation. Burroughs is said to have been a pleasant, unpretentious man

who liked to ride and play golf. Not one to compromise a
vivid unconscious with dim reality, he never set foot in Africa.

With a sense of recapturing childhood, I have just reread
several Tarzan books. It is fascinating to see how much one
recalls after a quarter century. At times the sense of *déjà vu*
is overpowering. It is equally interesting to discover that one's
memories of Tarzan of the Apes are mostly action scenes. The
plot had slipped one's mind . . . and a lot of plot there is.
The beginning is worthy of Conrad. "I had this story from one
who had no business to tell it to me, or to any other. I may
credit the seductive influence of an old vintage upon the narrator for the beginning of it, and my own skeptical incredul-
ity during the days that followed for the balance of the strange
tale." It is 1888. The young Lord and Lady Greystoke are
involved in a ship mutiny ("there was in the whole atmosphere
of the craft that undefinable something which presages disaster"). The peer and peeress are put ashore on the west coast
of Africa, where they promptly build a tree house. Here Burroughs is at his best. He tells you the size of the logs, the way
to hang a door when you have no hinges, the problems of
roofing. One of the best things about his books is the descriptions of making things. The Greystokes have a child, and
conveniently die. The "man-child" is discovered by Kala, a
Great Ape, who brings him up as a member of her tribe. As
anthropologist, Burroughs is pleasantly vague. His apes are
carnivorous, and they are able, he darkly suspects, to mate
with human beings.

Tarzan grows up as an ape, kills his first lion (with a full
nelson), teaches himself to read and write English by studying
some books found in the cabin. The method he used, sad to
say, is the currently fashionable "look-see." Though he can
read and write, he cannot speak any language except that of
the apes. He also gets on well with other members of the
animal kingdom, with Tantor the elephant, Ska the vulture,

Numa the lion (Kipling is among those whose grist found its way to the Burroughs dream mill). Then white folks arrive: Professor Archimedes Q. Porter and his daughter Jane. Also, a Frenchman named D'Arnot who teaches Tarzan to speak French, which is confusing. By an extraordinary coincidence, Jane's suitor is the current Lord Greystoke, who thinks the Greystoke baby is dead. Tarzan saves Jane from an ape. Then he puts on clothes and goes to Paris, where he drinks absinthe. Next stop, America. In Wisconsin, he saves Jane Porter from a forest fire: only to give her up nobly to Lord Greystoke, not revealing the fact that *he* is the real Lord Greystoke. Fortunately in the next volume, *The Return of Tarzan*, he marries Jane and they live happily ever after in Africa, raising a son John, who in turn grows up and has a son. Yet even as a grandfather, Tarzan continues to have adventures with people a foot high, with descendants of Atlantis, with the heirs of a Roman legion who think that Rome is still a success. All through these stories one gets the sense that one is daydreaming, too. Episode follows episode with no particular urgency. Tarzan is always knocked on the head and taken captive; he always escapes; there is always a beautiful princess or high priestess who loves him and assists him; there is always a loyal friend who fights beside him, very much in that Queequeg tradition which, Professor Leslie Fiedler assures us, is the urning in the fuel supply of the American psyche. But no matter how difficult the adventure, Tarzan, clad only in a loincloth with no weapon save a knife (the style is comforting to imitate), wins against all odds and returns to his shadowy wife.

Stylistically, Burroughs is — how shall I put it? — uneven. He has moments of ornate pomp, when the darkness is "Cimmerian"; of redundancy, "she was hideous and ugly"; of extraordinary dialogue: "Name of a name," shrieked Rokoff. "Pig, but you shall die for this!" Or Lady Greystoke to Lord G.: "Duty is duty, my husband, and no amount of sophistries may change it. I would be a poor wife for an Eng-

lish lord were I to be responsible for his shirking a plain duty."
Or the grandchild: "Muvver," he cried, "Dackie doe? Dackie
doe?" "Let him come along," urged Tarzan. "Dare!" exclaimed
the boy, turning triumphantly upon the governess, "Dackie do
doe yalk!" Burroughs's use of coincidence is shameless even
for a pulp writer. In one book he has three sets of characters
shipwrecked at exactly the same point on the shore of Africa.
Even Burroughs finds this a bit much. "Could it be possible
[muses Tarzan] that fate had thrown him up at the very thresh-
old of his own beloved jungle?" It was possible since anything can happen in a daydream.

Though Burroughs is innocent of literature and cannot reproduce human speech, he does have a gift very few writers
of any kind possess: he can describe action vividly. I give away
no trade secrets when I say that this is as difficult for a
Tolstoi as it is for a Burroughs (even William). Because it is
so hard, the craftier contemporary novelists usually prefer to
tell their stories in the first person, which is simply writing
dialogue. In character, as it were, the writer settles for an
impression of what happened rather than creating the sense of
the thing happening. In action Tarzan is excellent.

There is something basic in the appeal of the 1914 Tarzan
which makes me think that he can still hold his own as a daydream figure, despite the sophisticated challenge of his two
young competitors, James Bond and Mike Hammer. For most
adults, Tarzan (and John Carter of Mars) can hardly compete with the conspicuous consumer consumption of James
Bond or the sickly violence of Mike Hammer, but for children
and adolescents the old appeal continues. All of us need the
idea of a world alternative to this one. From Plato's Republic
to Opar to Bondland, at every level, the human imagination
has tried to imagine something better for itself than the existing society. Man left Eden when he got up off all fours, en-
dowing his descendants with nostalgia as well as chronic
backache. In its naïve way, the Tarzan legend returns us to

that Eden where, free of clothes and the inhibitions of an oppressive society, a man is able, as William Faulkner put it in his high Confederate style, to prevail as well as endure. The current fascination with LSD and nonaddictive drugs—not to mention alcohol—is all a result of a general sense of boredom. Since the individual's desire to dominate his environment is not a desirable trait in a society that every day grows more and more confining, the average man must take to daydreaming. James Bond, Mike Hammer, and Tarzan are all dream selves, and the aim of each is to establish personal primacy in a world that, more and more, diminishes the individual. Among adults, the current popularity of these lively fictions strikes me as a most significant and unbearably sad phenomenon.

[*Esquire,* December 1963]

Notes on Pornography

THE man and the woman make love; attain climax; fall separate. Then she whispers, "I'll tell you who I was thinking of if you'll tell me who you were thinking of." Like most sex jokes, the origins of this pleasant exchange are obscure. But whatever the source, it seldom fails to evoke a certain awful recognition, since few lovers are willing to admit that in the sexual act to create or maintain excitement they may need some mental image as erotic supplement to the body in attendance. One perverse contemporary maintains that when he is with A he thinks of B and when he is with B he thinks of A; each attracts him only to the degree that he is able simultaneously to evoke the image of the other. Also, for those who find the classic positions of "mature" lovemaking unsatisfactory yet dare not distress the beloved with odd requests, sexual fantasy becomes inevitable and the shy lover soon finds himself imposing mentally all sorts of wild images upon his unsuspecting partner, who may also be relying on an inner theater of the mind to keep things going; in which case, those popular writers who deplore "our lack of communication today" may have a point. Ritual and magic also have their devotees. In one of Kingsley Amis's fictions, a man mentally conjugates Latin verbs in order to delay orgasm as he waits chivalrously for his partner's predictably slow response. While another considerate lover (nonfictional) can only reduce tempo by thinking of a large loaf of sliced white bread, manufactured by Bond.

Sexual fantasy is as old as civilization (as opposed to as old as the race), and one of its outward and visible signs is pornographic literature, an entirely middle-class phenomenon, since we are assured by many investigators (Kinsey, Pomeroy, et al.) that the lower orders seldom rely upon sexual fantasy for extra-stimulus. As soon as possible, the uneducated man goes for the real thing. Consequently he seldom masturbates, but when he does he thinks, we are told, of *nothing at all*. This may be the last meaningful class distinction in the West. Nevertheless, the sex-in-the-head middle classes that D. H. Lawrence so despised are not the way they are because they want deliberately to be cerebral and anti-life; rather they are innocent victims of necessity and tribal law. For economic reasons they must delay marriage as long as possible. For tribal reasons they are taught that sex outside marriage is wrong. Consequently the man whose first contact with a woman occurs when he is twenty will have spent, ideally, the sexually most vigorous period of his life masturbating. Not unnaturally, in order to make that solitary act meaningful, the theater of his mind early becomes a Dionysian festival, and should he be a resourceful dramatist he may find actual love-making disappointing when he finally gets to it, as Bernard Shaw did. One wonders whether Shaw would have been a dramatist at all if he had first made love to a girl at fourteen, as nature intended, instead of at twenty-nine, as class required. Here, incidentally, is a whole new line of literary-psychological inquiry suitable for the master's degree: "Characteristics of the Onanist as Dramatist." Late coupling and prolonged chastity certainly help explain much of the rich dottiness of those Victorians whose peculiar habits planted thick many a quiet churchyard with Rose La Touches.

Until recently, pornography was a small cottage industry among the grinding mills of literature. But now that sex has taken the place of most other games (how many young people today learn bridge?), creating and packaging pornography has become big business, and though the high courts of the new American Empire cannot be said to be very happy about this state of affairs, they tend to agree that freedom of expression is as essential to our national life as freedom of meaningful political action is not. Also, despite our governors' paternalistic bias, there are signs that they are becoming less intolerant in sexual matters. This would be a good thing if one did not suspect that they may regard sex as our bread and circuses, a means of keeping us off the political streets, and in bed out of mischief. If this is so, we may yet observe President Johnson in his mad search for consensus settling for the consensual.

Among the publishers of pornography ("merchants of smut," as they say at the FBI), Maurice Girodias is uniquely eminent. For one thing, he is a second-generation peddler of dirty books (or "d.b.s," as they call them on Eighth Avenue). In the 1930's his English father, Jack Kahane, founded the Obelisk Press in Paris. Among Kahane's authors were Anaïs Nin, Lawrence Durrell, Cyril Connolly, and of course Henry Miller, whose books have been underground favorites for what seems like a century. Kahane died in 1939 and his son, Maurice Girodias (he took his mother's name for reasons not given), continued Kahane's brave work. After the war, Girodias sold Henry Miller in vast quantities to easily stimulated GIs. He also revived *Fanny Hill*. He published books in French. He prospered. Then the Terror began. Visionary dictatorships, whether of a single man or of the proletariat, tend to disapprove of irregular sex. Being profoundly immoral in public matters, dictators compensate by insisting upon what they think to be a rigorous morality in private affairs. General de Gaulle's private morality appears to be registered in his wife's name. In 1946 Girodias was prosecuted for publishing Henry Miller. It was France's first prosecution for obscenity since the trial of *Madame Bovary* in 1844. Happily, the world's writers rallied to Miller's defense, and since men of letters are taken solemnly in France, the government dropped its charges.

In a preface to the recently published *The Olympia Reader*, Girodias discusses his business arrangements at length; and though none of us is as candid about money as he is about sex, Girodias does admit that he lost his firm not as a result of legal persecution but through incompetence, a revelation that gives him avant-garde status in the new pornography of money. Girodias next founded the Olympia Press, devoted to the creation of pornography, both hard and soft core. His adventures as a merchant of smut make a most beguiling story. All sorts of writers, good and bad, were set to work turning out books, often written to order. He would think up a title (e.g., *With Open Mouth*) and advertise it; if there was sufficient response, he would then commission someone to write a book to go with the title. Most of his writers used pseudonyms. Terry Southern and Mason Hoffenberg wrote *Candy* under the name of Maxwell Kenton. Christopher Logue wrote *Lust* under the name of Count Palmiro Vicarion, while Alex Trocchi, as Miss Frances Lengel, wrote *Helen and Desire*. Girodias also published Samuel Beckett's *Watt*, Vladimir Nabokov's *Lolita*, and J. P. Donleavy's *The Ginger Man*; perversely, the last three authors chose not to use pseudonyms.

Reading of these happy years, one recalls a similar situation just after the Second War when a number of New York writers were commissioned at so many cents a page to write pornographic stories for a United States Senator. The solon, as they say in smutland, never actually met the writers but through a go-between he guided their stories: a bit more flagellation here, a touch of necrophilia there . . . The subsequent nervous breakdown of one of the Senator's pornographers, now a celebrated poet, was attributed to the strain of not knowing which of the ninety-six Senators he was writing for.

In 1958 the Fourth French Republic banned twenty-five of Girodias's books, among them *Lolita*. Girodias promptly sued the Ministry of the Interior and, amazingly, won. Unfortunately, five months later, the Great General saw fit to resume the grandeur of France. De Gaulle was back; and so was Madame de Gaulle. The Minister of the Interior appealed the now defunct Fourth Republic's decision and was upheld. Since then, censorship has been the rule in France. One by one Girodias's books, regardless of merit, have been banned. Inevitably, André Malraux was appealed to and, inevitably, he responded with that elevated double-talk which has been a characteristic of what one suspects will be a short-lived Republic. Girodias is currently in the United States, where he expects to flourish. Ever since our Puritan republic became a gaudy empire, pornography has been a big business for the simple reason that when freedom of expression is joined with the freedom to make a lot of money, the dream of those whose bloody footprints made vivid the snows of Valley Forge is close to fulfillment and that happiness which our Constitution commands us to pursue at hand.

The Olympia Reader is a collection of passages from various books published by Maurice Girodias since 1953. Reading it straight through is a curiously disjointed experience, like sitting through a program of movie trailers. As literature, most of the selections are junk, despite the presence of such celebrated contemporary figures as Nabokov, Genet and Queneau; and of the illustrious dead, Sade and Beardsley.

Pornography is usually defined as that which is calculated to arouse sexual excitement. Since what arouses X repels Y, no two people are apt to respond in quite the same way to the same stimulus. One man's meat, as they say, is another man's poison, a fact now recognized by the American judiciary, which must rule with wearisome frequency on obscenity. With unexpected good sense, a judge recently observed that since the books currently before him all involved ladies in black leather with whips, they could not be said to corrupt the generality, since a taste for being beaten is hardly common and those who are aroused by such fantasies are already "corrupted" and therefore exempt from laws designed to protect the young and usual. By their nature, pornographies cannot be said to proselytize, since they are written for the already hooked. The worst that can be said of pornography is that it leads not to "antisocial" sexual acts but to the reading of more pornography. As for corruption, the only immediate victim is English prose. Mr. Girodias himself writes like his worst authors ("Terry being at the time in acute financial need . . .") while his moral judgments are most peculiar. With reverence, he describes his hero Sir Roger Casement (a "superlative pederast," whatever that is) as "politically confused, emotionally unbalanced, maudlin when depressed and absurdly naïve when in his best form; but he was exceptionally generous, he had extraordinary courage and a simple human wisdom which sprang from his natural goodness." Here, Mr. Girodias demonstrates a harmony with the age in which he lives. He may or may not have described Sir Roger accurately, but he has certainly drawn a flattering portrait of the Serious American Novelist, 1966.

Of the forty selections Mr. Girodias has seen fit to collect, at least half are meant to be literature in the most ambitious sense, and to the extent that they succeed, they disappoint; Beckett's *Watt*, Queneau's *Zazie*, Donleavy's *The Ginger Man* are incapable of summoning up so much as the ghost of a rose, to appropriate Sir Thomas Browne's handsome phrase. There is also a good deal of Henry Miller, whose reputation as a pornographer is largely undeserved. Though he writes a lot about sex, the only object he seems ever to describe is his own phallus. As a result, unless one lusts specifically for the flesh of Henry Miller, his works cannot be regarded as truly edifying. Yet at Miller's best he makes one irritably conscious of what it is like to be inside his skin, no mean feat . . . the pornographic style, incidentally, is contagious: the stately platitude, the arch paraphrase, the innocent line which starts suddenly to buck with unintended double meanings.

Like the perfect host or madam, Mr. Girodias has tried to provide something for everyone. Naturally there is a good deal of straightforward heterosexual goings-on. Mr. Girodias gives us several examples, usually involving the seduction of an adolescent male by an older woman. For female masochists (and male sadists) he gives us *Story of O*. For homosexual sadists (and masochists) *The Gaudy Image*. For negrophiles (and phobes) *Pinktoes*, whose eloquent author, Chester Himes, new to me, has a sense of humor that sinks his work like a stone. For anal eroticists who like science fiction there are passages from William Burroughs's *Naked Lunch* and *The Soft Machine*, works that have appealed to Mary McCarthy. For devotees of camp, new to the scene, the thirty-three-year-old *The Young and Evil* by Charles Henri Ford and Parker Tyler is a pioneer work and reads surprisingly well today. Parenthetically, it is interesting to note the role that clothes play in most of these works, camp, kinky, and straight. Obviously, if there is to be something for everyone, the thoughtful entrepreneur must occasionally provide an old sock or pair of panties for the fetishist to get, as it were, his teeth into. But even writers not aiming at the fetishist audience make much of the ritual taking off and putting on of clothes, and it is significant that the bodies thus revealed are seldom described as meticulously as the clothes are.

Even Jean Genet, always lyric and vague when celebrating cock, becomes unusually naturalistic and detailed when he describes clothes in an excerpt from *The Thieves' Journal*. Apparently when he was a boy in Spain a lover made him dress up as a girl. The experiment was a failure because "Taste is required . . . I was already refusing to have any. I forbade myself to. Of course I would have shown a great deal of it." Nevertheless, despite an inadequate clothes sense, he still tells us far more about the *travesti manqué* than he ever tells us about the body of Stilitano for whom he lusted.

In most pornography, physical descriptions tend to be sketchy. Hard-core pornographers seldom particularize. Inevitably, genitals are massive, but since we never get a good look at the bodies to which they are attached, the effect is so impersonal that one soon longs to read about those more modest yet entirely tangible archetypes, the girl and boy next door, two creatures far more apt to figure in the heated theater of the mind than the voluptuous grotesques of the pulp writer's imagination. Yet by abstracting character and by keeping his human creatures faceless and vague, the pornographer does force the reader to draw upon personal experience in order to fill in the details, thereby achieving one of the ends of all literary art, that of making the reader collaborator.

As usual, it is the Marquis de Sade (here represented by a section from *Justine*) who has the most to say about sex — or rather the use of others as objects for one's own pleasure, preferably at the expense of theirs. In true eighteenth-century fashion, he explains and explains and explains. There is no God, only Nature, which is heedless of the Good as well as of the Bad. Since Nature requires that the strong violate the weak and since it is demonstrably true that Nature made women weak and men strong, therefore . . . and so on. The Marquis's vision — of which so much has been made in this century — is nothing but a rather simple-minded Manicheism, presented with more passion than logic. Yet in his endless self-justification (un-Natural this: Nature never apologizes, never explains) Sade's tirades often strike the Marlovian note: "It is Nature that I wish to outrage. I should like to spoil her plans, to block her advance, to halt the course of the stars, to throw down the globes that float in space — to destroy everything that serves her, to protect everything that harms her, to cultivate everything that irritates her — in a word to insult all her works." But he stops considerably short of his mark. He not only refused to destroy one of her more diverting creations, himself, but he also opposed capital punishment. Even for a French *philosophe*, Sade is remarkably inconsistent, which is why one prefers his letters to his formal argument. Off duty he is more natural and less Natural. While in the Bastille he described himself as possessing an "extreme tendency in everything to lose control of myself, a disordered imagination in sexual matters such as has never been known in this world, an atheist to the point of fanaticism — in two words there I am, and so once again kill me or take me like that, because I shall never change." Latter-day diabolists have tried to make of his "disordered imagination in sexual matters" a religion and, as religions go, it is no more absurd than that of the crucified tripartite man-god. But though Nature is indeed nonhuman and we are without significance except to ourselves, to make of that same indifferent Nature an ally in behavior which is, simply, harmful to human society is to be singularly vicious.

Yet it is interesting to note that throughout all pornography, one theme recurs: the man or woman who manages to capture another human being for use as an unwilling sexual object. Obviously this is one of the commonest of masturbatory daydreams. Sade's originality was to try, deliberately, to make his fantasies real. But he was no Gilles de Rais. He lacked the organizational sense, and his actual adventures were probably closer to farce than to tragedy, more Charlie Chaplin trying to drown Martha Raye than Ilse Koch castrating her paramours at Buchenwald. Incidentally, it is typical of our period that the makers of the play *Marat/Sade* were much admired for having perversely reduced a splendid comic idea to mere tragedy.

Mr. Girodias's sampler should provide future sociologists with a fair idea of what sex was like at the dawn of the age of science. They will no doubt be as amused as most of us are depressed by the extent to which superstition has perverted human nature (not to mention thwarted Nature). Officially the tribal norm continues. The family is the central unit of society. Man's function is to impregnate woman in order to make children. Any sexual act that does not lead to the making of a child is untribal, which is to say antisocial. But though these assumptions are still held by the mass of human society in the West, the pornographers by what they write (as well as by what they omit to mention) show that in actual fact the old laws are not only broken (as always) but are being questioned in a new way.

Until this generation, even nonreligious enemies of irregular sexuality could sensibly argue that promiscuity was bad because it led to venereal disease and to the making of unwanted babies. In addition, sex was a dirty business since bodies stank and why should any truly fastidious person want to compound the filth of his own body's corruption with that of another? Now science has changed all that. Venereal disease has been contained. Babies need not be the result of the sexual act ("I feel so happy and safe now I take the pill"), while improved bathing facilities together with the American Mom's relentless circumcision of boys has made the average human body a temptingly hygienic contraption suitable for all sorts of experiment. To which the moralists can only respond: Rome born again! Sexual license and excessive bathing, as everyone knows, made the Romans effete and unable to stand up to the stalwart puritan savages from the German forests whose sacred mission was to destroy a world gone rotten. This simplistic view of history is a popular one, particularly among those who do not read history. Yet there *is* a basic point at issue and one that should be pondered.

Our tribal standards are an uneasy combination of Mosaic law and the warrior sense of caste that characterized those savage tribesmen who did indeed engulf the world of cities. The contempt for people in trade one still finds amongst the Wasp aristocracy, the sense of honor (furtive but gnawing), the pride in family, the loyalty to class, and (though covert) the admiration for the military virtues and physical strength are all inherited not from our civilized predecessors who lived in the great cities but from their conquerors, the wandering tribesmen, who planted no grain, built no cities, conducted no trade, yet preyed successfully upon those who did these contemptible, unmanly things. Today of course we are all as mixed in values as in blood, but the unstated assumption that it is better to be physically strong than wise, violent than gentle, continent than sensual, landowner or coupon clipper than shopkeeper, lingers on as a memorial to those marauding tribes who broke into history at the start of the Bronze Age and whose values are with us still, as the Gallup Poll attested recently, when it revealed that the President's war in Vietnam is most popular in the South, the most "tribal" part of the United States. Yet the city is the glory of our race, and today in the West, though we are all city dwellers, we still accept as the true virtue the code of our wild conquerors, even though our actual lives do not conform to their laws, nor should they, nor should we feel guilty because they don't.

In ten thousand years we have learned how to lengthen human lives but we have found no way to delay human puberty. As a result, between the economics of the city and the taboos of the tribe we have created a monstrous sexual ethic. To mention the most notorious paradox: It is not economically convenient for the adolescent to marry; it is not tribally correct for him to have sex outside of marriage. Solutions to this man-made problem range from insistence upon total chastity to a vague permissiveness which, worriedly, allows some sexuality if those involved are "sincere" and "mature" and "loving." Until this generation, tribal moralists could argue with perfect conviction that there was only one correct sexual equation: man plus woman equals baby. All else was vice. But now that half the world lives with famine — and all the world by the year 2000, if Pope Paul's as yet unborn guests are allowed to attend (in his unhappy phrase) the "banquet of life," the old equation has been changed to read: man plus woman equals baby equals famine. If the human race is to survive, population will have to be reduced drastically, if not by atomic war then by law, an unhappy prospect for civil liberties but better than starving. In any case, it is no longer possible to maintain that those sexual acts which do not create (or simulate the creation of) a child are unnatural; unless, to strike the eschatological note, it is indeed Nature's will that we perish through overpopulation, in which case reliable hands again clutch the keys of Peter.

Fortunately, the pornographers appear to be on the side of survival. They make nothing of virginity deflowered, an important theme for two thousand years; they make nothing of it for the simple reason we make little of it. Straightforward adultery no longer fascinates the pornographer; the scarlet letter has faded. Incest, mysteriously, seldom figures in current pornographies. This is odd. The tribal taboo remains as strong as ever, even though we now know that when members of the same family mate the result is seldom more cretinous or more sickly than its parents. The decline of incest as a marketable theme is probably due to today's inadequate middle-class housing. In large Victorian houses with many rooms and heavy doors, the occupants could be mysterious and exciting to one another in a way that those who live in rackety developments can never hope to be. Not even the lust of a Lord Byron could survive the fact of Levittown.

Homosexuality is now taken entirely for granted by pornographers because we take it for granted. Yet though there is considerable awareness nowadays of what people actually do, the ancient somewhat ambivalent hostility of the tribe persists; witness *Time* magazine's recent diagnosis of homosexuality as a "pernicious sickness" like influenza or opposing the war in Vietnam. Yet from the beginning, tribal attitudes have been confused on this subject. On the one hand, nothing must be allowed to deflect man the father from his procreative duty. On the other hand, man the warrior is more apt than not to perform homosexual acts. What was undesirable in peace was often a virtue in war, as the Spartans recognized, inventing the buddy system at the expense of the family unit. In general, it would seem that the more warlike the tribe, the more opportunistic the sexual response. "You know where you can find your sex," said that sly chieftain Frederick the Great to his officers, "—in the barracks." Of all the tribes, significantly, the Jews alone were consistently opposed not only to homosexuality but to any acknowledgment of the male as an erotic figure (cf. II Maccabees 4:7–15). But in the great world of pre-Christian cities, it never occurred to anyone that a homosexual act was less "natural" than a heterosexual one. It was simply a matter of taste. From Archilochus to Apuleius, this acceptance of the way people actually are is implicit in what the writers wrote. Suetonius records that of his twelve emperors, eleven went with equal ease from boys to girls and back again without Suetonius ever finding anything remarkable in their "polymorphous perverse" behavior. But all that, as Stanley Kauffmann would say, happened in a "different context."

Nevertheless, despite contexts, we are bisexual. Opportunity and habit incline us toward this or that sexual object. Since additional children are no longer needed, it is impossible to say that some acts are "right" and others "wrong." Certainly to maintain that a homosexual act in itself is antisocial or neurotic is dangerous nonsense, of the sort that the astonishing Dr. Edmund Bergler used to purvey when he claimed that he would "cure" homosexuals, as if this was somehow desirable, like changing Jewish noses or straightening Negro hair in order to make it possible for those who have been so altered to pass more easily through a world of white Christians with snub noses.

Happily, in a single generation, science has changed many

old assumptions. Economics has changed others. A woman can now easily support herself, independent of a man. With the slamming of Nora's door, the family ceased to be the inevitable social unit. Also, the newly affluent middle class can now pursue other pleasures. In the film *The Collector*, a lower-class boy captures an educated girl and after alternately tormenting and boring her, he says balefully, "If more people had more time and money, there would be a lot more of this." This got an unintended laugh in the theater, but he is probably right. Sexual experiment is becoming more open. A placid Midwestern town was recently appalled to learn that its young married set was systematically swapping wives. In the cities, group sex is popular, particularly among the young. Yet despite the new freedoms that the pornographers reflect (sadly for them, since their craft must ultimately wither away), the world they show, though closer to human reality than that of the tribalists, reveals a new illness: the powerlessness that most people feel in an overpopulated and overorganized society. The sado-masochist books that dominate this year's pornography are not the result of a new enthusiasm for the *vice anglais* so much as a symptom of helplessness in a society where most of the male's aggressive-creative drive is thwarted. The will to prevail is a powerful one, and if it is not fulfilled in work or in battle, it may find an outlet in sex. The man who wants to act out fantasies of tying up or being tied up is imposing upon his sex life a power drive which became socially undesirable once he got onto that escalator at IBM which will take him by predictable stages to early retirement and the medically prolonged boredom of sunset years. Solution of this problem will not be easy, to say the least.

Meanwhile, effort must be made to bring what we think about sex and what we say about sex and what we do about sex into some kind of realistic relationship. Indirectly, the pornographers do this. They recognize that the only sexual norm is that there is none. Therefore, in a civilized society law should not function at all in the area of sex except to protect people from being "interfered with" against their will.

Unfortunately, even the most enlightened of the American state codes (Illinois) still assumes that since adultery is a tribal sin it must be regarded as a civil crime. It is not, and neither is prostitution, that most useful of human institutions. Traditionally, liberals have opposed prostitution on the ground that no one ought to be forced to sell his body because of poverty. Yet in our Affluency, prostitution continues to flourish for the simple reason that it is needed. If most men and women were forced to rely upon physical charm to attract lovers, their sexual lives would be not only meager but in a youth-worshiping country like America painfully brief. Recognizing this state of affairs, a Swedish psychologist recently proposed state brothels for women as well as for men, in recognition of the sad biological fact that the middle-aged woman is at her sexual peak at a time when she is no longer able to compete successfully with younger women. As for the prostitutes themselves, they practice an art as legitimate as any other, somewhere between that of masseur and psychiatrist. The best are natural healers and, contrary to tribal superstition, they often enjoy their work. It is to the credit of today's pornographer that intentionally or not, he is the one who tells us most about the extraordinary variety of human sexual response. In his way he shows us as we are, rather like those Fun House mirrors which, even as they distort and mock the human figure, never cease to reflect the real thing.

[*New York Review of Books,* March 31, 1966]

Sex and the Law

IN 1963 H. L. A. Hart, Oxford Professor of Jurisprudence, gave three lectures at Stanford University. In these lectures (published by the Stanford University Press as *Law, Liberty and Morality*) Professor Hart attempted to answer an old question: Is the fact that certain conduct is by common standards immoral a sufficient cause to punish that conduct by law? A question which leads him to what might be a paradox: "Is it morally permissible to enforce morality as such? Ought immorality as such to be a crime?" Philosophically, Professor Hart inclines to John Stuart Mill's celebrated negative. In *On Liberty*, Mill wrote, "The only purpose for which power can rightfully be exercised over any member of a civilized community against his will is to prevent harm to others"; and to forestall the arguments of the paternally minded, Mill added that a man's own good, either physical or moral, is not sufficient warrant. He cannot rightfully be compelled to do or forbear because it will be better for him to do so, because it will make him happier, because in the opinions of others, to do so would be wise or even right.

Now it would seem that at this late date in the Anglo-American society, the question of morality and its relation to the law has been pretty much decided. In general practice, if not in particular statute, our society tends to keep a proper distance between the two. Yet national crisis may, on occasion, bring out the worst in the citizenry. While our boys were Over There, a working majority of the Congress decided that drink was not only bad for morals but bad for health. The result was Prohibition. After a dozen years of living with the Great Experiment, the electorate finally realized that moral legislation on such a scale is impossible to enforce. A lesson was learned and one would have thought it unlikely that the forces which created the Volstead Act could ever again achieve a majority. But today strange things are happening in the American Empire, as well as in the Kingdom across the water where Professor Hart detects a revival of what he calls "legal moralism," and he finds alarming certain recent developments.

In the days of the Star Chamber, to conspire to corrupt public morals was a common-law offense. Needless to say, this vague catchall turned out to be a marvelous instrument of tyranny and it was not entirely abandoned in England until the eighteenth century. Now it has been suddenly revived as a result of the 1961 case *Shaw* v. *Director of Public Prosecutions*. Shaw was an enterprising pimp who published a magazine called *Ladies Directory*, which was just that. Despite this useful contribution to the gallantry of England, Shaw was found guilty of three offenses: publishing an obscene article, living on the earnings of prostitutes, and conspiring to corrupt public morals. The last offense delighted the legal moralists. There was much satisfied echoing of the eighteenth-century Lord Mansfield's statement, "Whatever is *contra bonos mores et decorum* the principles of our laws prohibit and the King's Court as the general censor and guardian of the public morals is bound to restrain and punish." As a result of the decision against Mr. Shaw, the possibilities of banning a book like *Lady Chatterley's Lover* on the imprecise grounds that it will corrupt public morals (themselves ill-defined) are endless and alarming. Though various American states still retain "conspiring to corrupt" statutes, they are largely cherished as relics of our legal origins in the theocratic code of Oliver Cromwell. The last serious invoking of this principle occurred in 1935 when the Nazis solemnly determined that anything was punishable if it was deserving of punishment according "to the fundamental conceptions of penal law and sound popular feeling."

Defining immorality is of course not an easy task, though English judges and American state legislatures seem not to mind taking it on. Lord Devlin, a leader of the legal moralists, has said that "the function of the criminal law is to enforce a moral principle and nothing else." How does Lord Devlin arrive at a moral principle? He appeals to the past. What is generally said to be wrong is wrong, while "a recognized morality is as necessary to society's existence as a recognized government." Good. But Lord Devlin does not acknowledge that there is always a considerable gap between what is officially recognized as good behavior and what is in actual fact countenanced and practiced. Though adultery in England is thought to be morally wrong, there are no statutes under which a man may be punished for sleeping with someone else's wife. Adultery is not a legal offense, nor does it presumably arouse in the public "intolerance, indignation, and disgust," the three emotions which Lord Devlin insists are inevitably evoked by those acts which offend the accepted morality. Whenever this triad is present, the law must punish. Yet how is one to measure "intolerance, indignation, and disgust"? Without an appeal to Dr. Gallup, it would be difficult to decide what, if anything, the general public really thinks about these matters. Without a referendum, it is anyone's guess to what degree promiscuity, say, arouses disgust in the public. Of course Lord Devlin is not really arguing for this sort of democracy. His sense of right and wrong is based on what he was brought up to believe was right and wrong, as prescribed by church and custom.

In the realm of sexual morals, all things take on a twilight shade. Off and on for centuries, homosexuality has aroused the triple demon in the eyes of many. But a majority? It would be surprising if it did, knowing what we now know about the extent — if not the quality — of human sexual behavior. In any case, why should homosexual acts between consenting adults be considered inimical to the public good? This sort of question raises much heat, and the invoking of "history." According to Lord Devlin, "the loosening of moral bonds is often the first stage of [national] disintegration." Is it? The periods in history which are most admired by legal moralists tend to be those vigorous warlike times when a nation is pursuing a successful and predatory course of military expansion, such as the adventures of the Spartans and Alexander, of Julius Caesar and Frederick of Prussia. Yet a reading of history ought to convince Lord Devlin that these militaristic societies were not only brutish and "immoral" by any standard but also startlingly homosexual. Yet what was morally desirable in a clean-limbed Spartan army officer is now punished in Leicester Square. Obviously public attitudes have changed since those vigorous days. Does that then mean that laws should alter as old prejudices are replaced by new? In response to public opinion, the Emperor Justinian made homosexuality a criminal offense on the grounds that buggery, as everyone knew, was the chief cause of earthquakes.

With the decline of Christianity, western moralists have more and more used the state to punish sin. One of Lord Devlin's allies, J. G. Stephen, in *Liberty, Equality, Fraternity,* comes straight to the point. Referring to moral offenders, he writes, "The feeling of hatred and the desire of vengeance are important elements to human nature which ought, in such cases, to be satisfied in a regular public and legal manner." There is the case not only for capital punishment but for public hangings, all in the name of the Old Testament God of vengeance. Or as Lord Goddard puts it, "I do not see how it can be either non-Christian, or other than praiseworthy, that the country should be willing to avenge crime." Yet Mr. Stephen also realizes that for practical purposes "you cannot punish anything which public opinion as expressed in the common practice of society does not strenuously and unequivocally condemn. To be able to punish a moral majority must be overwhelming." But is there such a thing as moral majority in sexual matters? Professor Hart thinks not. "The fact that there is lip service to an official sexual morality should not lead us to neglect the possibility that in sexual, as other matters, there may be a number of mutually tolerant moralities, and that even where there is some homogeneity of practice and belief, offenders may be viewed not with hatred or resentment, but with amused contempt or pity."

In the United States the laws determining correct human behavior are the work of the state legislatures. Over the years these solemn assemblies have managed to make a complete hash of things, pleasing no one. The present tangled codes go back to the founding of the country. When the Cromwells fell, the disgruntled Puritans left England for Holland, and not because they were persecuted for their religious beliefs but because they were forbidden to persecute others for *their* beliefs. Holland took them in, and promptly turned them out. Only North America was left. Here, as lords of the wilderness, they were free to create the sort of quasi-theocratic society they had dreamed of. Rigorously persecuting one another for religious heresies, witchcraft, sexual misbehavior, they formed that ugly polity whose descendants we are. As religious fundamentalists, they were irresistibly drawn to the Old Testament God at his most forbidding and cruel, while the sternness of St. Paul seemed to them far more agreeable than the occasional charity of Jesus. Since adultery was forbidden by the Seventh Commandment and fornication was condemned in two of St. Paul's memos, the Puritans made adultery and fornication criminal offenses even though no such laws existed in England, before or after Cromwell's reign. As new American states were formed, they modeled their codes on those of the original states. To this day, forty-three states will punish a single act of adulterous intercourse, while twenty-one states will punish fornication between unmarried people. In no other western country is fornication a criminal offense. As for adultery, England, Japan, and the Soviet Union have no such statutes. France and Italy will punish adultery under special conditions (e.g., if the man should establish the mistress in the family home). Germany and Switzerland punish adultery only if a court can prove that a marriage has been dissolved because of it.

In actual practice, the state laws are seldom invoked, although two hundred and forty-two Bostonians were arrested for adultery as recently as 1948. These statutes are considered "dead-letter laws" and there are those who argue that since they are so seldom invoked, why repeal them? One answer came in 1917 when a number of racketeers were arrested by the Federal government because they had taken girl friends to Florida, violating the Mann Act as well as the local fornication-adultery statutes. This case (*Caminetti* v. *U.S.*) set a dangerous precedent. Under a busy Attorney General, the "dead-letter laws" could be used to destroy all sorts of opponents, villainous or otherwise.

Rape is another offense much confused by state laws. During the thirties, out of 2,366 New York City indictments for rape, only eighteen per cent were for forcible rape. The remaining eighty-two per cent were for statutory rape, a peculiar and imprecise crime. For instance, in Colorado it is statutory rape if intercourse takes place between an unmarried girl under eighteen and a man over eighteen. In practice this means that a boy of nineteen who has an affair with a consenting girl of seventeen is guilty of statutory rape. All the girl needs to do is to accuse her lover of consensual relations and he can be imprisoned for as long as fifty years. There are thousands of "rapists" serving time because, for one reason or another, they were found guilty of sexual intercourse with a willing partner.

In nearly every state fellatio, cunnilingus, and anal intercourse are punished. Not only are these acts forbidden between men, they are forbidden between men and women,
within as well as without wedlock. As usual, the various state
laws are in wild disarray. Ohio deplores fellatio but tolerates
cunnilingus. In another state, sodomy is punished with a maximum twenty-year sentence, while fellatio calls for only three
years, a curious discrimination. Deviate sexual acts between
consenting adults are punished in most states, with sentences
running from three years to life imprisonment. Of the other
countries of the West, only the Federal German Republic
intrudes itself upon consenting adults.

Elsewhere in the field of moral legislation, twenty-seven
states forbid sexual relations and/or marriage between the
white race and its inferiors: Negroes, American Indians,
Orientals. And of course our narcotics laws are the scandal of
the world. With the passage in 1914 of the Harrison Act,
addiction to narcotics was found to be not the result of illness
or bad luck but of sin, and sin must of course be punished by
the state. For half a century the Federal government has had a
splendid time playing cops and robbers. And since you cannot
have cops without robbers, they have created the robbers by
maintaining that the sinful taking of drugs must be wiped out
by law. As a result, the government's severity boosts the price
of drugs, makes the game more desperate for addicts as well
as pushers, and encourages crime which in turn increases the
payroll of the Narcotics Bureau. This lunatic state of affairs
could exist only in a society still obsessed by the idea that the
punishing of sin is the responsibility of the state. Yet in those
countries where dope addiction is regarded as a matter for
the doctor and not the police, there can be no criminal traffic
in drugs. In all of England there are 550 drug addicts. In
New York City alone there are 23,000 addicts.

Theoretically, the American separation of church and state
should have left the individual's private life to his conscience.

But this was not to be the case. The states promptly took it upon themselves to regulate the private lives of the citizens, flouting, many lawyers believe, the spirit if not the letter of the Constitution. The result of this experiment is all around us. One in eight Americans is mentally disturbed, and everywhere psychiatry flourishes. Our per capita acts of violence are beyond anything known to the other countries of the West, making our streets unsafe for Peggy Goldwater and Mamie Eisenhower to walk. Clearly the unique attempt to make private morality answerable to law has not been a success. What to do?

On April 25, 1955, a committee of the American Law Institute presented a Model Penal Code (tentative draft No. 4) to the Institute, which was founded some forty years ago "to promote the clarification and simplification of the law and its better adaptation to social needs." This Code represented an attempt to make sense out of conflicting laws, to remove "dead-letter laws" which might, under pressure, be used for sinister ends, and to recognize that there is an area of private sexual morality which is no concern of the state. In this the Code echoed the recommendation of the British Wolfenden Report, which said: "Unless a deliberate attempt is to be made by society, acting through the agency of the law, to equate the sphere of crime with that of sin, there must remain a realm of private morality and immorality which is, in brief and crude terms, not the law's business."

The drafters of the Code proposed that adultery and sodomy between consenting adults be removed from the sphere of the law on the grounds that "the Code does not attempt to use the power of the state to enforce purely moral or religious standards. We deem it inappropriate for the government to attempt to control behavior that has no substantial significance except as to the morality of the actor. Such matters are best left to religious, educational and other influences." The Committee's recommendation on adultery was accepted. But there was a difference of opinion about sodomy. Judge John J. Parker spoke for the legal moralists: "There are many things that are denounced by the criminal civil code in order that society may know that the state disapproves. When we fly in the face of public opinion, as evidenced by the code of every state in this union, we are not proposing a code which will commend itself to the thoughtful." Judge Parker was answered by Judge Learned Hand, who said, "Criminal law which is not enforced practically is much worse than if it was not on the books at all. I think homosexuality is a matter of morals, a matter very largely of taste, and it is not a matter that people should be put in prison about." Judge Hand's position was upheld by the Institute.

As matters now stand, only the state of Illinois has attempted to modify its sex laws. As of 1962 there is no longer any penalty in Illinois for the committing of a deviate sexual act. On the other hand, an "open and notorious" adulterer can still be punished with a year in prison and fornication can be punished with six months in prison. So it is still taken for granted that the state has the right to regulate private behavior in the interest of public morality.

One postwar phenomenon has been the slowness of the liberal community to respond to those flaws in our society which might be corrected by concerted action. It is, of course, exhilarating to determine to what degree Hannah Arendt was responsible for Hitler. Yet it would seem to me that a change in the legal codes of the fifty American states might be almost as interesting an occupation for the liberally inclined as the fixing of past guilt and the analysis of old crimes. As they stand, the laws affect nearly everyone; implemented, they affect millions. Originally, the United States made a brave distinction between church and state. But then we put within the legal province of the states that which rightfully was religion's concern, and for those not susceptible to religious discipline, the concern of the moral conscience of the individual. The result has caused much suffering. The state laws are executed capriciously and though in time they may fade away, without some organized effort they could continue for generations. In fact, there are signs today that the legal conservatives are at work strengthening these laws. In Florida the administration has distributed an astonishing pamphlet denouncing homosexualists in terms of seventeenth-century grandeur. In Dallas a stripper named Candy Barr was given an unprecedented fifteen-year prison term, ostensibly because she was found with marijuana in her possession but actually because she was a sinful woman. In the words of a Dallas lawyer (Warren Leslie in *Dallas, Public and Private*), the jury was "showing the world they were in favor of God, heaven, and sending to hell-fire a girl who violated their sense of morality."

In these lowering days, there is a strong movement afoot to save society from sexual permissiveness. Guardians of the old-time virtue would maintain what they believe to be the status quo. They speak of "common decency" and "accepted opinion." But do such things really exist? And if they do, are they "right"? After all, there is no position so absurd that you cannot get a great many people to assume it. Lord Maugham, a former Lord Chancellor (where do they find them?), was convinced that the decline of the Roman Empire was the result of too frequent bathing. Justinian *knew* there was a causal link between buggery and earthquakes, while our grandparents, as Professor Steven Marcus recently reminded us, believed that masturbation caused insanity. I suspect that our own faith in psychiatry will seem as touchingly quaint to the future as our grandparents' belief in phrenology seems now to us. At any given moment, public opinion is a chaos of superstition, misinformation, and prejudice. Even if one could accurately interpret it, would that be a reason for basing the law upon a consensus?

Neither Professor Hart nor the legal moralists go that far. The conservatives are very much aware that they are living in an age of "moral decline." They wish to return to a stern morality like that of Cato or of Calvin. Failing that, they will settle for maintaining existing laws, the harsher the better. Professor Hart, on the other hand, believes that between what the law says people ought to do in their private lives and what they in fact do, there is a considerable division. To the degree that such laws ought, ideally, to conform with human practice, he is a democrat. In answering those who feel that despite what people actually do, they ought not to do it, he remarks that this may be true, yet "the use of legal punishment to freeze into immobility the morality dominant at a particular time in a society's existence may possibly succeed, but even where it does it contributes nothing to the survival of the animating spirit and formal values of social morality and may do much harm to them."

There is some evidence that by fits and starts the United States is achieving a civilization. Our record so far has not been distinguished, no doubt because we had a bad beginning. Yet it is always possible to make things better — as well as worse. Various groups are now at work trying to make sense of the fifty state codes. New York and California are expected to have improved codes by the end of this decade. But should there be a sudden renewal of legal moralism, attempts to modify and liberalize will fail. What is needed, specifically, is a test case before the Supreme Court which would establish in a single decision that "sin," where it does not disturb the public order, is not the concern of the state. This conception is implicit in our Constitution. But since it has never been tested, our laws continue to punish the sinful as though the state were still an arm of Church Militant. Although a Great Society is more easily attained in rhetoric than in fact, a good first step might be the removal from our statute books of that entirely misplaced scarlet letter.

[*Partisan Review*, Summer 1965]

The *Sexus* of Henry Miller

IN 1949 Henry Miller sent his friend Lawrence Durrell the two volumes of *Sexus* that together comprise one of the seven sections of his long-awaited masterwork, *The Rosy Crucifixion* (Rosicrucian?). The other parts are titled *Nexus*, *Plexus*, and presumably anything else that ends in "exus." Durrell's reaction to *Sexus* has been published in that amiable book, *Lawrence Durrell and Henry Miller: A Private Correspondence*: "I must confess I'm bitterly disappointed in [*Sexus*], despite the fact that it contains some of your very best writing to date. But, my dear Henry, the moral vulgarity of so much of it is artistically painful. These silly meaningless scenes which have no *raison d'être*, no humor, just childish explosions of obscenity—what a pity, what a terrible pity for a major artist not to have a critical sense enough to husband his force, to keep his talent aimed at the target. What on earth possessed you to leave so much twaddle in?"

Miller's response was serene and characteristic. "I said it before and I repeat it solemnly: I am writing exactly what I want to write and the way I want to do it. Perhaps it's twaddle, perhaps not. . . . I am trying to reproduce in words a block of my life which to me has the utmost significance—every bit of it. Not because I am infatuated with my own ego. You should be able to perceive that only a man without ego could write thus about himself. (Or else I am really crazy. In which case, pray for me.)"

Sexus is a very long book about a character named Henry Miller (though at times his first name mysteriously changes to Val) who lives in Brooklyn (circa 1925) with a wife and daughter; he works for the Cosmodemonic Telegraph Company of North America (Western Union) and conducts an affair with a dance-hall girl named Mara (whose first name changes to Mona halfway through and stays Mona). In the course of six hundred and thirty-four pages, the character Henry Miller performs the sexual act many times with many different women, including, perversely, his wife, whom he does not much like. By the end of the book he has obtained a divorce and Mara-Mona becomes his second or perhaps third wife, and he dreams of freedom in another land.

Because of Miller's hydraulic approach to sex and his dogged use of four-letter words, *Sexus* could not be published in the United States for twenty-four years. Happily, the governors of the new American Empire are not so frightened of words as were the custodians of the old Republic. *Sexus* can now be dispensed in our drugstores, and it will do no harm, even without prescription.

Right off, it must be noted that only a total egotist could have written a book which has no subject other than Henry Miller in all his sweet monotony. Like shadows in a solipsist's daydream, the other characters flit through the narrative, playing straight to the relentless old exhibitionist whose routine has not changed in nearly half a century. Pose one: Henry Miller, sexual athlete. Pose two: Henry Miller, literary genius and life force. Pose three: Henry Miller and the cosmos (they have an understanding). The narrative is haphazard. Things usually get going when Miller meets a New Person at a party. New Person immediately realizes that this is no ordinary man. In fact, New Person's whole life is often changed after expo-

sure to the hot radiance of Henry Miller. For opening the door
to Feeling, Miller is then praised by New Person in terms
which might turn the head of God — but not the head of
Henry Miller, who notes each compliment with the gravity of
the recording angel. If New Person is a woman, then she is due
for a double thrill. As a lover, Henry Miller is a national
resource, on the order of Yosemite National Park. Later,
exhausted by his unearthly potency, she realizes that for the
first time she has met a Man . . . one for whom *post coitum*
is not *triste* but rhetorical. When lesser men sleep, Miller talks
about the cosmos, the artist, the sterility of modern life. Or in
his own words: ". . . our conversations were like passages out
of *The Magic Mountain*, only more virulent, more exalted,
more sustained, more provocative, more inflammable, more
dangerous, more menacing, and much more, ever so much
more, exhausting."

Now there is nothing inherently wrong with this sort of
bookmaking. The literature of self-confession has always had
an enormous appeal, witness the not entirely dissimilar suc-
cesses of Saints Augustine and Genet. But to make art of
self-confession it is necessary to tell the truth. And unless
Henry Miller is indeed God (not to be ruled out for lack of
evidence to the contrary), he does not tell the truth. Everyone
he meets either likes or admires him, while not once in the
course of *Sexus* does he fail in bed. Hour after hour, orgasm
after orgasm, the great man goes about his priapic task. Yet
from Rousseau to Gide the true confessors have been aware
that not only is life mostly failure, but that in one's failure or
pettiness or wrongness exists the living drama of the self.
Henry Miller, by his own account, is never less than superb,
in life, in art, in bed. Not since the memoirs of Frank Harris has
there been such a record of success in the sack. Nor does
Miller provide us with any sort of relief. One could always
skip Frank Harris's erotic scenes in favor of literary and

political gossip. But Miller is much too important for gossip. People do not interest him. Why should they? They are mere wedding guests: he is Ancient Mariner.

At least half of *Sexus* consists of tributes to the wonder of Henry Miller. At a glance men realize that he *knows*. Women realize that he *is*. Mara-Mona: "I'm falling in love with the strangest man on earth. You frighten me, you're so gentle . . . I feel almost as if I were with a god." Even a complete stranger ("possibly the countess he had spoken of earlier") is his for the asking the moment she sees him. But, uniquely, they both prefer to chat. The subject? Let the countess speak for herself: "Whoever the woman is you love, I pity her . . . Nobody can hold you for long . . . You make friends easily, I'm sure. And yet there is no one whom you can really call your friend. You are alone. You will always be alone." She asks him to embrace her. He does, chastely. Her life is now changed. "You have helped, in a way . . . You always help, indirectly. You can't help radiating energy, and that is something. People lean on you, but you don't know why." After two more pages of this keen analysis, she tells him, "Your sexual virility is the only sign of a greater power, which you haven't begun to use." She never quite tells him what this power is, but it must be something pretty super because everyone else can also sense it humming away. As a painter friend (male) says, "I don't know any writer in America who has greater gifts than you. I've always believed in you—and I will even if you prove to be a failure." This is heady praise indeed, considering that the painter has yet to read anything Miller has written.

Miller is particularly irresistible to Jews: "You're no Goy. You're a black Jew. You're one of those fascinating Gentiles that every Jew wants to shine up to." Or during another first encounter with a Jew (Miller seems to do very well at first meetings, less well subsequently): "I see you are not an ordinary Gentile. You are one of those lost Gentiles—you are searching for something . . . With your kind we are never sure where we stand. You are like water — and we are rocks. You eat us away little by little — not with malice, but with kindness . . ." Even when Miller has been less than loyal in his relations with others, he is forgiven. Says a friend: "You don't seem to understand what it means to give and take. You're an intellectual hobo . . . You're a gangster, do you know that?" He chuckled. "Yes, Henry, that's what you are — you're a spiritual gangster." The chuckle saves the day for lovable Henry.

Yet Henry never seems to do anything for anyone, other than to provide moments of sexual glory which we must take on faith. He does, however, talk a lot and the people he knows are addicted to his conversation. "Don't stop talking now . . . please," begs a woman whose life is being changed, as Henry in a manic mood tells her all sorts of liberating things like "Nothing would be bad or ugly or evil — if we really let ourselves go. But it's hard to make people understand that." To which the only answer is that of another straight man in the text who says, "You said it, Henry. Jesus, having you around is like getting a shot in the arm." For a man who boasts of writing nothing but the truth, I find it more than odd that not once in the course of a long narrative does anyone say, "Henry, you're full of shit." It is possible, of course, that no one ever did, but I doubt it.

Interlarded with sexual bouts and testimonials are a series of prose poems in which the author works the cosmos for all it's worth. The style changes noticeably during these arias. Usually Miller's writing is old-fashioned American demotic, rather like the prose of one of those magazines Theodore Dreiser used to edit. But when Miller climbs onto the old cracker barrel, he gets very fancy indeed. Sentences swell and billow, engulfing syntax. Arcane words are put to use, often accurately: ectoplasmic, mandibular, anthropophagous, terrene, volupt, occipital, fatidical. Not since H. P. Lovecraft has there been such a lover of language. Then, lurking pale and wan in this jungle of rich prose, are the Thoughts: "Joy is founded on something too profound to be understood and communicated: To be joyous is to be a madman in a world of sad ghosts." Or: "Only the great, the truly distinctive individuals resemble one another. Brotherhood doesn't start at the bottom, but at the top." Or: "Sex and poverty go hand in hand." The interesting thing about the Thoughts is that they can be turned inside out and the effect is precisely the same: "Sex and affluence go hand in hand," and so on.

In nearly every scene of *Sexus* people beg Miller to give them The Answer, whisper The Secret, reveal The Cosmos; but though he does his best, when the rosy crucial moment comes he invariably veers off into platitude or invokes high mysteries that can be perceived only through Feeling, never through thought or words. In this respect he is very much in the American grain. From the beginning of the United States, writers of a certain kind, and not all bad, have been bursting with some terrible truth that they can never quite articulate. Most often it has to do with the virtue of feeling as opposed to the vice of thinking. Those who try to think out matters are arid, sterile, anti-life, while those who float about in a daffy daze enjoy copious orgasms and the happy knowledge that they are the salt of the earth. This may well be true but Miller is hard put to prove it, if only because to make a case of any kind, cerebration is necessary, thereby betraying the essential position. On the one hand, he preaches the freedom of the bird, without attachments or the need to justify anything in words, while on the other hand, he feels obligated to write long books in order to explain the cosmos to us. The paradox is that if he really meant what he writes, he would not write at all. But then he is not the first messiah to be crucified upon a contradiction.

It is significant that Miller has had a considerable effect on a number of writers better than himself — George Orwell, Anaïs Nin, Lawrence Durrell, to name three at random —

and one wonders why. Obviously his personality must play a part. In the letters to Durrell he is a most engaging figure. Also, it is difficult not to admire a writer who has so resolutely gone about his own business in his own way without the slightest concession to any fashion. And though time may have turned the Katzenjammer Kid into Foxy Grandpa, the old cheerful anarchy remains and beguiles.

Finally, Miller helped make a social revolution. Forty years ago it was not possible to write candidly of sexual matters. The door was shut. Then the hinges were sprung by D. H. Lawrence, and Miller helped kick it in. Now other doors need opening (death is the new obscenity). Nevertheless, at a certain time and in a certain way, Henry Miller fought the good fight, for which he deserves not only our gratitude but a permanent place of honor in that not inconsiderable company which includes such devoted figures as Havelock Ellis, Alfred M. Kinsey, and Marie C. Stopes.

[*Book Week*, August 1, 1965]

The City and the Pillar After
Twenty Years

I WAS twenty-one when I wrote *The City and the Pillar*. Although I had already published two novels, *Williwaw* and *In a Yellow Wood*, my talent was not precocious. I knew how to do a few things well, and I did them all in *Williwaw*. By the time I came to write *The City and the Pillar* I was bored with playing it safe. I wanted to take risks, to try something no American had done before. I decided to examine the homosexual underworld (which I knew rather less well than I pretended), and in the process show the "naturalness" of homosexual relations, as well as making the point — somewhat paradoxically — that there is of course no such thing as a homosexual. Despite current usage, the word is an adjective describing a sexual action, not a noun describing a recognizable type. All human beings are bisexual. Conditioning, opportunity, and habit account finally (and mysteriously) for sexual preference, and homosexual-ists are quite as difficult to generalize about as heterosexual-ists. They range from the transvestite who believes himself to be Bette Davis to the perfectly ordinary citizen who regards boys with the same uncomplicated lust that his brother regards girls.

When legal and social pressures against homosexuality are particularly severe, homosexual-ists can become neurotic, in much the same way that Jews and Negroes do in a hostile environment. Yet a man who enjoys sensual relations with his own sex is not, by definition, neurotic. In any event, categorizing is impossible. Particularly when one considers that most homosexual-ists marry and become fathers, which makes them, technically, bisexuals, a condition whose existence is firmly denied by at least one school of psychiatry on the odd ground that a man *must* be one thing or the other: which is demonstrably untrue. Admittedly, no two things are equal, and so a man is bound to prefer one specific to another, but that does not mean that under the right stimulus, and at another time, he might not accommodate himself to both. It is interesting to note that the current slang word for someone admirable is "swinger." And what is a swinger? One who swings both ways, who is able to take pleasure where he finds it, with either sex.

In 1946 when I wrote *The City and the Pillar*, it was a part of American folklore that homosexuality was a form of mental disease, confined for the most part to interior decorators and ballet dancers. Knowing this to be untrue, I set out to shatter the stereotype by taking as my protagonist a completely ordinary boy of the middle class and through his eyes observing the various strata of the underworld. This was a considerable act of imagination. I come from a political family. Jim Willard and I shared the same geography, but little else. Also, in the interest of verisimilitude I decided to tell the story in a flat gray prose reminiscent of one of James T. Farrell's social documents. There was to be nothing fancy in the writing. I wanted the prose plain and hard and, if I may say so, I succeeded.

Contemplating the American scene in the 1940's, Stephen Spender deplored the machinery of literary success, remarking sternly that "One has only to follow the whizzing comet of . . . Mr. Gore Vidal to see how quickly and effectively this transforming, diluting, disintegrating machinery can work." He then characterized *The City and the Pillar* as a work of sexual confession, quite plainly autobiography at its most artless. Transformed, diluted, disintegrated as I was, I found this description flattering. Mr. Spender had paid me a considerable compliment, for though I am the least autobiographical of novelists, apparently I had drawn the character of the athlete Jim Willard so convincingly that to this day aging pederasts are firmly convinced that I was once a male prostitute, with an excellent backhand at tennis. The truth, alas, is quite another matter.

When the book was published in 1948, it was received with shock and disbelief. How could that young war novelist (last observed in the pages of *Life* magazine posed like Jack London against a ship) turn into this? The New York *Times* refused to take advertising for the book, and most of the reviews were hostile. The press lectured me firmly on the delights of hetero-sexual love, while chiding the publishers for distributing such a lurid "memoir." Nevertheless, the book was a best seller, not only in the United States but in Europe, where it was taken seriously by critics, not all engaged. André Gide presented me with a copy of *Corydon*, as one prophet to another. E. M. Forster invited me to Cambridge and shyly confessed that he had written a somewhat similar book which he had never published, not wanting to embarrass family and friends. "Quite bold, actually," he said. In what way, I asked. Apparently there was a scene of two boys in bed. "And what," I asked, intrigued, "do they do?" Mr. Forster smiled. "They . . . *talk*," he said, with some satisfaction. Later that year, in a statistical report, Dr. Kinsey revealed what American men were actually up to, and I was somewhat exonerated for my candor. I even received a nice letter from the good Doctor, complimenting me on "your work in the field."

The world has changed a good deal since 1948. Sexual candor is now not only common but obligatory. Outright por-nography is published openly and I doubt if it does much harm. After all, Americans like how-to-do books. But, most significant, the young people today are in many ways more relaxed about sexual matters than we were in the 1940's. They have discovered that choice of sexual partner is a matter of taste, not of divine or even "natural" law. Also, I suspect that the psychological basis to most sex is not so much physical satisfaction as it is a will to power. This strikes me as implicit in *The City and the Pillar*, though I was perfectly unaware of it at the time. When a young man rejects the advances of another young man his motive, as often as not, is a fear of losing autonomy, of being used as a thing by the other, conquered instead of conquering.

Recently I reread *The City and the Pillar* for the first time since it was published, and I was startled to find that the book I had written was not at all the one I remembered. Midway through what I meant to be a commonsense redefinition of the homosexual-ist in American life, the narrative turned melodramatic. Nor was the actual theme of the book entirely clear. I intended Jim Willard to demonstrate the romantic fallacy. From too much looking back, he was destroyed, a naive Humbert Humbert trying to re-create an idyll that never truly existed except in his own imagination. Despite the title, this was never plain in the narrative. And of course the coda was unsatisfactory. At the time it was generally believed that the publishers forced me to tack on a cautionary ending in much the same way the Motion Picture Code insists that wickedness be punished. This was not true. I had always meant the end of the book to be black, but not as black as it turned out. I have now altered the last chapter considerably. In fact, I have rewritten the entire book (my desire to imitate the style of Farrell was perhaps too successful), though I have not changed the point of view nor the essential relationships.

In its slow way, our society is beginning to shed many of its superstitions about the sexual act. The idea that there is no such thing as "normality" is at last penetrating the tribal consciousness, although the religiously inclined still regard nonprocreative sex as "unnatural," while the statistically inclined regard as "normal" only what the majority does. Confident that most sexual acts are heterosexual, the consensus maintains that heterosexuality, as the preferred form of erotic expression, must be "right." However, following that line of reasoning to its logical conclusion, one would have to recognize that the most frequently performed sexual act is neither hetero- nor homosexual but onanistic, and surely, even in a total democracy, masturbation would not be declared the perfect norm from which all else is deviation. In any case, sex of any sort is neither right nor wrong. It is. And that seems to me to be the point to this novel, particularly in its revised form.

[Afterword to *The City and the Pillar Revised*, 1965]

On Revising One's Own Work

THE subject of Henry James's short story "The Middle Years" is a distinguished, aging novelist named Dencombe who goes to Bournemouth for his health, where we encounter him sitting in anonymous solitude on a terrace reading a first copy of his new novel *The Middle Years*, "recognizing," as he does, "his motive and surrendering to his talent." But he is not so bemused by his beautiful art that he does not make a number of corrections in the text. This attracts the notice of a young man who turns out to be — perfect Jamesian wish fulfillment — an ardent admirer of Dencombe. Sternly the young man reproaches what he takes to be a book reviewer. " 'I see you've been altering the text!' Dencombe was a passionate corrector, a fingerer of style; the last thing he ever arrived at was a form final for himself. His ideal would have been to publish secretly, and then, on the published text, treat himself to the terrified revise, sacrificing always a first edition and beginning for posterity and even for the collectors, poor dears, with a second. This morning, in *The Middle Years*, his pencil had pricked a dozen lights. He was amused at the effect of the young man's reproach; for an instant it made him change colour."

This year, three of my early novels,* considerably revised,

* *The City and the Pillar* (1948). *The Judgment of Paris* (1952). *Messiah* (1954).

have been published again, and I have been reproached for having pricked altogether too many lights. At worst, reviewers feel that an old novel is much like an old newspaper, suitable for its season in the bookstores and then oblivion. At best, whatever one's youthful faults, the original work ought to remain forever as it was, a pristine artifact, useful as evidence in any study of one's subsequent rise or decline. Henry James himself was a good deal censured when he revised his early novels for the New York edition. Like Dencombe, he was a fingerer of style. Like Jean Cocteau (in this if nothing else) he believed that a work of art was never finished, merely abandoned. At sixty, he was not about to abandon his early work without one final effort to get the thing said right. As F. W. Dupee wrote in his excellent study of Henry James, "Revision is a common practice among writers, and the rights and wrongs of it are a matter of tact and degree." On balance, Professor Dupee decided that most of the revisions James made were improvements.

But putting to one side the lesson of the tactful Master, the revision of books once published is *not* a common practice among American novelists, if only because very few of our writers are given the chance (no second acts in American lives, as they say). Also, American writers for the last fifty years have tended to be subjective and romantic. A book is torn from its author's flesh and flung at the reader, as if to say: Is this book not a part of me? and aren't I, like God, in all that I do? The thought of making an old text better would not occur to a romantic writer, if only because one's second thoughts tend to be intellectual rather than emotional (witness Auden's reworking of his early poems), and why would anyone want to alter the feelings of an early self?

I had the luck (both good and bad) of being published young. *Williwaw*, written at nineteen, was published in 1946 when I was twenty. By the time I was twenty-one I had written four novels, among them *The City and the Pillar* (1948), described by a recent critic as "the first American novel to represent openly and on a full scale homosexual experience and the homosexual subculture in contemporary society." In preparing the current edition, I found it necessary to rewrite the entire book, line by line. Sharp questions have since been raised. Why, if I was so much displeased with the original book, did I allow it to be republished? The answer to that is simple. The book has been in print for eighteen years. The publisher can—and does—reissue it whenever he chooses. Since I could not prevent a new printing, I did the next best thing, and rewrote the book.

I wanted particularly to change the original ending in which the protagonist, rebuffed, murders his first lover. It used to be said that this bit of melodrama was forced upon me by publishers who felt that homosexuality should be sternly punished. But the publishers were not at fault. Given the situation I chose to write about, physical violence was the only possible end to the story. In the new version the violence remains, but of a different kind. The original version was also weighted down with a good deal of solemn exposition about the nature of homosexuality, which that perceptive critic Steven Marcus now agrees was "hopelessly callow, in 1948 as much as today, and Mr. Vidal has, from one point of view, not hurt his novel by removing it." Mr. Marcus also finds the new ending "more plausible in the sense that it arises organically and consequentially out of the subject and textures of the novel, rather than escaping from it as the first ending did." But though Mr. Marcus regards the new version as "a neater, leaner, sharper book than the original it is not as interesting a book," because I have given to the world of 1948 the values of 1965, and imposed the second thoughts of my middle age upon the first warm responses of my youth. The charge of *aggiornamento* is inevitable, and to a degree Mr. Marcus is right. But I think the best of what existed in the early version remains and that one has honorably joined hands, to use a Jamesian image, with an old self across the years.

Certainly one knows more at forty than one did at twenty. And contrary to all American mythology, the novel is the rightful province not of the young but of the middle-aged. Neither genius nor talent is enough, as they are in poetry. The novelist must know a very great deal about the world he is living in. Also, like T. S. Eliot's ideal critic, he must be very intelligent, an innate faculty which needs constant exercise. Finally, he must come to terms with the idea of character as it is affected by time passing, and this takes, literally, time to achieve. In the case of Proust, half a life was lived before he was able to change that tea-soaked rusk into a madeleine.

In *The Judgment of Paris* (1952) and *Messiah* (1954), two novels reissued this year, I made a number of revisions, mostly technical. Though grammar and punctuation are seldom mentioned in discussions of literature, they are a matter of some concern on those occasions when one is not exquisitely forging symbols or working deep the vein of moral consciousness. It is difficult to write well. The national manner in prose changes over the years, and one changes, too, often without knowing it. I was startled to find how much I — and others—used the colon in the forties. Like a blare of French horns introducing a significant theme, the colon was used almost as much (and as irritatingly) as Sterne's dashes. The semicolon was also fashionable then; it is seldom used nowadays in the best prose but I am still loyal to it. As for commas, those of us brought up on Fowler used to allow them to swarm like gnats upon the page. Now the comma is used sparingly and I prefer the new economy.

Henry James regarded the rewriting of his books as a deliberate attempt to "redream one's career." I think this wish is not unnatural in an artist who has lived long enough to be able to see to what degree his own work is, finally, all of a piece, the comedy viewed from his particular place in shifting time. One certainly sees the process of redreaming in Proust, who wove and rewove the same themes year after year, reshaping early works, published and unpublished, in a desperate attempt to catch Time once and for all within the net of his formidable art. Even the prolific Balzac was prey to second thoughts, and often in galley proof hastily rewrote what he had hastily written. For some reason it is different with us. Fussing with an old book suggests that one is no longer "creative," and not to be creative is not to be American. Yet the old book is as much a part of a writer's work as a new one; the books interrelate; the new rests upon the old. There is also the matter of literary conscience. Even though one's novels may not be interesting to the future, they ought, certainly, to be as good as one can make them. Somewhere within the corpulence of *For Whom the Bell Tolls* there is a good novel waiting to be let out. But only the original author could have done it. No one else would know how, not even Somerset Maugham, who not long ago cut and edited ten great novels while serenely leaving untouched that obese hostage to fortune *Of Human Bondage*.

Finally, at forty, one should begin to set one's house in order. What's worth keeping should be made as good as possible. What ought to be suppressed should be dropped. I have disowned three out-of-print novels, knowing perfectly well that those three are certain to be exhumed, perhaps by the grandson of Steven Marcus, and their poor riddled mummies displayed beneath the self-reflecting gloss of doctoral prose as the only interesting work of that artful twentieth-century novelist who believed so naïvely that posterity might be prevented from making its usual error of taste, and perfectly failed.

[*New York Times Book Review,* November 14, 1965]

God's Country:
The American Empire's Beginning

OF the many words with which the mental therapists have enriched our language, "paranoia" is one of the most used if not useful. According to authority, a paranoiac is one who suffers from delusions of persecution or grandeur. Everyone, of course, has paranoid tendencies. In fact, a sizable minority of the people in the world maintain sanity by focusing their fears and sense of outrage upon some vague enemy usually referred to simply as "them." Once the source of distress has been identified as the Jews or the Communists or the Establishment, the moderate paranoiac is then able to function normally — until the magic word is said, as in that famous vaudeville sketch where mention of the town Kokomo makes mad the timid comic, who begins ominously to intone: "Then slowly I turned . . ."

If the poet of the paranoid style is Kafka, one of its best contemporary critics is Professor Richard Hofstadter, whose new book illuminates various aspects of a style which has always flourished in God's country, possibly because the North American continent was meant, literally, to be God's country, a haven for seventeenth-century Protestant fundamentalists who did not understand, as Hölderlin so sweetly put it, what a sin it is "to make the state a school of morals. The state has always been made a hell by man's wanting to make it his heaven." Into this heaven, *they* came: the secular-minded eighteenth-century skeptics who proceeded to organize the United States along freethinking lines. Since then, the paranoid style has been a constant in the affairs of the American Republic. Though it originated with Christian fundamentalists, who could not bear to see their heaven made hell by a national majority which now includes those very elements that caused them to flee the old world in the first place, the style is by no means peculiar to them. Western farmers denouncing Eastern banks, Jews trying to censor the film of *Oliver Twist*, uneasy heterosexuals fearful of a homosexual take-over — all demonstrate that the paranoid style has at one time or another been the preferred manner of nearly every one of the groups that comprise the nation, and in a most engaging essay Professor Hofstadter traces the main line of this illness from the persecution of the Bavarian Illuminati in the eighteenth century to the current obsession with the Communist conspiracy.

It is ironic that a nation which has never experienced a *coup d'état* should be so obsessed with the idea of conspiracy. From the John Birchers who regard General Eisenhower as a crypto-Communist to those liberals who find it thrilling to believe that Lyndon Johnson was responsible for Kennedy's murder, paranoid delusions afflict millions. Knowing this, even the most responsible of politicians finds it difficult not to play upon the collective madness of the electorate.

"There is a power somewhere so organized, so subtle, so watchful, so interlocked, so complete, so pervasive that they had better not speak above their breath when they speak in condemnation of it."

Although this sounds like Joseph McCarthy at his most eloquent, it is actually Woodrow Wilson at his least responsible, warning against "the special interests" (that what he was warning against might indeed exist to some degree is irrelevant; it is the manner in which he exploits the fears of the electorate that gives away the game).

According to Professor Hofstadter, the paranoid style is popular not only with that minority which is prone "to secularize a religiously derived view of the world," but also from time to time with the great majority which has never had any clear sense of national identity. For the American there is no motherland or fatherland to be shared with others of his tribe, for the excellent reason that he has no tribe; all that he holds in common with other United Statesmen is something called "the American way of life," an economic system involving the constant purchase of consumer goods on credit to maintain a high standard of living involving the constant purchase, etc. But though this materialistic, even sybaritic ethos does far less damage in the world than old-fashioned tribalism, it fails to satisfy all sorts of atavistic yearnings. A man might gladly give his life for a totem like the flag or the Cross, but who would give so much as a breath for a washing machine not yet paid for?

As a result, not only are the paranoid stylists of both Left and Right appalled by the soullessness of American society, but a good many nonparanoids are equally concerned by the lack of "national purpose," a phrase whose innocent implication is that a human society is like a factory with a quota to be met. Among the simple, this absence of traditional identity has let some strange obsessions flourish, particularly today when the national majority is made up of third-generation citizens uncertain of just what's expected of them. Not unnaturally, those of a passionate and idealistic nature are driven to displays of one hundred per cent Americanism, ranging from frequent hand-on-heart pledges of allegiance to the country's proto-Op-art flag to the joyous persecution of those suspected of being un-American (the only other society to have such a concept was Nazi Germany).

Analyzing the identity crisis, as the mental therapists would say, Professor Hofstadter makes a distinction between what he terms status politics and interest politics. In times of economic or military distress (that is to say, "normal" times), people vote their economic interests, and new deals are possible. But when the voters are affluent, they feel free to vote not their interests but their prejudices. The election of 1928 was such a time, and in an orgy of anti-Romanism the majority chose Herbert Hoover over Al Smith. Three years ago, when all seemed to be going smoothly for the nation, the Republicans nominated Barry Goldwater, quite aware that not only was he the most radical politician in the country (Supreme Court decisions are not, he declared, "necessarily the law of the land") but also the most consistent morally. Fiercely militant in the holy war against world Communism ("we will never reconcile ourselves to the Communist possession of power of any kind in any part of the world"), he was even more emphatic in his desire to repeal a hundred years of social legislation in order to create a society in which every man has the inalienable right *not* to give a sucker an even break. The fact that by living the "wrong" sort of economic life the United States had become incredibly rich did not disturb him; as a status politican he spoke for virtue, and the millions that heeded him were quite willing (or so they thought) to sacrifice their material prosperity in order to gain spiritual health by obeying the "natural law" of the marketplace.

According to Professor Hofstadter, those going up or down the social scale are the most prone to paranoia. When white Anglo-Saxon Protestants lose status, they often suspect a conspiracy aimed at depriving them of their ancient primacy, while Irish Catholics, moving up, are often disappointed to find that their new riches do not entitle them to more of a say in the governing of the country, and so suspect the Protestant old guard or the Jews of conspiring to deny them dignity. Religious (as well as ethnic) prejudices often decide the way these people vote. Since Americans lack an agreed-upon class system, status tends to originate in race and religion.

The fact that each of Professor Hofstadter's essays was

written for an occasion other than the present ought to have inspired him to make some sort of link from piece to piece. Unfortunately, he has not made the effort, even though the paranoid style would have provided a fine common denominator. Nevertheless, he is interesting on such subjects as "Cuba, the Philippines and Manifest Destiny": skillfully, he gives the background to the Spanish-American War, and shows how the paranoid style helped make possible the war, which gave birth to the American empire.

Like most empires, this one was the result of trouble at home. With the settling of California, the frontier shut down and there was no place new to go, a matter of poignant concern to a nomadic and adventurous people. Then came the depression of '93. To those of faint heart, the last best hope of earth appeared to be fading fast. At such times the shrewd politician can usually be counted upon to obscure domestic crises with foreign pageants. Or, as Henry Cabot Lodge confided to a friend, "Should there be a war, we will not hear much of the currency question in the election." Between Lodge's practicality and Theodore Roosevelt's vision of empire ("All the great masterful races have been fighting races. No triumph of peace is quite as great as the supreme triumphs of war!"), history required a war. But who was there to fight? Fortunately, Cuba wanted to be free of Spain; and so the United States, a Goliath posing as David, struck down Spain, a David hardly able to pose at all, and thus was Cuba freed to become a client state, the Philippines conquered and occupied, and westward the course of empire flowed. The Pacific Ocean, at first thought to be the end of the road, proved to be a new frontier whose end is not yet in sight, though it is heartening to know that downtown Hanoi is currently off limits.

The American empire began in a blaze of rhetoric, much of it paranoid. Witness Senator Albert J. Beveridge:

"God has been preparing the English-speaking and Teu-

tonic peoples for a thousand years [to be] master organizers of the world. He has made us adepts in government that we may administer government among savages and senile peoples."

Even thoughtful commentators felt that though "we risk Caesarism, Caesarism is preferable to anarchy." And so, to avoid anarchy (and socialism), the United States chose empire, and contrary to the famous witticism, empires are the deliberate creation of an adroit presence — not absence — of mind. Franklin Roosevelt, in his way, was quite as imperial as his cousin Theodore. Beneath a genuine high-mindedness (puzzling to foreigners who find the American nonparanoid style either hypocritical or unrealistic), American leaders have unconsciously accepted the "English-speaking, Teutonic" role of world conquerors for the world's good. With the result that the Americans are in this age the barbarian horde, as the English were in the last century.

Happily enough, it would also appear that the United States is destined to be the last empire on earth (in the best if not the apocalyptic sense), and there are now stirrings within the camp of the Great Khan at Washington to the effect that new necessities do not always require military force. Barring unexpected catastrophe, the hordes may soon achieve, if not peace, an uneasy stasis which, hopefully, should endure until the human race begins the infection of other worlds. For more and more do we resemble a proliferating virus, destructive of other organisms, incapable of arresting itself, and so destined — manifestly! — to prevail or vanish furiously in space and time.

[*New Statesman*, January 13, 1967]

Edmund Wilson, Tax Dodger

"BETWEEN the year 1946 and the year 1955, I did not file any income tax returns."

With that blunt statement, Edmund Wilson embarks on a most extraordinary polemic.* He tells us why he did not pay his taxes. Apparently he had never made much money. He was generally ignorant of the tax laws. In 1946, when his novel *Memoirs of Hecate County* was published, his income doubled. Then the book was suppressed by court order and the income stopped. While all this was going on, he was much distracted by a tangled private life. So what with one thing and another, Mr. Wilson never got around to filing a return.

"It may seem naïve, and even stupid, on the part of one who had worked for years on a journal which specialized in public affairs (the *New Republic*) that he should have paid so little attention to recent changes in the income tax laws . . ." It does indeed seem naïve and stupid, and one cannot help but think that our premier literary critic (who among other great tasks of illumination explained Marxian economics to a generation) is a bit of a dope. But with that harsh judgment out of the way, one can only admire his response to the American bureaucracy.

Mr. Wilson originally owed $20,000 in unpaid taxes. With interest and fines, the $20,000 became $60,000. The Internal Revenue Service then went into action, and Mr. Wilson learned at first hand just how much power the IRS exerts.

* *The Cold War and the Income Tax* (1963).

Royalties, trust funds, bank accounts can be attached; auto-
mobiles may be seized and sold at auction. Nothing belongs
to the victim until the case is settled. Meanwhile, his private
life is ruthlessly invaded in order to discover if he is of criminal intent (and therefore willfully bilking the nation of its
rightful revenue). In Mr. Wilson's case, much was made of
the fact that he had been married four times (a sign of un-
stable temperament); that he had written, Heaven help him,
books! In a passage of exquisite irony, Mr. Wilson describes
how one of the agents was put to work reading the master's
complete *œuvre* in order to prove that his not paying taxes
was part of a sinister design to subvert a great nation. Did
they find anything? Yes. In a journalistic piece, Mr. Wilson
seemed to admire a man who had, among other crimes, not
paid a Federal tax.

Even more unpleasant than the bureau's legitimate investigation was the unrelenting impertinence of the investigators.
Why did Mr. Wilson spend six dollars to buy a cushion for his
dog to sleep on? Why did he keep three places to live when
the investigator (who earned a virtuous $7,500 a year)
needed only one place to live in? Why was Mr. Wilson's daughter in a private school? Even worse than this sort of harass-
ment was the inefficiency and buck-passing of the bureau. No
one seemed able to make a decision. Regional office A had no
idea what regional office B had decided. Then, just as progress
was about to be made, a new investigator would be assigned
the case and everyone had to go back to "Start." Kafka inevitably comes to mind; also, the bureaucracy of the Soviet Union
which Mr. Wilson once contrasted — to his regret — unfavor-
ably with our own.

After describing his own particular predicament, Mr.
Wilson then discusses the general question of the income tax
and the free society. He records in detail the history of the tax
since the 1913 Constitutional amendment which made it legal
(in 1895 the Supreme Court had ruled that President Lin-

coln's wartime tax on personal income was unconstitutional).
Inexorably, the Federal tax has increased until today we pay
more tax than we did during the Second World War. And
there is no end in sight.

Mr. Wilson then asks a simple question: Why must we pay
so much? He notes the conventional answer: Since the cold
war, foreign aid, and defense account for seventy-nine per
cent of all Federal expenditures, putting the nation in permanent hock to that economic military complex President Eisenhower so movingly warned us against after eight years of
loyal service to it. There is of course some consolation in the
fact that we are not wasting our billions weakening the moral
fiber of the American yeoman by building him roads and
schools, or by giving him medical care and decent housing.
In public services, we lag behind all the industrialized nations
of the West, preferring that the public money go not to the
people but to big business. The result is a unique society in
which we have free enterprise for the poor and socialism for
the rich. This dazzling inequity is reflected in our tax system
where the man on salary pays more tax than the man who
lives on dividends, who in turn pays more tax than the wheeler-
dealer who makes a capital-gains deal.

How did we get into this jam? Admittedly, the Soviet is a
formidable enemy, and we have been well advised to protect
ourselves. Empires traditionally must buy not only weapons
but allies, and we are, like it or not, an empire. But there
is no evidence that we need spend as much as we do spend on
atomic overkill, on foreign aid, on chemical and bacteriological
warfare (we are now reactivating at great expense diseases
that the human race has spent centuries attempting to wipe
out).

Mr. Wilson is excellent at describing the mad uses to which
our tax money is being put ($30 billion to get a man on the
moon — literally lunatic), but he seems not to be aware of the
original policy behind the cold war. It was John Foster Dulles's

decision to engage the Soviet in an arms race. Dulles figured, reasonably enough, that the Soviet economy could not endure this sort of competition. It was also believed that even if they should achieve military parity, their people, hungering for consumer goods, would revolt. This policy was successful for a time. But it worked as much hardship on our free society as it did on their closed one. We have become a garrison state, frightened of our own government and bemused by a rhetoric in which all is appearance, nothing reality. Or, as Mr. Wilson puts it:

"The truth is that the people of the United States are at the present time dominated and driven by two kinds of officially propagated fear: fear of the Soviet Union and fear of the income tax.

"These two terrors have been adjusted so as to complement one another and thus to keep the citizen of our free society under the strain of a double pressure from which he finds himself unable to escape — like the man in the old Western story who, chased into a narrow ravine by a buffalo, is confronted with a grizzly bear. If we fail to accept the tax, the Russian buffalo will butt and trample us, and if we try to defy the tax, the Federal bear will crush us."

Is there a way out? Mr. Wilson is not optimistic. Opponents of the income tax tend to be of the Far Right, where they fear the buffalo even more than they do the bear. There is nothing quite so engaging in our public life today as to hear Barry Goldwater tell us how we can eventually eliminate the graduated income tax *while* increasing military expenditures. Also, the militant conservative, though he will go to the barricades to keep a Federal dollar from filtering down to a state school, sees nothing wrong with Federal billions subsidizing a corporation in which he owns stock. As for the politicians, they tend to be too much part of the system to try and change it. The most passionate Congressional budget cutter will do all that he can to get Federal money for his own district. Between the pork barrel and the terrible swift sword, Pentagon, Congress, and industry are locked together, and nothing short of a major popular revolt can shatter their embrace.

Mr. Wilson discusses in some detail various attempts made by individuals (mostly pacifists) to thwart the IRS. But the results have not been happy. The line between Thoreau and Poujade is a delicate one. Yet it is perfectly clear that it must one day be drawn if the United States is not to drift into a rigid Byzantine society where the individual is the state's creature (yes, liberals worry about this, too), his life the property of a permanent self-perpetuating bureaucracy, frozen in some vague never-ending cold war with an enemy who is merely a reflection of itself.

Edmund Wilson's personal conclusion is a sad one. He points out that at the age of sixty-eight he can never hope to pay the government what he owes. According to his settlement with the IRS, everything that he makes over a certain amount goes automatically toward settling the debt. On principle, he hopes to keep his income below the taxable level. More to the point, as a result of his experience with the New America, "I have finally come to feel that this country, whether or not I live in it, is no longer any place for me." That is a stunning indictment of us all. Edmund Wilson is our most distinguished man of letters. He has always been (though the bureaucrats may not know it) something of a cultural America Firster. To lose such a man is a warning signal that our society is approaching that shadow line which, once crossed, means an end to what the makers of the country had hoped would be a place in which happiness might be usefully pursued. Yet Mr. Wilson's grim pamphlet may be just the jolt we need. Not since Thomas Paine has the drum of polemic sounded with such urgency through the land, and it is to be hoped that every citizen of the United States will read this book.

[*Book Week*, November 3, 1963]

Public Television: A Meditation

ON February 28, 1967, the President addressed the Ninetieth Congress on matters of Health and Education, two
subjects close to the Great Socialite's heart. Sandwiched between a plea for the expansion of the Teachers' Corps and a
request for additional funds for biomedical research was this
statement: "I am convinced that a vital and self-sufficient noncommercial television system will not only instruct but inspire
and uplift our people." The fact that the President is an
owner not only of KTBC, Austin's one commercial television
station, but of Capital Cable, a program carrier, made all the
more resonant his plea for noncommercial television.

He recommended that the Congress make law the Public
Television Act of 1967, calling for (1) an increase in Federal
funds for television and radio construction to $10.5 million in
fiscal 1968; (2) "The creation of a corporation for public
television authorized to provide support to noncommercial
television and radio"; (3) "Provide $9 million in fiscal 1968
as initial funding for the company." Further, "Noncommercial television and radio in America, even though supported
by Federal funds, must be absolutely free from any Federal
Government interference over programming." Also, "The
strength of public television should lie in its diversity. Every
region and every community should be challenged to contribute its best." Finally, "One of the corporation's first tasks

should be to study the practicality and the economic advantages of using communication satellites to establish an educational television and radio network." With these words, the President set in motion what might yet become the most useful action of a most bloody reign, and though he deals somewhat gingerly with the key issues (freedom from Federal interference, regional diversity, satellite versus land-line interconnection), he gave the Congress (known to those it fascinates as the Nitwit Ninetieth), a chance to do something unusual and in the public interest.

On April 11, 1967, Senator John O. Pastore, chairman of the Senate Commerce Committee's Subcommittee on Communications, began hearings on Senate Bill 1160 which would make palpable the President's dream to inspire and uplift. The hearings were well conducted. A wide variety of interests, some candid, some not, were heard. The Senators who asked the questions (and sometimes answered them) were unusually dedicated and, all in all, the Upper House could be observed at its judicious best, particularly when the bill finally came to a vote on May 17 and was passed. The bill then went to the Lower House, the chamber more susceptible to special interests. On September 22, after a stormy time in committee (at one point the entire Republican membership voted against setting up *any* public television corporation), the House of Representatives passed the bill, suitably weakened. Since then, the two Houses have worked out a joint bill which the President signed on November 7, 1967.

Meanwhile, the first nationwide attempt at conventionally interconnected noncommercial television was made November 5 by the Public Broadcasting Laboratory, a creation of the Ford Foundation. Beneficiary of a grant of $10 million and some autonomy, PBL put on the first of what will be forty-five news programs this year. Executive director for news is Av Westin, formerly of CBS. He is aided (or hindered) by an editorial board composed of a number of Establishment worthies headed by an academic from (where else?) Columbia. Behind the entire operation looms the somber Foundation, whose chief mover for television is the turbulent Fred W. Friendly, until recently president of CBS News. Though not much in public view these days, Mr. Friendly is as responsible as anyone for what has now come to pass.

The theme of the first program was the matter of race in the United States and how it affected the mayoral elections in Boston, Cleveland, and Gary. Of the 125 stations that were supposed to receive the program, thirty-five chose not to show it. Cleveland thought they should wait until after the election, while Tallahassee, Florida, and all of South Carolina decided to wait until hell froze over. Boston ran the program at the last minute but offered free time for those who felt they had been unfairly treated. All in all, the nervousness the first program caused is a tribute to the adventurousness of Mr. Westin and his staff. At least half of the first program was excellent television. The other half, *Day of Absence* (a fantasy about the disappearance of all the Negroes in a Southern town) simply proved that to write plays it is not enough to be beautiful and black. Interestingly enough, the editorial board had objected to the play on aesthetic grounds, but the newsmen pushed it through as relevant comment and nearly wrecked the evening. It is never a good idea to mix fiction and reality. PBL would be better advised to prepare dialogues on various issues, to be written for the occasion and spoken by actors. From Plato to Camus the form has been effective on the page; on camera it could be marvelous. Nevertheless, the program's good things outweighed the bad. The showing of a meeting between white waffling liberals and booming black rhetoricians was chilling. Coverage of the candidates in the three cities was also excellent. Yet watching Louise Day Hicks snub a black Boston voter, one could not help but think that, though it was a good thing to show up the lady racist in all her soft simplicity and sweet malice, the same technique could be used quite as effectively to show a noble candidate at a bad moment in order to give the impression that he was a rogue. After all, *Time* magazine makes its fortune that way. The same approach in the iciest of mediums could be fatal to the good. Television with a point of view is all very well . . . but whose? Everything depends, finally, on the men who will make up the corporation.

At the moment PBL is on the spot. If the news reporting is sharp and to the point, the politicians will be alarmed since they are the inevitable victims of close scrutiny; if alarmed, they are certain not to support the new network. On the other hand, should the programs be bland and tactful, then there will be no need for the government to subsidize that which neither inspires nor uplifts. To be unable to win no matter what one does is a familiar television dilemma. In the "Golden Age" of television drama, the advertisers believed that the ideal play for television must not be too boring or the viewer would switch to another channel, nor too interesting or the viewer would resent the commercial break. Happily for all concerned, this truly golden mean was achieved more often than not.

To understand the forces currently at work to discredit the idea of public television, one must consider the state of commercial television in the United States today. As a document, Friendly's recent memoir, *Due to Circumstances Beyond Our Control*, is instructive, though one often has the sense that he does not begin to say half of what he knows. Nevertheless, the story he does tell is interesting, and sad. Although commercial television has never been devoted to the public interest, the private interests which control it often used to allow good things to be done. They could afford to. In the 1950's an advertising minute of prime time (evening) cost $1,000. Today that minute can cost as much as $60,000. It was possible in the 1950's to do seven new plays a week. It was also possible to do reasonably controversial news reports and show them at times when "opinion makers" were watching. But human beings tend to take the good as much for granted as the bad. Gradually, without public protest, costs rose (also profits) and quality declined; by the 1960's commercial television had lost the intelligent viewer, and gained the world. It also lost Fred W. Friendly.

From 1937 to 1941 Friendly was a radio producer-reporter in Providence. During the war he worked on an army newspaper in the China-Burma-India Theater. In 1947 he met Edward R. Murrow, and together they produced the record, "I Can Hear It Now." Out of this association came a partnership. The two men complemented each other. Murrow was a respectable journalist made famous by his radio reports from wartime London. Friendly was an eager technician who made up in energy and, at times, boldness what he lacked in style and wisdom. Murrow thought and gravely spoke in measured popular cadence while Friendly promoted and probed and organized. Their first broadcasting venture together was the CBS radio news program "Hear It Now," which promptly became television's "See It Now," sponsored each week by the Aluminum Company of America. In the seven years that Murrow and Friendly produced "See It Now," a time span equivalent in television to the Wars of the Roses, they were able to strike an occasional blow for sanity in a country which was behaving with more than its usual irrationality. Senator McCarthy and television came into prominence together, and it is a nice irony that a medium so perfectly made to order for a demagogue should have proved to be the means of his undoing, thanks as much to Murrow and Friendly as to the Senator's own extraordinary capers.

The first foray of "See It Now" into the shadow area of paranoid politics is worth recalling, if only as a reminder that nothing like it will ever again be done on commercial television. In 1953 an Air Force lieutenant named Milo Radulovich was asked to resign his commission because his sister and father had been secretly denounced for holding "radical" political beliefs. This sort of thing was common in the McCarthy era, and though it still goes on, means of redress are somewhat easier. After considerable investigation, Murrow and Friendly decided that the charges against the two relatives were probably groundless and, in any case, there existed no valid reason for the lieutenant's dismissal. They reported the matter to the public. The result was an eloquent television program, much applauded by the press (with the usual right-wing exceptions). Best of all, after some backing and filling, the Air Force restored Radulovich to active duty, and all was well in the land . . . except that Murrow and Friendly had broken CBS's first rule of news reporting: "Ideally, in the case of controversial issues, the audience should be left with no impression as to which side the analyst himself actually favors." The magnates of CBS were plainly not happy. As Friendly puts it in his flat way: "I never heard a word from any company executives [sic] about the Radulovich broadcast other than about the mail count, which continued to run in Murrow's favor." In Friendly's book those company executives are like gods, irrational and superb, as apt to cast a thunderbolt as to reach out a healing hand.

The two principal network deities are Chairman William Paley, the founder of CBS, and Dr. Frank Stanton, who "operate CBS much like father and son, with all the complexities and nuances of such a relationship." Since the Chairman is only seven years older than the Doctor, the father-son aspect must be a trying one for both. Friendly's love-hate for these two men (rather more love for the Chairman, more hate for the Doctor) makes fascinating reading, if only because of what he does not say — after all, should something go wrong with his current plans he might one day want to return to CBS. The fact that there are only three major networks gives a certain poignancy to his account of life with the two magnificoes. Yet he is particularly revealing of Dr. Stanton when he writes: "I believe that he despaired of the broadcast schedule about 1960; thereafter he did not bother to watch much of it except for news and special programs." The fact that the two television proprietors seldom watch their own programs was a significant factor in the termination of Friendly's career at CBS, thus, by indirection, helping to make possible what might yet prove to be a splendid alternative.

During the 1950's, "See It Now" was allowed considerable autonomy, because of the prestige of Murrow and the corporate pluckiness of the sponsor. In the course of two hundred programs a large number of interesting topics were dealt with (school integration 1954, cigarettes and lung cancer, Oppenheimer post-pillorying, recognition of Red China, and, inevitably, "a wonderful week with Carl and Paula Sandburg in Flat Rock, North Carolina"). Of the lot, the most famous was the March 9, 1954, report on Senator McCarthy, then at his peak. At this time over half the American people in their wisdom approved his investigations. The great magnates of television and the press were as intimidated by the Senator as his fellow politicians, eight of whom he was to "purge" from the Senate in 1954. It was not the best of times. Simply by showing the Senator in action Murrow caused a storm.

In the interest of fairness, the network allowed McCarthy to reply on April 6. Although the Senator's rambling accusations were ineptly presented, there was something, as always, in his mucker manner which had the power to cause to beat faster that black heart of America which is ever responsive to the idea of conspiracy. By the time the Senator had finished, a third of the audience was convinced that he had proved Murrow to be a Communist or fellow traveler. Dr. Stanton was distressed. So were others, but on quite different grounds. After seeing the two programs, the television reviewer Gilbert Seldes wrote: "I got the impression that the giant Murrow had been fighting a pygmy. Intellectually this may be right; politically I remain as frightened as if I had seen a ghost—the ghost of Hitler to be specific." Despite Mr. Seldes's over-wrought analogy, the point was well taken. It might indeed be in the public interest to bring down a McCarthy or a Louise Day Hicks. But suppose a network in the hands of devils decided to destroy a good President or candidate? Even though equal time were to be offered the victim, it is doubtful that he could ever in his own defense (and, right off, to defend is to be at a disadvantage) compete with the professionalism of network technicians, presided over by a famous and trusted television personality. This problem of responsibility may prove to be insoluble (significantly, Friendly opposed the broadcasting of Xerox's pro-U. N. programs on the ground that now a sponsor is at liberty to create an anti-U. N. series).

On June 1, 1955, "The $64,000 Question" was born and commercial television was never the same again. The mass audience wanted to see money given away in the course of simple-minded guessing games, and the networks joyously gave them what they wanted. After all, as Dr. Stanton so wisely expressed it, "A program in which a large part of the audience is interested is by that very fact . . . in the public interest." After 1955, in the public's interest, the drama pro-grams were axed while "See It Now" ceased to be a half-hour weekly show and became an hour program scheduled at irregular intervals. Nevertheless, Murrow and Friendly sol-diered on. They could still stir things up from time to time, but it was getting more and more difficult to convince the management that intelligent controversy was the surest way to increase sales. By March 1958, the game was over. "See It Now" was killed, and Murrow, in a denunciation of the entire network ethos, declared that he was "frightened by the im-balance, the constant striving to reach the largest possible audience for everything."

But that habit, once contracted, is not easily broken. In any case, Murrow and the management were no longer com-patible. A new program — "CBS Reports" — went to Friendly alone. The career of the great broadcaster was at an end. But his sort of news program still continued though in a somewhat less emphatic way, for already there were those who wanted to eliminate news analysis entirely. The new president of the company, James Aubrey, was more than intrigued by the fact that the six commercial minutes of a CBS "Report" could be sold in an entertainment package for $40,000 a minute. Even more to the point, a news program at prime time invariably causes a loss of rating for the show that follows it — a dreadful situation known to the trade as "depression." The commercial argument for eliminating the "Reports" was impeccable. Nor were the programs quite so vivid as the "See It Now" commentaries. As Friendly puts it, "Looking back now, I suppose that I was subtly influenced to do controversial subjects in a noncontroversial manner . . . in balancing arguments rather than objectively weighing them, we were sacrificing one ingredient of good journalism." Yet with or without the proper ingredients the "Reports" were to remain on the air for seven years. Both the Doctor and the Chairman were adamant on that score, for as the Chairman once told Friendly, "You have in your hands the most sacred trust that CBS has. Your job is to keep CBS news holy — and I expect you to do it."

But no commercial network can exist part profane and part holy. By 1966 television had become, in Friendly's phrase, a "profit machine whose only admitted function was to purvey six one-minute commercials every half hour." Gone were the high ideals of the 1930's when the young William Paley was able to tell the FCC that CBS Radio devoted "approximately 75 per cent of our time on the air to public service, as contrasted with sponsored programming." Now everything was sacrificed to wringing as much money as possible from advertisers. A holy act such as the showing of the McCarthy-Army hearings was simply no longer possible. Nothing of national or world significance seemed to the accountants to be worth interrupting the flow of profits from those filmed half-hour situation comedies which, run and re-run, fill the national air with canned laughter and grotesque images. To their credit, however, they took a dim view of Friendly's full coverage of the Pope's visit to New York, and did not agree with him that "the mass that night at a special altar over second base at Yankee Stadium was an inspirational television program, and I was proud of television's part in such an epic." For once Mammon had better taste.

Last February Friendly, now president of CBS News, decided to show live the Senate Foreign Affairs Committee's hearings on Vietnam. Despite Dr. Stanton's warnings that the network would lose revenue by covering the debate live, Friendly persevered. He showed General Gavin's testimony to the committee, and the result was electrifying. For a moment the United States were suddenly linked. A complex matter of state was at last being discussed by everyone. The national assembly existed, and had been convened. Characteristically, CBS's finest hour was not watched by Dr. Stanton, while the most mysterious of all the gods and the one least apt to interfere in human affairs, Chairman Paley, did not know about the program until the next day. The accountants, however, were on the job: they knew exactly how much money had been lost.

When Friendly requested permission to telecast George Kennan's testimony before the committee, the network gods simply dematerialized. In their place news officials and management consultants together decided not to show the hearings live. Instead a fifth rerun of "I Love Lucy" filled the air that historic morning. This decision, which was "clearly one of business over journalism, of dollar editing over the professional judgment of an entire news organization," caused Friendly, somewhat late in the day, to resign.

Now as television consultant to the Ford Foundation's all-purpose hero McGeorge Bundy, Friendly has been involved in the planning of what will, in effect, be a new network, without advertising. The bill just signed is in large part a response to his efforts as well as to those of the Ford Foundation, the Carnegie Commission, et al. The fact that so many dominions and powers (among them the owner of KTBC-TV) agree that such a network is needed is proof that nothing can be done about commercial television. There is no way to improve it, nor has there been since the 1950's, when the networks abdicated most of their programming to advertisers. The networks became sellers of time, displayers of "packages" assembled by advertisers. Needless to say, this alliance is highly profitable: CBS stockholders' equity has increased 250 per cent in the last decade; 485 per cent since 1951.

Even in a semicapitalist society, it would be cruel and unnatural to force such extraordinary moneymaking machines to reform themselves in the public interest. On the other hand, they ought to be forced to contribute in some way to setting up a noncommercial network. For instance, it has been suggested that the commercial television stations pay for the privilege of broadcasting. After all, the man who wants to drive his own taxicab in New York must pay nearly $30,000 for the dubious privilege of serving the public. Yet the broadcaster who wants to use the national air to make millions of dollars for himself pays nothing at all for an FCC license. Fees paid for licenses could go to the public network. In addition, the Carnegie Commission believes that a tax of between two and five per cent on television sets would more than adequately subsidize the network's year-to-year programming. As legal precedent for this tax, they point to the Migratory Bird Conservation Fund: fees to hunt birds go into a fund to protect birds — a happy paradox which opens up all sorts of attractive vistas.

Both the Report of the Carnegie Commission on Educational Television of January, 1967, and the general line of thinking at the Ford Foundation agree in principle to set up an independent public television corporation with financing from Federal as well as private sources (something like $200 million will be needed). They also favor a national linking of the various new stations into one network. The 126 educational stations now in operation are not linked. That is to say, they cannot receive the same program simultaneously. They cannot afford to use the landlines (a combination of coaxial cable and microwave relays from tower to tower) which interconnect the commercial networks. To repeat a program initiated by any one of the NET stations, the original tape must first be sent to Ann Arbor to be copied. Not only is this a laborious and lengthy process, but that immediacy which is television's peculiar virtue is lost.

The business of interconnection is most tangled. The Carnegie Report favors using the present landline system, thereby enormously profiting the American Telephone and Telegraph Company, among others. There is some evidence that a majority of the House of Representatives believes that what is good for A.T. & T. is good for the American economy. The Ford Foundation, however, demurs. On December 12, 1966, the Foundation made known to the FCC its preference for the use of satellites and the eventual abandoning of landlines. Three or four satellites "hung" in the world's common sky would cut transmission costs by half. The Carnegie Commission's response to what it termed the "ingenious Ford proposal" has been wary, while the response of Comsat was less than ambiguous: satellite-to-home television, though suitable for "underdeveloped nations," was not desirable in a highly developed country like the United States.

Meanwhile, the House of Representatives is caught in the middle. Some Representatives are devoted to the telephone interest; others are responsive to Comsat; a few no doubt take pride in the technological discoveries of Hughes Aircraft and its affiliate TelePrompTer. None is indifferent. All members of Congress must deal with local television stations, if only as performers, while perhaps as much as a fourth of the total Congressional delegation is financially interested in broadcasting.

The serious issue, however, is not whether A.T. & T. and the other conventional interconnectors continue to make money. Rather it is the question of what the President refers to as "diversity" in television. Satellites will make for cheaper transmission, and the millions of dollars saved by the commercial networks could, theoretically, go into the public television account, as noted by Ford. This is all to the good. But what happens to the country's 337 public television stations (the optimum number proposed by Carnegie) when they find themselves simply passive receivers of some central organization's programs? The whole point to public television has been the encouragement of experimental programming at the local level. Interconnection would exist only to transmit the occasional extraordinary event. Yet with cheap satellite transmission, the role of the regional station is bound to be minimized. In fact, satellites can make irrelevant the ground station by simply transmitting directly to the viewer's set.

The dangers of central programming are obvious, not only artistically but politically. Defenders of the proposed new order point out that no public television station need take everything that is transmitted. The station can pick and choose. But there is little doubt that the viewers, aware that there is a choice between a locally initiated program and a national one, will choose the national one. After all, given the present choice between an educational program and a commercial one, the audience has proved altogether too emphatically that it prefers the fifth rerun of "I Love Lucy" to even the most spirited rendering of a Strindberg play. That of course is the majority's right, but if public television does not provide for the minority audience too, then it ought not to exist. Decisions now being made are crucial. Many right-minded people may end by doing the wrong thing. For instance, it is possible that those well-meaning idealists who serve the satellite will end by creating a supernetwork even more dreadful and ubiquitous than the ones we have at present. The whole matter needs a good deal of airing, and should satellite transmission come to pass it ought to be guarded around with many checks and balances. Diversity, no matter how banal, is preferable to the monolithic, no matter how excellent.

Conceivably, regional television stations might revolutionize the political as well as the aesthetic life of the country. Technical means now exist for viewers to "meet" on the air, and to register their approval or disapproval of men and issues — no doubt a dangerous experiment in democracy (face to face, Reagan would always defeat Humphrey), but then the charm of democracy is the constant risk the nation runs of being derailed by the will of the majority. Politics would lose all savor without the constant tension between the shrewd few acting upon the foolish many. Television could at least make the process plain for all to see, and be a part of. Also, television could offer citizens with a grievance the opportunity to face whoever or whatever it is that gives them pain, with a local ombudsman to mediate the encounter. The police, in particular, might be kept in line by this sort of constant exposure.

It will also be possible in the future to transmit newspapers and books through television, a final victory for linear type and a good joke on the Canadian prophet. For those who find distressing the passivity of television viewing, an MIT professor has proposed that the viewer at home be allowed to select which camera he wants to see through at a sporting event or in an art gallery. As for plays, the viewer will be both director and playwright, choosing events as well as camera angles and thereby, in the professor's pleasant phrase, "interactively participating." This sort of participation should solve once and for all the problem of the West's continuing cultural decline: if everyone is an artist then no one is, and the matter's finished. In any event, E. M. Forster's vision of the Machine is now reality and it will be a long time before there is a stopping.

[*New York Review of Books,* December 7, 1967]

Byzantium's Fall

ONE of the laws of physics as yet unrevised by the masters of the second of the two cultures is that in nature there can be no action without reaction. This law also appears to hold true in human nature. Praise Aristides too much for his justice and people will think him unjust. Evoke once too often a vision of golden youths listening to wise old men in the green shade of Academe and someone will snarl that those Athenian youths were a dreary lot taught by self-serving proto-fascists of whom Plato was the worst. Depict Byzantium as the last custodian of the Greek heritage, destroyed by barbarous Turks, and Professor H. Trevor-Roper will promptly ask the readers of the *New Statesman*: "As a living political system was the Byzantine Empire, at least in its decline, really better than the Ottoman Empire in its heyday?" Though Professor Trevor-Roper indicates that his own answer to the question is negative, the question itself is a useful one to ask, particularly now.

During the last forty years the attitude of the West toward Byzantium (best expressed by Gibbon) has changed from indifferent contempt to a fascinated admiration for that complex and resourceful society which endured for a thousand years, governed by Roman Emperors in direct political descent from Constantine the Great who transformed the ruined village of Byzantium at the juncture of Europe and Asia into the New Rome. When the Western Empire broke up in the fifth century, Constantinople alone maintained the reality and the mystique of the Caesars. The city's long, perilous success story has so aroused the admiration of recent scholars that there is indeed a tendency to glorify Byzantium at the expense of the Ottoman Turks and, as Professor Trevor-Roper suggests, the Turks must have had virtues quite as notable as the legendary vices of the Byzantines. Fortunately, a partial answer to Professor Trevor-Roper's question is provided by the book he was reviewing when he asked it, *The Fall of Constantinople, 1453,* by Sir Steven Runciman, a contemporary writer of history peculiarly unaffected by an age in which scholars quite as much as popularizers delight in publicity and perverse argument. Was Hitler mad? Evil? Neither, maintains one usually responsible historian: he was simply a better than average politician who nearly won a war made inevitable by a generation of political blunderers. Elsewhere, historians not content with telling what happened now reveal exactly *why* it happened, ordering events in such a way as to fit some overall and to them entirely satisfying theory of history. Alongside the publicists and grand designers, Sir Steven looks to be curiously demure. He tells his story plain. Since God has not revealed any master plan to him, he does not feel impelled to preach "truth" to us. He does make judgments but only after he has made his case. He likes a fact and distrusts a theory. He is always pleasurable to read, and his new book describing the conquest of Constantinople by the Turks is one of his best.

The end of the Byzantine Empire began in 1204, when the Crusaders seized Constantinople and divided much of the Empire amongst themselves. This terrible deed was particularly dishonorable since the Crusade's pious object had been the freeing of the Holy Sepulcher and the turning back of the Moslems. Instead, the Crusaders greedily seized what belonged to their fellow Christians while making practical accommodations with the Infidel. Simultaneously, the Pope did his best to bring the "schismatic" Greek church back into the fold. Not until 1264 were our ancestors ("those dark and wandering tribes . . . among whom neither grace nor muse takes shelter") driven out of Constantinople by Michael Palae-ologus, founder of the last dynasty. But despite the vigor of that dynasty's domestic and foreign policies and the sudden artistic revival in the capital and at Mistra, the Empire never recovered from the Fourth Crusade. By the end of the four-teenth century, only a part of the Morea, the cities of Con-stantinople and Thessalonica, and a few odd holdings re-mained to the Roman Emperors who, possibly as a result of their experience with contemporary Romans, took note at last that their culture as well as language was entirely Greek. Proudly, as Hellenes and not *Romaioi*, the last Byzantines now presented themselves to the world.

Two centuries after the Byzantine Hellenic revival under the Comneni and the Angeli, the Western Renaissance began and with it a new interest in matters Greek, both contemporary and ancient, as well as a new and perhaps guilty sympathy for the beleaguered Emperor. Much of this sympathy was due to the gradual dispersal of Byzantine scholars to Europe, a "brain drain" which began at least a generation before the city fell. As the bookish Pius II remarked, any man with a pre-tension to learning must not only know Greek but he would be well advised to say that he had attended the University of Constantinople.

At the beginning of the thirteenth century, Tartar victories in the East caused a great removal of Turks from Anatolia to the Balkans. By 1410 there were more Turks in Europe than in Asia Minor, further isolating the city from its old Empire. Finally, with the fall of Thessalonica in 1430, it was plain that barring divine intervention, the absorption of Constan-tinople was only a matter of time. Although divine interven-tion was never entirely ruled out, human intervention was sought, particularly by John VIII Palaeologus, who made the round of European capitals, begging for aid. Although he was received respectfully, even warmly, his mission was a failure.

For one thing, the Holy See had made it plain that the price of a new Crusade would be the submission of the Greek church to Rome. Sir Steven is particularly illuminating as he describes the various wranglings at Constantinople for and against union, including the celebrated remark Lucas Notaras is supposed to have made: "Better the Sultan's turban than a Cardinal's hat."

In 1448 John VIII died and was succeeded by his forty-four-year-old brother Constantine XI, a shadowy figure whose fate it was to be the last Emperor of the East. At the time it was considered ominous that the new ruler's name was Constantine and that his mother's name was Helena; that the first and the last rulers of the city should have the same name is tribute to that neatness to which history is prone (the fact that the current King of the Hellenes is also named Constantine must give pause to the superstitious). Lacking money for mercenaries and a land empire for ordinary recruitment, the Emperor engaged in a desperate diplomacy to obtain Western aid, while spending the resources he did have on fortifying the city. Again the Pope insisted that the Greek church submit to Rome. For a time there was stalemate. Then Murad II, that most civilized of Sultans, died in 1451 to be succeeded by his son Mehmet II, a fierce youth of nineteen. When Mehmet's Vizier came to him with gifts, the new Sultan pushed them aside and said, "Only one thing I want. Give me Constantinople."

The siege began April 2, 1453. Four months earlier, Constantine had finally submitted to the Pope, but no aid came from Italy. Every advantage was now with the Turks, including a Hungarian armorer named Urban who had previously offered his services to the Emperor, who could not afford them. Urban then presented himself to the Sultan, who engaged him to build the cannon that shattered the walls. When the siege began, Mehmet's army numbered some eighty thousand men; the defenders numbered less than seven thousand.

Nevertheless, the Christians fought valiantly and not until May 29 did the Turks break into the city through a gate left open by accident. Although Constantine's advisers wanted him to withdraw to the Morea, he chose to remain with the city. And so he vanishes, literally, from history, his body never found. "The last Christian Emperor standing in the breach," as Sir Steven records it, "abandoned by his Western allies, holding the infidel at bay until their numbers overpowered him and he died, with the Empire as his winding sheet."

It is a marvelous story, marvelously told. Sir Steven takes the traditional view that the fall of the city was indeed a great and significant event, and not merely a minor happening in some vast cyclic drama. But though his view is traditional, it is hardly romantic. He reminds us that the Turks though cruel conquerors were sensible governors. Unlike the Roman Catholics, they did not persecute others for their religion. By submitting politically to the Sultan, the Greek church was able to survive until the present day, while the Hellenic community, though politically enslaved, continued to maintain its identity in a way which might have proved impossible had the Westerners once more "saved" Constantinople. Much of the old Byzantine Empire accepted the rule of the Sultans without protest, preferring political and economic stability to the sad and dangerous comings and goings of bankrupt Despots. Particularly in Thessaly was Turkish rule welcomed. It is at this point that one wishes that Sir Steven had gone into fuller detail. For it was at Thessalonica in the 1340's that the first recognizable class war of our era took place between aristocrats on the one hand and a well-organized communist-minded working class on the other, while a divided but powerful middle class representing "democratic" virtues vacillated between extremes. Significantly, the Palaeologi sided with the middle class, put down the revolution, and so maintained their dynasty for another century.

To read an historian like Sir Steven is to be reminded that history is a literary art quite equal to that of the novel. The historian must be a master not only of general narrative but of particular detail. He must understand human character. He must be able to describe physical action, a difficult task for any writer; and, finally, he must be, in the best sense, a moralist. Yet today the historian is not accorded the same artistic rank as the "serious" novelist. I suspect that much of this is due to the high value we place on "creativity," a vague activity that somehow has got mixed up with the idea of procreation. One ought to make something unique out of oneself, as opposed to assembling bits and pieces like Baron Frankenstein. Yet the art of a Runciman is certainly as creative as the art of the sort of novelist who tells us how his wife betrayed him with his best friend last summer. Both historian and novelist are describing actual events. Each must interpret those events in his own way. Yet which is of greater significance: the work of private grievance or the work of history, which attempts to order fact in such a way as to show us what actually happened in the past and how what happened affects us still? Naturally, there is a place for both kinds of writing, but I consider it a sad commentary on our period that in the literary arts we tend to prefer gossip to analysis, personality to character, "creative writing" even at its worst to historical writing at its best. Happily, works like *The Fall of Constantinople, 1453* continue to illuminate the present by recreating the past. For instance, when Zoë, the niece of Constantine XI, married the Grand Prince of Moscow, the masters of the Kremlin became not only defenders of the Greek Orthodox faith but by styling themselves Caesar (Tsar), they made it plain that as Emperors of the East they must one day liberate that imperial city to the south which they regarded as their rightful capital. And still do.

[*The Reporter*, October 7, 1965]

The Holy Family

*The Gospel according to Arthur, Paul, Pierre, and William
and several minor apostles*

FROM the beginning of the Republic, Americans have enjoyed accusing the first magistrate of kingly ambition. Sometimes seriously but more often derisively, the President is denounced as a would-be king, subverting the Constitution for personal ends. From General Washington to the present incumbent, the wielder of power has usually been regarded with suspicion, a disagreeable but not unhealthy state of affairs for both governor and governed. Few Presidents, however, have been accused of wanting to establish family dynasties, if only because most Presidents have found it impossible to select a successor of any sort, much less promote a relative. Each of the Adamses and the Harrisons reigned at an interval of not less than a political generation from the other, while the two Roosevelts were close neither in blood nor in politics. But now something new is happening in the Republic, and as the Chinese say, we are living "in interesting times."

In 1960, with the election of the thirty-fifth President, the famous ambition of Joseph P. Kennedy seemed at last fulfilled. He himself had come a long way from obscurity to great wealth and prominence; now his eldest surviving son, according to primogeniture, had gone the full distance and become President. It was a triumph for the patriarch. It was also a splendid moment for at least half the nation. What doubts one may have had about the Kennedys were obscured by the charm and intelligence of John F. Kennedy. He appeared to be beautifully on to himself; he was also on to us; there is even evidence that he was on to the family, too. As a result, there were few intellectuals in 1960 who were not beguiled by the spectacle of a President who seemed always to be standing at a certain remove from himself, watching with amusement his own performance. He was an ironist in a profession where the prize usually goes to the apparent cornball. With such a man as chief of state, all things were possible. He would "get America moving again."

But then mysteriously the thing went wrong. Despite fine rhetoric and wise commentary, despite the glamor of his presence, we did not move, and if historians are correct when they tell us that Presidents are "made" in their first eighteen months in office, then one can assume that the Kennedy administration would never have fulfilled our hopes, much less his own. Kennedy was of course ill-fated from the beginning. The Bay of Pigs used up much of his credit in the bank of public opinion, while his attempts at social legislation were resolutely blocked by a more than usually obstructive Congress. In foreign affairs he was overwhelmed by the masterful Khrushchev and not until the Cuban missile crisis did he achieve tactical parity with that sly gambler. His administration's one achievement was the test-ban treaty, an encouraging footnote to the cold war.

Yet today Kennedy dead has infinitely more force than Kennedy living. Though his administration was not a success, he himself has become a world touchstone of political excellence. Part of this phenomenon is attributable to the race's need for heroes, even in deflationary times. But mostly the legend is the deliberate creation of the Kennedy family and its clients. Wanting to regain power, it is now necessary to show that once upon a time there was indeed a Camelot beside the Potomac, a golden age forever lost unless a second Kennedy should become the President. And so, to insure the restoration of that lovely time, the past must be transformed, dull facts transcended, and the dead hero extolled in films, through memorials, and in the pages of books.

The most notorious of the books has been William Manchester's *The Death of a President*. Hoping to stop Jim Bishop from writing one of his ghoulish *The Day They Shot* sagas, the Kennedys decided to "hire" Mr. Manchester to write their version of what happened at Dallas. Unfortunately, they have never understood that treason is the natural business of clerks. Mr. Manchester's use of Mrs. Kennedy's taped recollections did not please the family. The famous comedy of errors that ensued not only insured the book's success but also made current certain intimate details which the family preferred for the electorate not to know, such as the President's selection of Mrs. Kennedy's dress on that last day in order, as he put it, "to show up those cheap Texas broads," a remark not calculated to give pleasure to the clients of Neiman-Marcus. Also, the family's irrational dislike of President Johnson came through all too plainly, creating an unexpected amount of sympathy for that least sympathetic of magistrates. Aware of what was at stake, Mrs. Kennedy tried to alter a book which neither she nor her brothers-in-law had read. Not since Mary Todd Lincoln has a President's widow been so fiercely engaged with legend if not history.

But then, legend making is necessary to the Kennedy future. As a result, most of the recent books about the late President are not so much political in approach as religious. There is the ritual beginning of the book which is the end: the death at Dallas. Then the witness goes back in time to the moment when he first met the Kennedys. He finds them strenuous but fun. Along with riotous good times, there is the constant question: How are we to elect Jack President? This sort of talk was in the open after 1956, but as long ago as 1943, as he tells us in *The Pleasure of His Company*, Paul B. Fay, Jr., made a bet that one day Jack would be JFK.

From the beginning the godhead shone for those who had the eyes to see. The witness then gives us his synoptic version of the making of the President. Once again we visit cold Wisconsin and dangerous West Virginia (can a young Catholic war hero defeat a Protestant accused of being a draft dodger in a poor mining state where primary votes are bought and sold?). From triumph to triumph the hero proceeds to the convention at Los Angeles, where the god is recognized. The only shadow upon that perfect day is cast, significantly, by Lyndon B. Johnson. Like Lucifer he challenged the god at the convention, and was struck down only to be raised again as son of morning. The deal to make Johnson Vice-President still causes violent argument among the new theologians. Pierre Salinger in *With Kennedy* quotes JFK as observing glumly, "The whole story will never be known, and it's just as well that it won't be." Then the campaign itself. The great television debates (Quemoy and Matsu) in which Nixon's obvious lack of class, as classy Jack duly noted, did him in — barely. The narrowness of the electoral victory was swiftly erased by the splendor of the inaugural ("It all began in the cold": Arthur M. Schlesinger, Jr., *A Thousand Days*). From this point on, the thousand days unfold in familiar sequence and, though details differ from gospel to gospel, the story already possesses the quality of a passion play: disaster at Cuba One, triumph at Cuba Two; the eloquent speeches; the fine pageantry; and always the crowds and the glory, ending at Dallas.

With Lucifer now rampant upon the heights, the surviving Kennedys are again at work to regain the lost paradise, which means that books must be written not only about the new incarnation of the Kennedy godhead but the old. For it is the dead hero's magic that makes legitimate the family's pretensions. As an Osiris-Adonis-Christ figure, JFK is already the subject of a cult that may persist, through the machinery of publicity, long after all memory of his administration has been absorbed by the golden myth now being created in a thousand books to the single end of maintaining in power our extraordinary holy family.

The most recent batch of books about JFK, though hagiographies, at times cannot help but illuminate the three themes which dominate any telling of the sacred story: money, image-making, family. That is the trinity without which nothing. Mr. Salinger, the late President's press secretary, is necessarily concerned with the second theme, though he touches on the other two. Paul B. Fay, Jr., (a wartime buddy of JFK and Under Secretary of the Navy) is interesting on every count, and since he seems not to know what he is saying, his book is the least calculated and the most lifelike of the ones so far published. Other books at hand are Richard J. Whalen's *The Founding Father* (particularly good on money and family) and Evelyn Lincoln's *My Twelve Years with John F. Kennedy,* which in its simple way tells us a good deal about those who are drawn to the Kennedys.

While on the clerical staff of a Georgia Congressman, Mrs. Lincoln decided in 1952 that she wanted to work for "someone in Congress who seemed to have what it takes to be President"; after a careful canvass, she picked the Representative from the Massachusetts Eleventh District. Like the other witnesses under review, she never says *why* she wants to work for a future President; it is taken for granted that anyone would, an interesting commentary on all the witnesses from Schlesinger (whose *A Thousand Days* is the best political novel since *Coningsby*) to Theodore Sorensen's dour *Kennedy.* Needless to say, in all the books there is not only love and awe for the fallen hero who was, in most cases, the witness's single claim to public attention, but there are also a remarkable number of tributes to the holy family. From Jacqueline (Isis-Aphrodite-Madonna) to Bobby (Ares and perhaps Christ-to-be) the Kennedys appear at the very least as demigods, larger than life. Bobby's hard-working staff seldom complained, as Mr. Salinger put it, "because we all knew that

Bob was working just a little harder than we were." For the same reason "we could accept without complaint [JFK's] bristling temper, his cold sarcasm, and his demands for always higher standards of excellence because we knew he was driving himself harder than he was driving us—despite great and persistent physical pain and personal tragedy." Mrs. Lincoln surprisingly finds the late President "humble"—doubtless since the popular wisdom requires all great men to be humble. She refers often to his "deep low voice" [sic], "his proud head held high, his eyes fixed firmly on the goals— sometimes seemingly impossible goals—he set for himself and all those around him." Mr. Schlesinger's moving threnody at the close of *his* gospel makes it plain that we will not see JFK's like again, at least not until the administration of Kennedy II.

Of the lot, only Mr. Fay seems not to be writing a book with an eye to holding office in the next Kennedy administration. He is garrulous and indiscreet (the Kennedys are still displeased with his memoirs even though thousands of words were cut from the manuscript on the narrow theological ground that since certain things he witnessed fail to enhance the image, they must be apocrypha). On the subject of the Kennedys and money, Mr. Fay tells a most revealing story. In December, 1959, the family was assembled at Palm Beach; someone mentioned money, "causing Mr. Kennedy to plunge in, fire blazing from his eyes. 'I don't know what is going to happen to this family when I die,' Mr. Kennedy said. 'There is no one in the entire family, except Joan and Teddy, who is living within their means. No one appears to have the slightest concern for how much they spend.'" The tirade ended with a Kennedy sister running from the room in tears, her extravagance condemned in open family session. Characteristically, Jack deflected the progenitor's wrath with the comment that the only "solution is to have Dad work harder." A story which contradicts, incidentally, Mr. Salinger's pious "Despite his great wealth and his generosity in contributing all of his salaries as Congressman, Senator and President to charities, the President was not a man to waste pennies."

But for all the founding father's grumbling, the children's attitude toward money — like so much else — is pretty much what he wanted it to be. It is now a familiar part of the sacred story of how Zeus made each of the nine Olympians individually wealthy, creating trust funds which now total some ten million dollars per god or goddess. Also at the disposal of the celestials is the great fortune itself, estimated at a hundred, two hundred, three hundred, or whatever hundred millions of dollars, administered from an office on Park Avenue, to which the Kennedys send their bills, for we are told in *The Founding Father*, "the childhood habit of dependence persisted in adult life. As grown men and women the younger Kennedys still look to their father's staff of accountants to keep track of their expenditures and see to their personal finances." There are, of course, obvious limitations to not understanding the role of money in the lives of the majority. The late President was aware of this limitation and he was forever asking his working friends how much money they made. On occasion, he was at a disadvantage because he did not understand the trader's mentality. He missed the point to Khrushchev at Vienna and took offense at what, after all, was simply the boorishness of the marketplace. His father, an old hand in Hollywood, would have understood better the mogul's bluffing.

It will probably never be known how much money Joe Kennedy has spent for the political promotion of his sons. At the moment, an estimated million dollars a year is being spent on Bobby's behalf, and this sum can be matched year after year until 1972, and longer. Needless to say, the sons are sensitive to the charge that their elections are bought. As JFK said of his 1952 election to the Senate, "People say 'Kennedy bought the election. Kennedy could never have been elected if his father hadn't been a millionaire.' Well, it wasn't the Kennedy name and the Kennedy money that won that election. I beat Lodge because I hustled for three years," (quoted in *The Founding Father*). But of course without the Kennedy name and the Kennedy money, he would not even have been a contender. Not only was a vast amount of money spent for his election in the usual ways, but a great deal was spent in not so usual ways. For instance, according to Richard J. Whalen, right after the pro-Lodge Boston *Post* unexpectedly endorsed Jack Kennedy for the Senate, Joe Kennedy loaned the paper's publisher $500,000.

But the most expensive legitimate item in today's politics is the making of the image. Highly paid technicians are able to determine with alarming accuracy just what sort of characteristics the public desires at any given moment in a national figure, and with adroit handling a personable candidate can be made to seem whatever the Zeitgeist demands. The Kennedys are not of course responsible for applying to politics the techniques of advertising (the two have always gone hand in hand), but of contemporary politicians (the Rockefellers excepted) the Kennedys alone possess the money to maintain one of the most remarkable self-publicizing machines in the history of advertising, a machine which for a time had the resources of the Federal government at its disposal.

It is in describing the activities of a chief press officer at the White House that Mr. Salinger is most interesting. A talented image maker, he was responsible, among other things, for the televised press conferences in which the President was seen at his best, responding to simple questions with careful and often charming answers. That these press conferences were not very informative was hardly the fault of Mr. Salinger or the President. If it is true that the medium is the message and television is the coolest of all media and to be cool is desirable, then the televised thirty-fifth President was positively glacial in his effectiveness. He was a natural for this time and place, largely because of his obsession with the appearance of things. In fact, much of his political timidity was the result of a quite uncanny ability to sense how others would respond to what he said or did, and if he foresaw a negative response, he was apt to avoid action altogether. There were times, however, when his superb sense of occasion led him astray. In the course of a speech to the Cuban refugees in Miami, he was so over-whelmed by the drama of the situation that he practically launched on the spot a second invasion of that beleaguered island. Yet generally he was cool. He enjoyed the game of pleasing others, which is the actor's art.

He was also aware that vanity is perhaps the strongest of human emotions, particularly the closer one comes to the top of the slippery pole. Mrs. Kennedy once told me that the last thing Mrs. Eisenhower had done before leaving the White House was to hang a portrait of herself in the entrance hall. The first thing Mrs. Kennedy had done on moving in was to put the portrait in the basement, on aesthetic, not political grounds. Overhearing this, the President told an usher to re-store the painting to its original place. "The Eisenhowers are coming to lunch tomorrow," he explained patiently to his wife, "and that's the first thing she'll look for." Mrs. Lincoln records that before the new Cabinet met, the President and Bobby were about to enter the Cabinet room when the Presi-dent "said to his brother, 'Why don't you go through the other door?' The President waited until the Attorney Gen-eral entered the Cabinet room from the hall door, and then he walked into the room from my office."

In its relaxed way Mr. Fay's book illuminates the actual man much better than the other books if only because he was a friend to the President, and not just an employee. He is particularly interesting on the early days when Jack could discuss openly the uses to which he was being put by his father's ambition. Early in 1945 the future President told Mr. Fay how much he envied Fay his postwar life in sunny Cali-fornia while "I'll be back here with Dad trying to parlay a lost PT boat and a bad back into a political advantage. I tell you, Dad is ready right now and can't understand why Johnny boy isn't 'all engines full ahead.'" Yet the exploitation of son by father had begun long before the war. In 1940 a thesis written by Jack at Harvard was published under the title *Why England Slept*, with a foreword by longtime, balding, family friend Henry Luce. The book became a best seller and (Richard J. Whalen tells us) as Joe wrote at the time in a letter to his son, "You would be surprised how a book that really makes the grade with high-class people stands you in good stead for years to come."

Joe was right of course and bookmaking is now an important part of the holy family's home industry. As Mrs. Lincoln observed, when JFK's collection of political sketches "won the Pulitzer prize for biography in 1957, the Senator's prominence as a scholar and statesman grew. As his book continued to be a best seller, he climbed higher upon public-opinion polls and moved into a leading position among Presidential possibilities for 1960." Later Bobby would "write" a book about how he almost nailed Jimmy Hoffa; and so great was the impact of this work that many people had the impression that Bobby had indeed put an end to the career of that turbulent figure.

Most interesting of all the myth making was the creation of Jack the war hero. John Hersey first described for the *New Yorker* how Jack's Navy boat was wrecked after colliding with a Japanese ship; in the course of a long swim, the young skipper saved the life of a crewman, an admirable thing to do. Later they were all rescued. Since the officer who survived was Ambassador Kennedy's son, the story was deliberately told and retold as an example of heroism unequaled in war's history. Through constant repetition the simple facts of the story merged into a blurred impression that somehow at some point a unique act of heroism had been committed by Jack Kennedy. The last telling of the story was a film starring Cliff

Robertson as JFK (the President had wanted Warren Beatty for the part, but the producer thought Beatty's image was "too mixed up").

So the image was created early: the high-class book that made the grade; the much-publicized heroism at war; the election to the House of Representatives in 1946. From that point on, the publicity was constant and though the Congressman's record of service was unimpressive, he himself was photogenic and appealing. Then came the Senate, the marriage, the illnesses, the second high-class book, and the rest is history. But though it was Joe Kennedy who paid the bills and to a certain extent managed the politics, the recipient of all this attention was meanwhile developing into a shrewd psychologist. Mr. Fay quotes a letter written him by the new Senator in 1953. The tone is jocular (part of the charm of Mr. Fay's book is that it captures as no one else has the preppish side to JFK's character; he was droll, particularly about himself, in a splendid W. C. Fields way): "I gave everything a good deal of thought. I am getting married this fall. This means the end of a promising political career, as it has been based up to now almost completely on the old sex appeal." After a few more sentences in this vein the groom-to-be comes straight to the point. "Let me know the general reaction to this in the Bay area." He did indeed want to know, like a romantic film star, what effect marriage would have on his career. But then most of his life was governed, as Mrs. Lincoln wrote of the year 1959, "by the public-opinion polls. We were not unlike the people who check their horoscope each day before venturing out." And when they did venture out, it was always to create an illusion. As Mrs. Lincoln remarks in her guileless way: after Senator Kennedy returned to Washington from a four-week tour of Europe, "it was obvious that his stature as a Senator had grown, for he came back as an authority on the current situation in Poland."

It is not to denigrate the late President or the writers of his gospel that neither he nor they ever seemed at all concerned by the bland phoniness of so much of what he did and said. Of course politicians have been pretty much the same since the beginning of history, and part of the game is creating illusion. In fact, the late President himself shortly after Cuba One summed up what might very well have been not only his political philosophy but that of the age in which we live. When asked whether or not the Soviet's placement of missiles in Cuba would have actually shifted the balance of world power, he indicated that he thought not. "But it would have politically changed the balance of power. It would have appeared to, and appearances contribute to reality."

From the beginning, the holy family has tried to make itself appear to be what it thinks people want rather than what the realities of any situation might require. Since Bobby is thought by some to be ruthless, he must therefore be photographed as often as possible with children, smiling and happy and athletic, in every way a boy's ideal man. Politically, he must *seem* to be at odds with the present administration without ever actually taking any important position that President Johnson does not already hold. Bobby's Vietnamese war dance was particularly illustrative of the technique. A step to the Left (let's talk to the Viet Cong), followed by two steps to the Right, simultaneously giving "the beards" — as he calls them — the sense that he is for peace in Vietnam while maintaining his brother's war policy. Characteristically, the world at large believes that if JFK were alive there would be no war in Vietnam. The myth makers have obscured the fact that it was JFK who began our active participation in the war when, in 1961, he added to the six hundred American observers the first of a gradual buildup of American troops, which reached twenty thousand at the time of his assassination. And there is no evidence that he would not have persisted in that war, for, as he said to a friend shortly before he died, "I have to go all the way with this one." He could not suffer a second Cuba and hope to maintain the appearance of Defender of the Free World at the ballot box in 1964.

The authors of the latest Kennedy books are usually at their most interesting when they write about themselves. They are cautious, of course (except for the jaunty Mr. Fay), and most are thinking ahead to Kennedy II. Yet despite a hope of future preferment, Mr. Salinger's self-portrait is a most curious one. He veers between a coarse unawareness of what it was all about (he never, for instance, expresses an opinion of the war in Vietnam), and a solemn bogusness that is most putting off. Like an after-dinner speaker, he characterizes everyone ("Clark Clifford, the brilliant Washington lawyer"); he pays heavy tribute to his office staff; he praises Rusk and the State Department, remarking that "JFK had more effective liaison with the State Department than any President in history," which would have come as news to the late President. Firmly Mr. Salinger puts Arthur Schlesinger, Jr., in his place, saying that he himself never heard the President express a lack of confidence in Rusk. Mr. Salinger also remarks that though Schlesinger was "a strong friend" of the President (something Mr. Salinger, incidentally, was not), "JFK occasionally was impatient with their [Schlesinger's memoranda] length and frequency." Mrs. Lincoln also weighs in on the subject of the historian-in-residence. Apparently JFK's "relationship with Schlesinger was never that close. He admired Schlesinger's brilliant mind, his enormous store of information . . . but Schlesinger was never more than an ally and assistant."

It is a tribute to Kennedy's gift for compartmentalizing the people in his life that none knew to what extent he saw the others. Mr. Fay was an after-hours buddy. Mrs. Lincoln was the girl in the office. Mr. Salinger was a technician and not a part of the President's social or private or even, as Mr. Salinger himself admits, political life. Contrasting his role with that of James Hagerty, Mr. Salinger writes, "My only policy duties were in the information field. While Jim had a voice in deciding what the administration would do, I was responsible only for presenting that decision to the public in a way and at a time that would generate the best possible reception." His book is valuable only when he discusses the relations between press and government. And of course when he writes about himself. His 1964 campaign for the Senate is nicely told and it is good to know that he lost because he came out firmly for fair housing on the ground that "morally I had no choice — not after sweating out Birmingham and Oxford with John F. Kennedy." This is splendid but it might have made his present book more interesting had he told us something about that crucial period of sweating out. Although he devotes a chapter to telling how he did not take a fifty-mile hike, he never discusses Birmingham, Oxford, or the Negro revolution.

All in all, his book is pretty much what one might expect of a PR man. He papers over personalities with the reflexive and usually inaccurate phrase (Eisenhower and Kennedy "had deep respect for each other"; Mrs. Kennedy has "a keen understanding of the problems which beset mankind"). Yet for all his gift at creating images for others, Mr. Salinger seems not to have found his own. Uneasily he plays at being U.S. Senator, fat boy at court, thoughtful emissary to Khrushchev. Lately there has been a report in the press that he is contemplating writing a novel. If he does, Harold Robbins may be in the sort of danger that George Murphy never was. The evidence at hand shows that he has the gift. Describing his divorce from "Nancy, my wife of eight years," Mr. Salinger manages in a few lines to say everything. "An extremely artistic woman, she was determined to live a quieter life in which she could pursue her skills as a ceramicist. And we both knew that I could not be happy unless I was on the move. It was this difference in philosophies, not a lack of respect, that led to our decision to obtain a divorce. But a vacation in Palm Springs, as Frank Sinatra's guest, did much to revive my spirits."

Mr. Fay emerges as very much his own man, and it is apparent that he amused the President at a level which was more that of a playmate escorting the actress Angie Dickinson to the Inaugural than as serious companion to the prince. Unlike the other witnesses, Mr. Fay has no pretensions about himself. He tells how "the President then began showing us the new paintings on the wall. 'Those two are Renoirs and that's a Cézanne', he told us. Knowing next to nothing about painters or paintings, I asked, 'Who are they?' The President's response was predictable, 'My God, if you ask a question like that, do it in a whisper or wait till we get outside. We're trying to give this administration a semblance of class.'" The President saw the joke; he also saw the image which must at all times be projected. Parenthetically, a majority of the recorded anecdotes about Kennedy involve keeping up appearances; he was compulsively given to emphasizing, often with great charm, the division between how things must be made to seem, as opposed to the way they are. This division is noticeable, even in the censored version of Mr. Manchester's *The Death of a President*. The author records that when Kennedy spoke at Houston's coliseum, Jack Valenti, crouched below the lectern, was able to observe the extraordinary tremor of the President's hands, and the artful way in which he managed to conceal them from the audience. This tension between the serene appearance and that taut reality add to the poignancy of the true legend, so unlike the Parson Weems version Mrs. Kennedy would like the world to accept.

Money, image, family: the three are extraordinarily intertwined. The origin of the Kennedy sense of family is the holy land of Ireland, priest-ridden, superstitious, clannish. While most of the West in the nineteenth century was industrialized and urbanized, Ireland remained a famine-ridden agrarian country, in thrall to politicians, homegrown and British, priest and lay. In 1848, the first Kennedy set up shop in Boston, where the Irish were exploited and patronized by the

Wasps; not unnaturally, the Irish grew bitter and vengeful and finally asserted themselves at the ballot box. But the old resentment remained as late as Joe Kennedy's generation and with it flourished a powerful sense that the family is the only unit that could withstand the enemy, as long as each member remained loyal to the others, "regarding life as a joint venture between one generation and the next." In *The Fruitful Bough*, a privately printed cluster of tributes to the Elder Kennedy (collected by Edward M. Kennedy) we are told, in Bobby's words, that to Joe Kennedy "the most important thing . . . was the advancement of his children . . . except for his influence and encouragement, my brother Jack might not have run for the Senate in 1952." (So much for JFK's comment that it was his own "hustling" that got him Lodge's seat.)

The father is of course a far more interesting figure than any of his sons if only because his will to impose himself upon a society which he felt had snubbed him has been in the most extraordinary way fulfilled. He drove his sons to "win, win, win." But never at any point did he pause to ask himself or them just what it was they were supposed to win. He taught them to regard life as a game of Monopoly (a family favorite): you put up as many hotels as you can on Ventnor Avenue and win. Consequently, some of the failure of his son's administration can be ascribed to the family philosophy. All his life Jack Kennedy was driven by his father and then by himself to be first in politics, which meant to be the President. But once that goal had been achieved, he had no future, no place else to go. This absence of any sense of the whole emerged in the famous exchange between him and James Reston, who asked the newly elected President what his philosophy was, what vision did he have of the good life. Mr. Reston got a blank stare for answer. Kennedy apologists are quick to use this exchange as proof of their man's essentially pragmatic nature ("pragmatic" was a favorite word of the era, even though its political meaning is opportunist). As they saw it: give the President a specific problem and he will solve it through intelligence and expertise. A "philosophy" was simply of no use to a man of action. For a time, actual philosophers were charmed by the thought of an intelligent young empiricist fashioning a New Frontier.

Not until the second year of his administration did it become plain that Kennedy was not about to do much of anything. Since his concern was so much with the appearance of things, he was at his worst when confronted with those issues where a moral commitment might have informed his political response not only with passion but with shrewdness. Had he challenged the Congress in the Truman manner on such bills as Medicare and Civil Rights, he might at least have inspired the country, if not the Congress, to follow his lead. But he was reluctant to rock the boat, and it is significant that he often quoted Hotspur on summoning spirits from the deep: any man can summon, but will the spirits come? JFK never found out; he would not take the chance. His excuse in private for his lack of force, particularly in dealing with the Congress, was the narrow electoral victory of 1960. The second term, he declared, would be the one in which all things might be accomplished. With a solid majority behind him, he could work wonders. But knowing his character, it is doubtful that the second term would have been much more useful than the first. After all, he would have been constitutionally a lame duck President, perhaps interested in holding the franchise for his brother. The family, finally, was his only commitment and it colored all his deeds and judgment.

In 1960, after listening to him denounce Eleanor Roosevelt at some length, I asked him why he thought she was so much opposed to his candidacy. The answer was quick: "She hated my father and she can't stand it that his children turned out so much better than hers." I was startled at how little he understood Mrs. Roosevelt, who, to be fair, did not at all understand him, though at the end she was won by his personal

charm. Yet it was significant that he could not take seriously
any of her political objections to him (e.g., his attitude to
McCarthyism); he merely assumed that she, like himself, was
essentially concerned with family and, envying the father,
would want to thwart the son. He was, finally, very much his
father's son even though, as all the witnesses are at pains to
remind us, he did not share that magnate's political philosophy — which goes without saying, since anyone who did
could not be elected to anything except possibly the Chamber
of Commerce. But *The Founding Father*'s confidence in his
own wisdom ("I know more about Europe than anybody else
in this country," he said in 1940, "because I've been closer to
it longer") and the assumption that he alone knew the absolute
inside story about everything is a trait inherited by the sons,
particularly Bobby, whose principal objection to the "talking
liberals" is that they never know what's really going on, as
he in his privileged place does but may not tell. The Kennedy
children have always observed our world from the heights.

The distinguished jurist Francis Morrissey tells in *The
Fruitful Bough* a most revealing story of life upon Olympus.
"During the Lodge campaign, the Ambassador told [Jack and
me] clearly that the campaign . . . would be the toughest fight
he could think of, but there was no question that Lodge would
be beaten, and if that should come to pass Jack would be
nominated and elected President. . . . In that clear and com-
manding voice of his he said to Jack, 'I will work out the
plans to elect you President. It will not be any more difficult
for you to be elected President than it will be to win the
Lodge fight . . . you will need to get about twenty key men in
the country to get the nomination for it is these men who will
control the convention. . . .' "

One of the most fascinating aspects of politician-watching
is trying to determine to what extent any politician believes
what he says. Most of course never do, regarding public statements as necessary noises to soothe the electorate or deflect

the wrath of the passionate, who are forever mucking things up for the man who wants decently and normally to rise. Yet there are cases of politicians who have swayed themselves by their own speeches. Take a man of conservative disposition and force him to give liberal speeches for a few years in order to be elected and he will, often as not, come to believe himself. There is evidence that JFK often spellbound himself. Bobby is something else again. Andrew Kopkind in the *New Republic* once described Bobby's career as a series of "happenings": the McCarthy friend and fellow traveler of one year emerges as an intense New York liberal in another, and between these two happenings there is no thread at all to give a clue as to what the man actually thinks or who he really is. That consistency which liberals so furiously demanded of the hapless Nixon need not apply to any Kennedy.

After all, as the recent gospels point out, JFK himself was slow to become a liberal, to the extent he ever was (in our society no working politician can be radical). As JFK said to James MacGregor Burns, "Some people have their liberalism 'made' by the time they reach their late twenties. I didn't. I was caught in crosscurrents and eddies. It was only later that I got into the stream of things." His comment made liberalism sound rather like something run up by a tailor, a necessary garment which he regrets that he never had time in his youth to be fitted for. Elsewhere (in William Manchester's *Portrait of a President*) he explains those "currents and eddies." Of his somewhat reactionary career in the House of Representatives he said, "I'd just come out of my father's house at the time, and these were the things I knew." It is of course a truism that character is formed in one's father's house. Ideas may change but the attitude toward others does not. A father who teaches his sons that the only thing that matters is to be first, not second, not third, is obviously (should his example be followed) going to be rewarded with energetic sons. Yet it is hardly surprising that to date one cannot determine where the junior Senator from New York stands on such a straight-forward issue (morally if not politically) as the American adventure in Vietnam. Differing with the President as to which cities ought to be bombed in the North does not constitute an alternative policy. His sophisticated liberal admirers, however, do not seem in the least distressed by his lack of a position; instead they delight in the *uses* to which he has put the war in Vietnam in order to embarrass the usurper in the White House.

The cold-blooded jauntiness of the Kennedys in politics has a remarkable appeal for those who also want to rise and who find annoying — to the extent they are aware of it at all — the moral sense. Also, the success of the three Kennedy brothers nicely makes hash of the old American belief that by working hard and being good one will deserve (and if fortunate, receive) promotion. A mediocre Representative, an absentee Senator, through wealth and family connections, becomes the President while his youngest brother inherits the Senate seat. Now Bobby is about to become RFK because he is Bobby. It is as if the United States had suddenly reverted to the eighteenth century, when the politics of many states were family affairs. In those days, if one wanted a political career in New York one had best be born a Livingston, a Clinton, or a Schuyler; failing that, one must marry into the family, as Alexander Hamilton did, or go to work for them. In a way, the whole Kennedy episode is a fascinating throwback to an earlier phase of civilization. Because the Irish maintained the ancient village sense of the family longer than most places in the West and to the extent that the sons of Joe Kennedy reflect those values and prejudices, they are an anachronism in an urbanized non-family-minded society. Yet the fact that they are so plainly not of this time makes them fascinating; their family story is a glamorous continuing soap opera whose appeal few can resist, including the liberals, who, though they may suspect that the Kennedys are not with them at heart, believe that the two boys are educable. At this very moment beside the river Charles a thousand Aristotles dream of their young Alexanders, and the coming heady conquest of the earth.

Meanwhile, the source of the holy family's power is the legend of the dead brother, who did not much resemble the hero of the books under review. Yet the myth that JFK was a philosopher-king will continue as long as the Kennedys remain in politics. And much of the power they exert over the national imagination is a direct result of the ghastliness of what happened at Dallas. But though the world's grief and shock were genuine, they were not entirely for JFK himself. The death of a young leader necessarily strikes an atavistic chord. For thousands of years the man-god was sacrificed to ensure with blood the harvest, and there is always an element of ecstasy as well as awe in our collective grief. Also, Jack Kennedy was a television star, more seen by most people than their friends or relatives. His death in public was all the more stunning because he was not an abstraction called The President, but a man the people thought they knew. At the risk of *lèse-divinité*, however, the assassination of President Nixon at, let us say, Cambridge by what at first was thought to be a member of the ADA but later turned out to be a dotty Bircher would have occasioned quite as much national horror, mourning, and even hagiography. But in time the terrible deed would have been forgotten, for there are no Nixon heirs.

Beyond what one thinks of the Kennedys themselves, there remains the large question: What sort of men ought we to be governed by in the coming years? With the high cost of politics and image making, it is plain that only the very wealthy or those allied with the very wealthy can afford the top prizes. And among the rich, only those who are able to please the people on television are Presidential. With the decline of the religions, the moral sense has become confused, to say the least, and intellectual or political commitments that go beyond the merely expedient are regarded with cheerful contempt not only by the great operators themselves but also by their admirers and, perhaps, by the electorate itself. Also, to be fair, politicians working within a system like ours can never be much more than what the system will allow. Hypocrisy and self-deception are the traditional characteristics of the middle class in any place and time, and the United States today is the paradigmatic middle-class society. Therefore we can hardly blame our political gamesmen for being, literally, representative. Any public man has every right to try and trick us, not only for his own good but, if he is honorable, for ours as well. However, if he himself is not aware of what he is doing or to what end he is playing the game, then to entrust him with the first magistracy of what may be the last empire on earth is to endanger us all. One does not necessarily demand of our leaders passion (Hitler supplied the age with quite enough for this century) or reforming zeal (Mao Tse-tung is incomparable), but one does insist that they possess a sense of community larger than simply personal power for its own sake, being first because it's fun. Finally, in an age of supercommunications, one must have a clear sense of the way things are, as opposed to the way they have been made to seem. Since the politics of the Kennedys are so often the work of publicists, it is necessary to keep trying to find out just who they are and what they really mean. If only because should *they* be confused as to the realities of Cuba, say, or Vietnam, then the world's end is at hand.

At one time in the United States, the popular wisdom maintained that there was no better work for a man to do than to set in motion some idea whose time had not yet arrived, even at the risk of becoming as unpopular as those politicians JFK so much admired in print and so little emulated in life. It may well be that it is now impossible for such men to rise to the top in our present system. If so, this is a tragedy. Meanwhile, in their unimaginative fierce way, the Kennedys continue to play successfully the game as they found it. They create illusions and call them facts, and between what they are said to be and what they are falls the shadow of all the useful words not spoken, of all the actual deeds not done. But if it is true that in a rough way nations deserve the leadership they get, then a frivolous and apathetic electorate combined with a vain and greedy intellectual establishment will most certainly restore to power the illusion-making Kennedys. Holy family and bedazzled nation, in their faults at least, are well matched. In any case, the age of the commune in which we have lived since the time of Jackson is drawing to a close and if historical analogies are at all relevant, the rise of the *signori* is about to begin, and we may soon find ourselves enjoying a strange new era in which all our lives and dreams are presided over by smiling, interchangeable, initialed gods.

[*Esquire*, April 1967]

POSTSCRIPT: JUNE 6, 1968

It is curious how often one prefers his enemies to his friends. Although I certainly never wanted Bobby to be President, I had lately come to accept him as a useful figure on the scene — and now that he is gone I find that I genuinely miss him. Nevertheless, I still think "The Holy Family" worth reprinting partly for what it has to say about that doomed family, partly for what it has to say about the way in which our political system has become a game for the very rich.

Unlike most Americans I do not think that to be rich is automatically to be virtuous. More to the point, I think it tragic that the poor man has almost no chance to rise unless he is willing to put himself in thrall to moneyed interests. Unless drastic reforms are made, we must accept the fact that every four years the United States will be up for sale, and the richest man or family will buy it.

The Manchester Book

AT ANY given moment only a handful of people are known to almost everyone in the world. Mr. and Mrs. Richard Burton, the Kennedys . . . and the list is already near its end. There are of course those who enjoy reading about the late Sir Winston Churchill and the never-late General de Gaulle, but their fans are relatively few. Interest in Lyndon Johnson the Man (as opposed to the Warrior) is alarmingly slight; in fact, of the world's chiefs of state, only the enigmatic Mao Tse-tung can be said to intrigue the masses. There is something perversely gratifying in the fact that in an age of intense gossip and global publicity so few people are known to both the alert Malaysian and the average American. Things were different of course in the small world of Europe's Middle Ages. Numerous heroes were much sung about, while everyone was imbued with the Christian ethos. As a result, painters had a subject, scholars had something to argue about, poets had a point of departure. But the idea of Christendom died in Darwin's study, and now perhaps the only thing that we may all be said to hold in common is Bobby and Teddy and Jackie, and the memory of the dead President. Is it enough?

William Manchester thinks so, and his testament, *The Death of a President*, is very much a work of love, even passion. As we learned in the course of his notorious agony last year, the sun set for him when John Kennedy died. Happily, the sun has since risen and Mr. Manchester can now take satisfaction in knowing that he too is part of history, a permanent footnote to an administration which is beginning to look as if it may itself be simply a glamorous footnote to that voluminous text the Age of Johnson. But whether or not Camelot will continue to exert its spell (and perhaps, like Brigadoon, rematerialize), Mr. Manchester has written a book hard to resist reading, despite its inordinate length. The narrative is compelling even though one knows in advance everything that is going to happen. Breakfast in Fort Worth. Flight to Dallas. Governor Connally. The roses. The sun. The friendly crowds. The Governor's wife: "Well, you can't say Dallas doesn't love you, Mr. President." And then one hopes that for once the story will be different — the car swerves, the bullets miss, and the splendid progress continues. But each time, like a recurrent nightmare, the handsome head is shattered. It is probably the only story that everyone in the world knows by heart. Therefore it is, in the truest sense, legend, and like all legends it can bear much repetition and reinterpretation. In classical times, every Greek playgoer knew that sooner or later Electra would recognize Orestes, but the manner of recognition varied significantly from teller to teller.

Mr. Manchester's final telling of the death of Kennedy is most moving; it is also less controversial than one had been led to believe by those who read the original manuscript and found the portrait of President Johnson unflattering. According to the current text, Johnson seems a bit inadequate but hardly villainous. The Kennedys, on the other hand, blaze with light; the author's love is apparent on every page. That love, however, did his writing little service, for the prose of the book is not good — the result, no doubt, of the strain under which the author was compelled to work. Certainly the style shows none of the ease which marked his first book on Kennedy, nor is there any trace of that elegance with which he once portrayed H. L. Mencken. Yet the crowded, overwritten narrative holds. Mr. Manchester is perhaps too haughty in his dismissal of the plot theory, and altogether too confident in analyzing Oswald's character ("In fact, he was going mad"). Nevertheless, if the best the detractors of the book can come up with is a photograph proving that, contrary to what Mr. Manchester has written, a number of Kennedy courtiers did indeed attend the swearing-in of the new President, then it is safe to assume that he has apparently accomplished what he set out to do: describe accurately what happened at Dallas, and immediately after.

Apparently. For there is a certain mystery about the origins of the book. It is known that the Kennedys approached Mr. Manchester and asked him to write the "official" version of the assassination. But in this age of image making, politicians are never motivated simply. Whatever the moment's purpose, everything must serve it. Certainly nothing must get out of hand, as the Kennedys know better than anyone, for they were stung once before by a writer. Preparing for 1960, they gave Professor James MacGregor Burns a free hand to write what, in effect, was to be a campaign biography of John Kennedy. The result was a work of some candor which still remains the best analysis of the thirty-fifth President's character, but the candor which gave the book its distinction did not at all please its subject or his family. References to Joe Kennedy's exuberant anti-Semitic outbursts combined with a shrewd analysis of John Kennedy's ambivalent attitude toward McCarthy caused irritation. Therefore the next writer must be tractable. The starry-eyed Mr. Manchester seemed made to order: he was willing to swear loyalty; more important, he was willing to sign agreements. With some confidence, Launcelot and Guinevere confided him the task of celebrating the fallen hero.

The comedy began. Right off, there was the matter of President Johnson. Whatever Mr. Manchester's original feelings about Johnson, he could not have spent all those hours com-

muning with members of the exiled court and not get the sense
of what a disaster it was for the country to have that vulgar,
inept boor in Jack's place. The Kennedys have always been
particularly cruel about Johnson, and their personal disdain is
reflected and magnified by those around them, particularly their
literary apologists, of whom Mr. Manchester was now one.
When at last he submitted his work to the family, they proved
too great and too sensitive to read it for themselves. Instead
friends were chosen to pass on the contents of the book. The
friends found the anti-Johnson tone dangerous in the political
context of the moment. They said so, and Mr. Manchester
obediently made changes.

But Mr. Manchester's true ordeal did not begin until Richard Goodwin, a former aide to President Johnson, read the
manuscript and found fault. He alarmed Mrs. Kennedy with
tales of how what she had said looked in cold print. As a
result, she threatened to sue if large cuts were not made. Some
were made. Some were not. At last the publishers grew weary:
the text could not be further altered. To their amazement,
Mrs. Kennedy brought suit against them; meanwhile, in com-
municating her displeasure to Mr. Manchester, she reminded
him that so secure was she in the pantheon of American
heroines, no one could hope to cross her and survive — "unless I run off with Eddie Fisher," she added drolly. Needless
to say, Mrs. Kennedy had her way, as the world knows.

It is now reasonable to assume that Mr. Manchester is not
the same man he was before he got involved with the Kennedys. But though one's sympathy is with him, one must examine
the matter from the Kennedy point of view. They are playing
a great and dangerous game: they want the Presidency of the
United States and they will do quite a lot to obtain it. By reflecting accurately their view of Johnson, Mr. Manchester
placed in jeopardy their immediate political future. Put
simply, they do not want, in 1967, to split fatally the Democratic Party. Unhappily for them, Mr. Manchester's sense

of history did not accommodate this necessary fact; nevertheless, since he was, in their eyes, a "hired" writer, he must tell
the story their way or not at all. As it turned out, he did
pretty much what they wanted him to do. But, in the process of
publicly strong-arming Mr. Manchester and the various
publishers involved, the Kennedys gave some substance to
those "vicious" rumors (so often resorted to by polemicists)
that they are ruthless and perhaps not very lovable after all.
As a result, Mr. Manchester's contribution to history may
prove not to be the writing of this book so much as being the
unwitting agent who allowed the innocent millions an unexpected glimpse of a preternaturally ambitious family furiously at work manipulating history in order that they might
rise.

It was inevitable that sooner or later popular opinion would
go against this remarkable family. In nature there is no action
without reaction, no raising up without a throwing down. It
does not take a particularly astute political observer to detect
the public's change of mood toward the Kennedys. Overt
ambition has always caused unease in the Republic, while
excessive busyness makes for fatigue. Since our electorate is
as easily alarmed as it is bored, political ascent has always been
hazardous, and the way strewn with discarded idols. Mrs.
Kennedy, in particular, is a victim of the public's fickleness;
undeserving of their love, she is equally undeserving of their
dislike. But then it is a most terrible thing to live out a legend,
and one wonders to what extent the Kennedys themselves
understand just what was set in motion for them by their
father's will that they be great. Theirs is indeed *the* story of
our time, and, if it did nothing else, the noisy quarrel with
Mr. Manchester made vivid for everyone not only their ar-
rogance but their poignancy. They are unique in our history,
and the day they depart the public scene will be a sad one; for
not only will we have lost a family as much our own as it is
theirs, we shall have also lost one of the first shy hints since

Christianity's decline that there may indeed be such a thing as fate, and that tragedy is not merely a literary form of little relevance in the age of common men but a continuing fact of the human condition, requiring that the overreacher be struck down and in his fall, we, the chorus, experience awe, and some pity.

[*Book Week,* April 9, 1967]

A Passage to Egypt

"ARE you German, sir?" A small, dark youth stepped from behind a palm tree into the full light of the setting sun which turned scarlet the white shirt and albino red the black eyes. He had been watching me watch the sun set across the Nile, now blood-red and still except for sailboats tacking in a hot, slow breeze. I told him that I was American but was used to being mistaken for a German: in this year of the mid-century, Germans are everywhere, and to Arab eyes we all look alike. He showed only a moment's disappointment.

"I have many German friends," he said. "Two German friends. *West* German friends. Perhaps you know them?" He pulled a notebook out of his pocket and read off two names. Then, not waiting for an answer, all in a rush, he told me that he was a teacher of Arabic grammar, that he was going to Germany, *West* Germany (he emphasized the *West* significantly), to write a book. What sort of book? A book about West Germany. The theme? He responded with some irritation: "A Book About West Germany." That was what the book would be about. He was a poet. His name was Ahmed. "Welcome," he said, "welcome!" His crooked face broke into a smile. "Welcome to Luxor!" He invited me to his house for mint tea.

As we turned from the bank of the Nile, a long, haunting cry sounded across the water. I had heard this same exotic cry for several evenings, and I was certain that it must be of ancient origin, a hymn perhaps to Ikhnaton's falling sun. I asked Ahmed what this lovely aria meant. He listened a moment and then said, "It's this man on the other side who says: will the ferryboat please pick him up?" So much for magic.

Ahmed led the way through narrow streets to the primary school where he taught. It was a handsome modern building, much like its counterparts in Scarsdale or Darien. He took me inside. "You must see what the children make themselves. Their beautiful arts." On the entrance-hall table their beautiful arts were exhibited: clay figures, carved wood, needlework, all surrounding a foot-long enlargement in clay of the bilharzia, a parasite which is carried by snails in the irrigation ditches; once it invades the human bloodstream, lungs and liver are attacked and the victim wastes away; some ninety per cent of the fellahin suffer from bilharzia. "Beautiful?" he asked. "Beautiful," I said.

On the wall hung the exhibit's masterpiece, a larger than life-size portrait of Nasser, painted in colors recalling Lazarus on the fourth day. A somewhat more talented drawing next to it showed students marching with banners in a street. I asked Ahmed to translate the words on the banners. "Our heads for Nasser," he said with satisfaction. I asked him if Nasser was popular with the young. He looked at me as though I had questioned the next day's sunrise. Of course Nasser was loved. Had I ever been in Egypt before? Yes, during the winter of 1948, in the time of the bad fat King. Had things improved? I told him honestly that they had indeed. Cairo had changed from a nineteenth-century French provincial capital surrounded by a casbah to a glittering modern city, only partially surrounded by a casbah. He asked me what I was doing in Egypt, and I told him I was a tourist, not mentioning that I had an appointment to interview Nasser the following week for *Look* magazine.

Ahmed's house is a large one, four stories high; here he

lives with some twenty members of his family. The parlor is a square room with a high ceiling from which hangs a single unshaded light bulb. Two broken beds serve as sofas. I sat on one of the beds while Ahmed, somewhat nervously, ordered mint tea from a sister who never emerged from the dark hall. Then I learned that his father was also a teacher, and that an uncle worked in Nasser's office; obviously a prosperous family by Luxor standards.

I was offered the ceremonial cigarette. I refused; he lit up. He was sorry his father was not there to meet me. But then again, puffing his cigarette, he was glad, for it is disrespectful to smoke in front of one's father. Only recently the father had come unexpectedly into the parlor. "I was smoking a cigarette and when he came in, oh! I bit it hard, like this, and have to swallow it down! Oh, I was sick!" We chuckled at the thought.

When the mint tea arrived (passed to us on a tray from the dark hall, only bare arms visible), Ahmed suggested we sit outside where it was cool. Moonlight blazed through a wooden trellis covered with blossoming wisteria. We sat on stiff wooden chairs. He switched on a light momentarily to show me a photograph of the girl he was to marry. She was pretty and plump and could easily have been the editor of the yearbook in any American high school. He turned off the light. "We modern now. No more arranged marriages. Love is everything. Love is why we marry. Love is all." He repeated this several times, with a sharp intake of breath after each statement. It was very contagious, and I soon found myself doing it. Then he said, "Welcome," and I said, "Thank you."

Ahmed apologized for the unseasonable heat. This was the hottest spring in years, as I had discovered that day in the Valley of the Kings where the temperature had been over a hundred and the blaze of sun on white limestone blinding. "After June, Luxor is *impossible!*" he said proudly. "We all go who can go. If I stay too long, I turn dark as a black in the sun." Interestingly enough, there is racial discrimination in

Egypt. "The blacks" are second-class citizens: laborers, servants, minor government functionaries. They are the lowest level of Egyptian society in every way except one: there are no Negro beggars. That is an Arab monopoly. Almsgivers are blessed by the Koran, if not by Nasser, who has tried to discourage the vast, well-organized hordes of beggars.

"To begin with, I had naturally a very light complexion," said Ahmed, making a careful point, "like the rest of my family, but one day when I was small the nurse upset boiling milk on me and ever since that day I have been somewhat dark." I commiserated briefly. Then I tried a new tack. I asked him about his military service. Had he been called up yet? A new decree proposed universal military service, and I thought a discussion of it might get us onto politics. He said that he had not been called up because of a *very interesting story*. My heart sank, but I leaned forward with an air of sympathetic interest. Suddenly, I realized I was impersonating someone. But who? Then when he began to talk and I to respond with small nods and intakes of breath, I realized that it was E. M. Forster. I was the Forster of *A Passage to India* and this was Dr. Aziz. Now that I had the range, my fingers imperceptibly lengthened into Forsterian claws; my eyes developed an uncharacteristic twinkle; my upper lip sprouted a ragged gray moustache, while all else turned to tweed.

"When the British attacked us at Suez, I and these boys from our school, we took guns and together we marched from Alexandria to Suez to help our country. We march for many days and nights in the desert. We have no food, no water. Then we find we are lost and we don't know where we are. Several die. Finally, half dead, we go back to Alexandria and we march in the street to the place where Nasser is. We ask to see him, to cheer him, half dead all of us. But they don't let us see him. Finally, my uncle hears I am there and he and Nasser come out and, ah, Nasser congratulates us, we are heroes! Then I collapse and am unconscious one month. That

is why I have *not* to do military service." I was impressed and
said so, especially at their getting lost in the desert, which
contributed to my developing theory that the Arabs are
disaster-prone: they *would* get lost, or else arrive days late for
the wrong battle.

Ahmed told me another story of military service, involving
friends. "Each year in the army they have these . . . these . . ."
We searched jointly — hopelessly — for the right word until
E. M. Forster came up with "maneuvers," which was correct.
I could feel my eyes twinkling in the moonlight.

"So these friends of mine are in this maneuvers with guns
in the desert and they have orders: *shoot to kill.* Now one of
them was Ibrahim, my friend. Ibrahim goes to this outpost
in the dark. They make him stop and ask him for the password
and he . . ." Sharp intake of breath. "He has *forgotten* the
password. So they say, 'He must be the enemy.'" I asked if this
took place in wartime. "No, no, *maneuvers.* My friend Ibrahim say, 'Look, I forget. I *did* know but now I forget the password but you know me, anyway, you know it's Ibrahim.' And
he's right. They do know it was Ibrahim. They recognize his
voice but since he cannot say the password they shot him."

I let E. M. Forster slip to the floor. "Shot him? Dead?"

"Dead," said my host with melancholy satisfaction. "Oh,
they were very sorry because they knew it was Ibrahim, but,
you see, *he did not know the password,* and while he was
dying in the tent they took him to, he said it was all right.
They were right to kill him."

I found this story hard to interpret. Did Ahmed approve
or disapprove what was done? He was inscrutable. There was
silence. Then he said, "Welcome," and I said, "Thank you."
And we drank more mint tea in the moonlight.

I tried again to get the subject around to politics. But beyond high praise for everything Nasser has done, he would
volunteer nothing. He did point to certain tangible results of
the new regime. For one thing, Luxor was now a center of

education. There were many new schools. All the children were being educated. In fact he had something interesting to show me. He turned on the lamp and opened a large scrapbook conveniently at hand. It contained photographs of boys and girls, with a scholastic history for each. Money had to be raised to educate them further. It *could* be done. Each teacher was obliged to solicit funds. "Look what my West German friends have given," he said, indicating amounts and names. Thus I was had, in a good cause. I paid and walked back to the hotel.

On the way back, I took a shortcut down a residential street. I had walked no more than a few feet when an old man came rushing after me. "Bad street!" he kept repeating. I agreed politely, but continued on my way. After all, the street was well lit. There were few people abroad. A shout from an upstairs window indicated that I should halt. I looked up. The man in the window indicated I was to wait until he came downstairs. I did. He was suspicious. He was from the police. *Why* was I in that street? I said that I was taking a walk. This made no sense to him. He pointed toward my hotel, which was in a slightly different direction. That was where I was supposed to go. I said yes, but I wanted to continue in *this* street, I liked to walk. He frowned. Since arrest was imminent, I turned back. At the hotel I asked the concierge why what appeared to be a main street should be forbidden to foreigners. "Oh, 'they' might be rude," he said vaguely. "You know . . ." I did not know.

In the diner on the train south to Aswan I had breakfast with a young government official from the Sudan. He was on his way home to Khartoum. He had a fine smile and blue-black skin. On each cheek there were three deep scars, the ritual mark of his tribe — which I recognized, for I had seen his face only the day before on the wall of the Temple of Luxor. Amenhotep III had captured one of his ancestors in Nubia; five thousand years ago the ritual scars were the same as they are now. In matters of religion Africans are profound conservatives. But otherwise he was a man of our time and world. He was dressed in the latest French fashion. He had been for two years on an economic mission in France. He spoke English, learned at the British school in Khartoum.

We breakfasted on musty-tasting dwarfish eggs as dust filtered slowly in through closed windows, covering table, plates, eggs with a film of grit. A fan stirred the dusty air. Parched, I drank three Coca-Colas — the national drink — and sweated. The heat outside was already 110 degrees, and rising. For a while we watched the depressing countryside and spoke very little. At some points the irrigated land was less than a mile wide on our side of the river: a thin ribbon of dusty green ending abruptly in a blaze of desert where nothing at all grew, a world of gray sand as far as the eye could see. Villages of dried-mud houses were built at the desert's edge so as not to use up precious land. The fellahin in their ragged clothes moved slowly about their tasks, quite unaware of the extent of their slow but continual decline. In the fifth century B.C., Herodotus was able to write: "As things are at present these people get their harvest with less labor than anyone else in the world; they have no need to work with plow or hoe, or to use any other of the ordinary methods of cultivating their land; they merely wait for the river of its own accord to flood the fields." But all that has changed. Nearly thirty million people now live in a country whose agriculture cannot support half that number.

"I used to think," said the Sudanese at last, "that Egypt was a fine place, much better than the Sudan. A big country. Rich. But now I know how lucky we are. There is no one at home poor like this." He pointed to several ragged men in a field. Two lay listlessly in the sun. The others worked slowly in the field, narcotized by the heat; the diet of the fellahin is bread and stewed tea and not much of that. I asked him what he thought of Nasser's attacks on his government (recently there had been a disagreement over Nile water rights and Nasser had attacked the Sudanese President with characteristic fury). "Oh, we just laugh at him. We just laugh at him," he repeated as though to convince himself. I asked him why Nasser was continuously on the offensive not only against the West but against the rest of the Arab world. He shrugged. "To impress his own people, I suppose. We don't like it, of course. But perhaps it makes him feel big. Makes them . . ." He pointed to a group of villagers drawing water from a canal. "Makes them forget."

Aswan is the busiest and most optimistic of Egypt's cities. On its outskirts a brand-new chemical factory employs several thousand people. There is a sense of urgency in the city's life, for it is here that all of Egypt's hopes are concentrated: the High Dam is being built. When the dam — the world's largest — is completed in 1970, vast tracts of desert will be made arable and electrical power will be supplied cheaply for the whole country. It should be recalled that the United States had originally agreed to finance a part of the dam, but in 1956 John Foster Dulles withdrew our support and the Soviet obligingly filled the vacuum. Not only are the Russians now financing the dam, but their engineers are building it.

The government had arranged that I be shown around by one of the Egyptian engineers, a cautious, amiable man who spoke not only English but Russian. "I like the Russians very much," he announced firmly as we got into his car. He would show me everything, he said. Nothing to hide.

It was sundown as we approached the barren hills where a huge channel is being cut contiguous to the Nile. Ten thousand men work three eight-hour shifts. Most of the heavy work is done in the cool of the night. Off to the left of the road I noticed a fenced-in compound containing a number of small, modern apartment houses. "The Russians," said my guide. It was a pleasant scene: women chatted in the doorways while through uncurtained windows one could see modern kitchens where dinners were cooking. A large sign forbade the taking of photographs.

"How many Russians are there in Aswan?" I asked. He looked at me bewildered. "What you say?" He took refuge in pidgin English. I repeated the question very slowly and distinctly. He looked puzzled. He lost all his English until I made it impossible for him not to understand me.

"You mean how many Russians altogether? Or how many Russian *engineers*?" he countered, playing for time. "After all, there are wives and children, and sometimes visitors and . . ." I told him carefully and slowly that I would like to know, first, how many Russians altogether; then I would like to know how many of those were engineers. Of course he had thought that what I wanted to know was the actual number of technicians, and in what categories. After all, there were civil engineers, electrical engineers, and so on, but none of *that* was secret. "We have no secrets! Everything open! Anything you want to know we tell you!" He beamed expansively and parked the car in front of a small circular building. Not until I got out did I realize he had not answered the question.

We now stood on a low hill with a long view of the digging. It was a startling sight. Beneath us was the vast channel already cut from the rock. The sun was gone by now, and the channel — more like a crater — was lit by hundreds of electric lights strung on poles. A perpetual haze of dust obscured the view. Russian diesel trucks roared up and down the sides of the crater, adding to the shrill chatter of drills in stone. Behind us a whole town of new buildings had been somewhat casually assembled: machine shops, technical schools, a hospital. In the desert beyond these buildings, a thousand low black tents were pitched, each with its own campfire. Here the workers lived in stern, nomadic contrast to the modern world they were making.

We entered the circular building which contained a large

detailed model of the completed dam. On the walls, diagrams, maps, photographs demonstrated the work's progress and dramatized the fertile Egypt-to-be. I met more Egyptian engineers.

We studied the models and I tried unsuccessfully to sound knowledgeable about turbines. I asked how the workers were recruited. Were they local? How quickly could people who had never used machinery be trained? I was told that the fellahin were surprisingly adaptable. They were trained in schools on the spot. Most of the workers are recruited locally. "But the main thing," said my guide, "is that they know how important all this is. And they do."

I had been told that the dam was some forty weeks behind in its current schedule. But not being an expert in these matters, I could not tell from looking at what I was shown if things were going well or badly, behind or on schedule. The most I could gather was that the engineers were genuinely enthusiastic about their work. Morale is high. And I am ready to testify that they have dug a fine big hole.

We drove to the center of the channel, a good mile from the exhibition hall and at least a hundred yards below the surface of the desert. The air in the crater is almost unbreathable: part dust, part exhaust. A constant haze dims the lights on their poles. The noise is continual and deafening. Hundreds of drills in long, chattering rows break the sandstone floor of the crater, while Russian steam shovels tear at the cliff. I noticed that all the Russian machines looked improvised. No two steam shovels were alike.

We made our way to the entrance of a tunnel cut into a sandstone hill. This was a shortcut to the place where the first turbines were to be set up. At the entrance of the tunnel we were stopped by the only Russian I was to see: a gray, middle-aged man with a tired face. After a long discussion, he gave permission for me to enter the tunnel. "With every

Egyptian engineer," said my guide, "there is also a Russian engineer." It was obvious who was in charge.

The tunnel was brightly lit; the noise of drilling was stunningly amplified by stone walls. I was surprised to see occasional puddles of water on the tunnel floor. I daydreamed: The diggers had struck underground springs. That meant there was water in the desert, deep down, and if there was water deep down, all of Egypt's problems were solved. Obviously no one else had figured out the true meaning of the puddles. I turned to my guide. We shouted at one another and I learned that the puddles were caused not by springs but by seepage from the nearby Nile. The nightmare of the dam builders is that the Nile's water might begin to seep at too great a rate through the sandy walls of the crater, wrecking not only the project but possibly diverting the river's course as well.

Finally, lungs protesting, I said that I had seen enough. This time two engineers drove me back to the hotel, where we drank a ceremonial beer together and I complimented them not only on their enthusiasm but on their courage. At the earliest, the dam will be completed in 1970, which means that these men are dedicating their professional lives to a single project. "But we do this, as Nasser says, for the good of our people," said my original guide solemnly. The other engineer was equally solemn "No, for the good of all humanity." Taking advantage of this suddenly warm mood, I asked again how many Russians were working on the dam. I got two blank looks this time. "What you say?" And I was no wiser when they left.

The next day in Aswan I was able to obtain an unofficial view of what is really going on. There is a good deal of friction between Egyptians and Russians. Much of it is due to the language barrier. The Russians speak only Russian, the Egyptians speak English or French, sometimes both, but few

have learned Russian. The professional interpreters are hopeless because, though they can cope with ordinary conversation, they do not know the technical terms of either language.
"We use sign language mostly," said one technician glumly.
"Everything is too slow."

Another problem is machinery. It is well known that the
Soviet has always had a somewhat mystical attitude toward
that sine qua non of the machine age: the interchangeable
part. It seems to go against the Slavic grain to standardize.
Consequently, when a machine breaks down (usually in six
months' time) it must be replaced entirely. Efforts to "canni-
balize," as the mechanics put it, are futile since a part from
one drill will not fit another drill. As a result, Swedish drills
are now being imported, at considerable cost.

Humanly, the Russians are praised for their ability to
survive without complaint the terrible heat. "But," said one
Egyptian, "heat is bad for their babies. They turn all red
and get sick, so they have to send them home." The Russians
keep almost entirely to themselves. One of the livelier engineers was the most critical: "They don't go out; they don't
dance; they don't do nothing. Just eat and drink!" He shook his
head disapprovingly, for the Egyptian with any money is a
happy fellow who wants to have a good time in whatever is
the going way: alcohol has lately caught on, despite the
Prophet's injunction, while the smoking of hashish and kif
has gone into decline, the result of stringent new laws against
their sale and use. Also the emancipation of women is pro-
gressing nicely and women are to be seen in public places.
Dancing is popular. In fact, the twist was the rage of Cairo's
nightclubs until Nasser banned it.

Sooner or later every Egyptian connected with the High
Dam denounces John Foster Dulles. He is the principal demon in the Egyptian hell, largely because the engineers still
wish the Americans would come in on the dam — speaking
only as technicians, they add quickly, reminding one that they

are, after all, Western-trained and used to Western machinery
and procedures. Also they find Western life sympathetic. But
what's done is done . . . and we would look sadly at one another . . . such is Allah's will. The Soviet is committed to the
dam to the end. I suspect that they wish they were out of it:
spending four hundred million dollars to build the largest dam
in the world in the midst of a desert is a venture more apt than
not to leave all participants exhausted and disenchanted with
one another. And there, but for the grace of John Foster
Dulles, go we.

At my hotel in Cairo I found a message from the President's
office. My appointment was canceled, but His Excellency
would see me in the next few days. I telephoned the Appointments Secretary. When? They would let me know. I was to
stand by. Meanwhile, there were many people in and out of
the Cabinet I could see. Name anyone. I picked Mohammed
Hassanein Heikal. He is editor of Cairo's chief newspaper,
Al Ahram. He is supposed to have written *The Philosophy of
the Revolution*, Nasser's *Mein Kampf* (a rather touching work
reminiscent more of Pirandello than of Hitler). Heikal is the
President's alter ego. An appointment was made for late that
afternoon.

I had a drink in a nearby hotel bar with an English
journalist who had been some years in Egypt. He is a short,
red-faced man who speaks Arabic; he demonstrates the usual
love-hate for Nasser which one soon gets used to. "He's a
dictator, but then they all are. They have to be. He's personally
honest, which few of them are. But the main thing is he's the
first man ever to try to do anything for the people here. *The
first*. Ever! And it's not just demagoguery. He means it. But
the problems! He's inherited the old bureaucracy, the most
corrupt in the world. On top of that there aren't enough
trained people to run the country, much less all the new
businesses he confiscated last year. The foreigners who used
to manage things are gone. Alexandria's a ghost town. Even

so, in spite of everything, he's made these people proud to be Egyptians." I said that I thought nationalistic pride, of de Gaulle's *la gloire* sort, too luxurious an emotion in a dangerous world.

"That's not the point. This isn't manifest-destiny stuff. It's that these people really believed they were inferior to everybody else. They thought they really were scum . . . wogs. For centuries. Well, Nasser's changed all that. He's shown them they're like anybody else. We said Egyptians could never run the Suez Canal. Remember? Well, they run it a lot better than we ever did." I asked him about Arab imperialism. Nasser has proposed himself as leader of the Arab world, a new Saladin. Through his radio and through the thousands of Cairo-trained schoolteachers sent out to the various Arab countries, Nasser has tried to incite the people to overthrow their "reactionary" governments and to unite with him in some vague but potent hegemony.

The Englishman laughed. "The joke of course is the Egyptians aren't Arab at all. The Arabs conquered Egypt and stayed. But so have a lot of other races. Nasser himself is only part Arab. The Copts have no Arab blood, while everyone else is a mixture. The Egyptians used to be contemptuous of the Arabs. In fact, their word for Arab means a nomad, a wild man, a . . ." "Hick?" I supplied, and he nodded. "Now everyone's trying to claim pure Arab descent."

We spoke of the more ruthless side of Nasser's reign. Egypt is a police state. Arrests are often indiscriminate. Currently, a journalist is in jail for having provided an American newspaper with the information — accurate — that Nasser is a diabetic. There is nothing resembling representative government. The middle class is in a state of panic.

I asked him about Nasser personally. What sort of a man was he? I got the familiar estimate: great personal charm, most reasonable in conversation, entirely lacking in personal vanity and ostentation . . . he still lives at Heliopolis in the house he owned as a colonel. He tends to be nervous with foreigners, especially with the British and the French. They put him on the defensive. He is a devoted family man, a puritan who was profoundly shocked during his first Cairo meeting with Indonesia's President Sukarno, who gaily asked, "Now, where are the girls?" He worries about gaining weight. He admires Tito because he "showed me how to get help from both sides — without joining either." Nasser in his passion for Egypt has also declared, "I will treat with the devil himself if I have to for my country." But he is wary of foreign commitments. He has said: "An alliance between a big and a small power is an alliance between the wolf and the sheep, and it is bound to end with the wolf devouring the sheep." His relations with the Soviet are correct but not warm. He has imprisoned every Egyptian Communist he can find. He took advantage of a Soviet offer to give technical training to Egyptian students, but when he discovered that their first six months in Moscow were devoted to learning Marxist theory, he withdrew the students and rerouted them to the West. He is thought to be genuinely religious. He is obsessed, as well he might be, by the thought of sudden death.

"He's at the Barrage right now. That's his place downriver. You may as well know you're going to have a hard time seeing him." He looked about to make sure that the ubiquitous barman — a government informer — was out of earshot. Then he whispered: "Nasser was shot at yesterday." I contained my surprise and the Englishman played this dramatic scene with admirable offhandedness. "Complete censorship, of course. It won't hit the papers. He wasn't hurt, but his bodyguard was killed. So he's holed up at the Barrage for the rest of this week." Who shot at him? The Englishmen shrugged. Saudi Arabia, Yemen, Syria, Iraq, Israel — any number of governments would like Nasser dead.

I sat in the anteroom of the editor of *Al Ahram*. His secretary went on with her work. I glanced at her desk (I can read upside down if the type is sufficiently large) and noted a copy of the American magazine *Daedalus*. Seeing my interest, she gave it to me. It featured an article on birth control. Heikal himself had made many marginal notes. "A problem, isn't it?" I said. She nodded. "A problem."

I was shown into the editor's office. Heikal is a short, lean man, handsome in the way that certain actors of the thirties who played suave villains with pencil moustaches were handsome. He smokes cigars. He gives an impression of great energy. He shook my hand; then he darted back to his desk, where he was correcting proofs of an editorial. Would I mind? He always liked to go over them at the last minute. He made marginal notes. He puffed cigar smoke. He is an actor, I decided, giving a performance: Malraux without genius. He has the half-challenging, half-placating manner of those men who are close to a prince.

I waited patiently for quite a few minutes. Finally, he slapped his pencil down with a flourish. He was mine. I asked him how many printer's errors he had found. "Eight," he said precisely, "but mostly I like to change at the last minute." I mentioned *Daedalus* and birth control. "A problem," he said. They were doing their best, of course, but it would take twenty years to educate the people. It was a formidable task.

I then made the error of referring to *The Philosophy of the Revolution* as *his* book. "My book? *My* book? It is Nasser's book." I said that I had thought it was at least a joint effort. "You've been reading Robert St. John's *The Boss*," which indeed I had: it is one of the better books about Nasser. "Well, that is not the only mistake in that book," he said drily. I remarked that it was neither shameful nor unusual for politicians to be helped in their literary work. Even President Kennedy had once been accused — falsely, as it turned out — of having used a ghost to write an entire book. "Yes," said Heikal knowledgeably, "but Sorensen works for Kennedy. I don't work for Nasser. He is my friend. My leader. But I don't work for him." He discussed American politics for a moment; he was the only Egyptian politician or editor I met who knew much about American affairs. I mentioned the recent letter Kennedy had written to Nasser, a personal letter whose contents were more or less known to everyone. Nasser had been sufficiently moved to answer Kennedy personally, not going through the usual Foreign Office machinery. This exchange had been much discussed in Cairo. It was believed that a new era had begun; that the two young Presidents would understand one another. But the crux to the renewed dialogue was unchanged: What about Israel? Was there a solution to the Arab-Israel conflict?

"None," said Heikal firmly, ending all debate. "How can there be?" Before I could stop him, he was off in full tirade. I was reminded of 1948, of the seven hundred thousand Arabs driven from their Palestinian homes, of the predatoriness of Israeli foreign policy, and how it is written on the wall of the Knesset that there would one day be a Jewish empire from the Mediterranean to the Euphrates. He spoke of Jewish ingratitude. "The Arabs are the only people *never* to persecute Jews," he said with some accuracy. "English, French, Germans, Spanish, at one time or another every country in Europe persecuted them, but never we. During the last war, we were friends to them. Then they do this! They dispossess Arabs from their homes. They move into a land which isn't theirs. The Jews," he said, with a note of triumph, "are not a race, they're a religion." There is nothing quite so chilling as to hear a familiar phrase in a new context. I relished it. "They are *Europeans*," he said grimly, coming to the point, "setting themselves up in *our* world. No, there is no solution!" But then he became reasonable. "The real fault of course is our weakness, and their strength. Our policy now is to build up

Egypt. Perhaps when we are stronger economically there will be less to fear from the Israelis." This seems to be current Egyptian policy.

We discussed Nasser's "Arab socialism." Heikal was emphatic: it was not doctrinaire socialism. It was improvisational. Point-to-point navigation, as it were. I said that despite some of the methods used to expropriate businesses, there was no doubt that some kind of socialism was inevitable for Egypt and that Nasser had merely done the inevitable. But Heikal would not accept this small compliment. "Methods? Methods? You make us sound like Stalin, with your 'methods'!" I said I had not meant to compare Nasser to Stalin. He cut me off. "What we do is legal. Open. It is for the people. How can you accuse us of 'methods' . . ." This time I cut *him* off. With some irritation, I told him that I had no intention of repeating the various horror stories told me by those who had been ruined by his government, their businesses seized, their livelihoods ended. Even allowing for the natural exaggeration of victims, such methods were not apt to please those who were ruined by them. Nor was it only the large corporations which had been nationalized. Innumerable small businesses had also been taken over. An owner would come to work one morning to find an army officer sitting at his desk, directing what had been his business the day before.

Heikal was scornful. "So we take their money. So they are not happy. So what? At least they are still alive! That's something!" He felt this showed great restraint on the part of the government and perhaps he was right. I was reminded of Joseph Stalin's answer to Lady Astor when she asked him, "When are you going to stop killing people?" "The undesirable classes," said the tyrant, turning upon her his coldest eye, "never liquidate themselves."

Wanting to needle Heikal — an irresistible impulse — I said I didn't think that the endlessly vituperative style of

Egypt's newspapers was very apt to win them any friends. Israel is the principal victim of these attacks, but any government which does not momentarily please Nasser will get the full treatment from the Arab press and radio.

Heikal took my question personally, as well he might. His voice slipped automatically into the singsong of rhetoric and denunciation. "We write this way because we feel this way. How can we help it? How can we be asked not to say what we feel so strongly? Take the British, *I hate the British*. I can't help it. I saw them. I know them. Their contempt for us. Their treachery. And over Suez they were not . . . kind." This was an unexpected word. "You came into Suez with force." "They," I murmured. "You tried to destroy us." "They," I said somewhat more loudly. "All right," he said irritably, the tide of his rhetoric briefly stemmed. "*They* wanted to destroy us. So how can we feel anything but hate for them? Look what they did to the Arab world after 1918. They brought back the kings, the sheiks, to keep us medieval. As if we were to occupy England and restore the lords, break the country up into Saxon kingdoms. So how can we express ourselves in any way except the way we do?" Like most rhetorical questions, no answer was desired.

Actually, the fulminating style is inherent in the language (*vide* the Old Testament). Semitic languages are curiously suited to the emotional tirade, even when the speaker is not himself an emotional man. By nature Nasser is an unemotional speaker. As a rule he will bore his audiences for an hour or two, droning on sensibly about the state of the nation. Then when he is in danger of losing them entirely, he allows the language to do its natural work; he proposes that all Egypt's enemies "choke in their rage" as well as other gaudy sentiments calculated to keep his torpid audience awake. Yet to give Nasser his due he is, verbally, one of the most continent of Arab leaders.

Heikal reverted to Israel. Did I realize that thirty-eight per cent of their budget went for the military as opposed to thirteen per cent of Egypt's budget? Having spent several days poring over the Egyptian budget, I was surprised that anyone could have come up with any figure for any department. The only ascertainable fact is that Egypt is flat broke. But I accepted his figures. I did remark that it must be distressing for Israel — for any country — to be reminded daily that its neighbors, once they awaken from their "deep slumber," will drive them into the sea. After all, no one wants to be drowned. Heikal shook his head sadly: didn't I realize that the Israeli military expenditure was for offense, not defense? I asked him point-blank: "Do you think Israel is planning an offensive war against Egypt?" he shrugged. I then mentioned his own press's continual reminder of Israel's financial dependence on the United States. This being true, did he really think that the United States would permit Israel to embark on a military adventure? We had effectively stopped Israel, France, and England at the time of Suez. Did he honestly believe that we would now allow Israel, by itself, to launch an attack on Egypt? He edged away. No, he did not think the United States would allow a unilateral action. "But," he added quickly, "you can't blame us for being on guard." Then again he reverted to what is the government's present line: we must strengthen Egypt, concentrate on home problems, create "Arab socialism," become a model for the rest of the Arab world.

As I left, I told him that if I saw Nasser at the end of the week I was perfectly willing to present to the American public Egypt's case against Israel, just as Egypt would like it presented. Partly out of a sense of mischief (we hear altogether too much of the other side) and partly out of a sense of justice, I thought that the Arab case *should* be given attention in the American press. As of now it has been disregarded. In fact, a few years ago the Egyptians, despairing of ever seeing their cause presented impartially in the usual news columns, tried to buy an advertisement in the New York *Times*. They were turned down. As a result, the Egyptians are somewhat cynical about our "free press." They are also quite aware that when Israel was being founded in 1948 and the Arabs protested to Harry Truman, he told them with characteristic bluntness: "I do not have hundreds of thousands of Arabs among my constituents." Heikal laughed when I told him that the Arab point of view might one day be given in the American national press. "Your press would never let you," he said with finality, as one journalist to another. "Don't even try."

Another week passed. More appointments were made with Nasser. Each was broken at the last minute, and I was advised to be patient. He would see me soon. But then the Syrian comedy began, disrupting Nasser's schedule. The President of Syria was removed by some army colonels in Damascus. A few days later the young captains in Aleppo tried to overthrow the older officers in Damascus who had overthrown the President. The young men in Aleppo declared that they were for Nasser; they wanted union again with Egypt. Was Nasser behind this plot? Some think yes. Some think no. I suspect no. As one of his closest advisers said, with what seemed candor: "We don't even know these boys in Aleppo. They're much younger than our group." It is protocol in the Middle East that only colonels may start revolutions. Generals are too old, captains too young. In any case, the colonels in Damascus triumphed over the captains in Aleppo and then in a marvelous gesture of frustration the colonels restored the President they had overthrown in the first place. There was no one else, apparently, available for the job. But by the time this comedy had run its course I had fled Egypt, though just as I was getting on the plane to Beirut there was yet another telephone message from the President's office: "His Excellency will definitely see you tomorrow." But I was ready to go, shamefully demonstrating the difference between the amateur and the professional journalist. The professional would have remained, as Hans Von Kaltenborn once remained six weeks, to obtain an interview with Nasser. The amateur moves on.

"The Arabs are their own worst enemies," said a foreign diplomat in Beirut. "They can't present anything to anyone without undermining themselves. They are self-destructive. In fact, many of them actually believe that since this world is a mess, why bother to alter it when what really matters is the Paradise to come." I was reminded of the Koran, where it is written that "The life of the world is only play and idle talk and pageantry."

The Arabs' religion contributes greatly to the difficulties they are experiencing in the modern world. Americans tend to believe, in a vague, soupy way, that all religion is A Good Thing. Richard Nixon was much applauded when he said that a man's religion should never be a matter of concern in politics, *unless of course he had no religion.* Nixon shook his head gravely on that one. Yet some religions are more useful than others, and some religions are downright dangerous to the human spirit and to the building of a good society.

To understand the Arab world one must understand the Koran, a work Goethe described as "A holy book which, however often we approach it, always disgusts us anew, but then attracts, and astonishes and finally compels us to respect it." It is a remarkable work which I shall not go into here except to note that its Five Pillars are: (1) the creed; (2) the prayer; (3) the fast; (4) the pilgrimage to Mecca; (5) almsgiving. One unfortunate result of the last: the holiness which accrues to almsgivers has fostered a demoralizing tradition of beggars. Also, in requesting aid of other countries, the Arab nations are profoundly self-righteous and demanding, on the high moral ground that they are doing the giver a favor by taking his money and making him more holy. The result has been that until very recently American aid to Egypt was almost never acknowledged in the press or noted in any other way, except by complaints that the giver, if he weren't so selfish, ought to come through with ever more cash, making himself that much worthier in Allah's eyes. In any event, no quo for the quid is Arab policy, as both the Soviet and ourselves have discovered.

I found myself continually asking diplomats, journalists, and old Arab hands: Why should we give *any* aid to Egypt? What do we gain by it? What should we get from it? Answers were never very precise. Naturally, there was "the Soviet threat." If we don't help Egypt, the Russians will and the Middle East will come into "the Soviet sphere." For a number of reasons this is not likely to happen. Soviet policy in the Arab world has been even more unsuccessful than our own. In 1956, after jailing the local Communists (while accepting Soviet aid for the High Dam), Nasser said quite explicitly: "The Communists have lost faith in religion, which in their opinion is a myth. . . . Our final conclusion is that we shall never repudiate it in exchange for the Communist doctrine." The Moslem world and the Marxist world are an eternity apart. Paradise here and now on earth, as the result of hard work and self-sacrifice, is not a congenial doctrine to the Arab. Also, of some importance is the Egyptian's human response to the Russians: they find them austere, dogmatic, and rather alarming.

One is also reminded that whether Nasser chooses to be incorporated in the Soviet bloc or not, in a time of chaos the Soviets *might* move in and take the country by force. This drastic shift in the world balance of power is not easy to visualize. The Soviets, already overextended financially, are not apt to take on (any more than we are) the burden of governing a starving Egypt. But if they did, it is unlikely that they would then shut down the Suez Canal (England's old nightmare), since, after cotton, the canal is the main source of Egypt's revenue. I would suggest that the strategic value of Egypt to the West is very small, and it merely turns Nasser's head and feeds his sense of unreality for us to pretend that Egypt is of great consequence. Yet it is of *some* consequence, especially now.

The principal source of irritation between Nasser and the United States is Israel, a nation in which we have a large economic and emotional interest. But I got the impression from members of the Egyptian government that the continual tirades against Israel are largely for home consumption. Nations traditionally must have the Enemy to prod them into action. President Kennedy finds it difficult to get any large appropriation bill through our Congress unless he can first prove that it will contribute to the holy war against Communism. Once he has established that he is indeed striking a blow at the Enemy, he can get any money he needs, whether it is to explore the moon or to give assistance to the public schools. In the same way, Nasser needs the idea of Israel to goad his own people into the twentieth century.

Nasser once said to Miles Copeland, "If you want the cooperation of any Middle Eastern leader you must first understand his limitations — those limitations placed on him by the emotions and suspicions of the people he leads — and be reconciled to the fact that you can never ask him to go beyond those limitations. If you feel you *must* have him go beyond them, you must be prepared to help him lessen the limitations." A most rational statement of any politician's dilemma; and one which Dulles in his blithely righteous way ignored, causing Nasser to observe with some bitterness in 1956: "Dulles asked me to commit suicide." National leaders are always followers of public opinion. No matter how well-intentioned they might be privately, they are limited by those they govern. Paradoxically, this is truest of dictators.

Our current policy toward Nasser is sympathetic. It is hard to say to what extent he can or will respond, but it is evident he is trying. His value to us is much greater now that he has, temporarily, given up hope of leading the Arab world, of becoming the new Saladin. He must make Egypt work first. He is perfectly — sadly — aware that Algeria and Morocco, two Arab nations potentially richer and politically more sophisticated than Egypt, may well provide new leadership for the Moslem world. His only remaining hope is to make "Arab socialism" a success. If it is, then the kings and the sheiks will eventually fall of their own corruption and incompetence, and Nasser's way will be the Arab's way.

What is our role? Since 1952 our assistance to Egypt has totaled $705,000,000. Over half this amount was given or loaned in the last three years. So far the Egyptian government has been most scrupulous in its interest payments, etc. However, since July, 1961, when Nasser seized most of the nation's industries and businesses, he has opposed all private investment. The only assistance he will accept (the weak must be firm!) is government-to-government, with no political strings. Again, why should we help him?

"Because," said an American economist, "any aid ties him to us, whether he likes it or not, whether he acknowledges it or not. If we help him build the new power plant in Cairo (with Westinghouse assistance), he will have to come to us in the future for parts and technicians. That's good business for us. That keeps *our* economy expanding." This, of course, is the standard rationale for America's foreign-aid program, and up to a point it is valid. Today's empires are held not with the sword but the dollar. It is the nature of the national organism to expand and proliferate. We truly believe that we never wanted a world empire simply because we don't suffer (since Teddy Roosevelt, at least) from a desire to see Old Glory waving over the parliaments of enslaved nations. But we do want to make a buck. We do want to maintain our standard of living. For good or ill, we have no other true national purpose. There is no passion in America for military glory, at least outside of Texas and Arizona. Our materialistic ethos is made quite plain in the phrase "the American way of life." I submit that our lack of commitment to any great mystique of national destiny is the healthiest thing about us and the reason for our current success. We are simple materialists, not bent on setting fire to the earth as a matter of holy principle, unlike the True Believers with their fierce Either-Ors, their Red or Dead absolutes, when the truth is that the world need be neither, just comfortably pink and lively. Even aid to such a disagreeable and unreliable nation as Nasser's Egypt increases our sphere of influence, expands our markets, maintains our worldly empire. And we are an empire. Americans who would not have it so had best recall Pericles' admonition to those Athenians who wished to shirk imperial responsibilities. We may have been wrong to acquire an empire, Pericles said, but now that we possess one, it is not safe for us to let it go. Nor is it safe for the United States to opt out now. Luckily, our passion for trade and moneymaking and our relatively unromantic view of ourselves has made us surprisingly attractive to the rest of the world, especially to those countries whose rulers suffer from *folie de grandeur*.

Historians often look to the Roman Empire to find analogies with the United States. They flatter us. We live not under the Pax Americana, but the Pax Frigida. I should not look to Rome for comparison but rather to the Most Serene Venetian Republic, a pedestrian state devoted to wealth, comfort, trade, and keeping the peace, especially after inheriting the wreck of the Byzantine Empire, as we have inherited the wreck of the British Empire. Venice was not inspiring but it worked. Ultimately, our danger comes not from the idea of Communism, which (as an Archbishop of Canterbury remarked) is a "Christian heresy" whose materialistic aims (as opposed to means) vary little from our own; rather, it will come from the increasing wealth and skill of other Serene Republics which, taking advantage of our increasing moral and intellectual fatness, will try to seize our markets in the world. If we are to end, it will not be with a Bomb but a bigger Buck. Fortunately, under that sanctimoniousness so characteristic of the American selling something, our governors know that we are fighting not for "the free world" but to hold onto an economic empire not safe or pleasant to let go. The Arab world — or as salesmen would say, "territory" — is almost ours, and we must persevere in landing that account. It will be a big one some day.

[*Esquire,* October 1963]

The Liberal Dilemma

IT seems only fifty-nine minutes ago that John Kenneth Galbraith's liberal hour struck.* Freed of narrow prejudice, uninspired by the conventional wisdom, willing to institute reforms tending in the direction of a greater democracy, the American leadership had finally made its "long-term commitment to the realities." Dissenters from liberalism were few and predictable: right-wingers obsessed with conspiracy and mistrustful of fluorine. Except for an occasional eccentric, the educated, the energetic, and the hopeful were dedicated to making things better. Everyone was pragmatic and no one was dogmatic; the New Frontier could be crossed and the Great Society built. But as the thirty-sixth President learned the hard way, there is no lasting consensus this side of the grave.

The liberal Center did not hold, and for some time now liberalism has been at bay. At alarmingly regular intervals that most liberal of professional public servants, Dean Rusk, has been picketed by the educated, the energetic, and the hopeful because, as one of them explained recently at an ad hoc meeting in New York's Bryant Park: "We're demonstrating against the American establishment, against the liberal fascists." The

* The Liberal Hour (1960).

phrase "liberal fascist" is almost as unthinkable as "Christian atheist." Admittedly Mr. Rusk's dream of making Southeast Asia safe for liberalism has called into question certain of his methods, but to question so cruelly the ultimate worthiness of his ideals and the generosity of his vision would have been unthinkable a few seconds ago. After all, Dean Rusk is a former foundation head.

Some try to discount these attacks as signs of "immaturity" among the young (not to mention Communist infiltration), and so disregard them. But lately the attacks on liberalism have been mounted from other, more respectable quarters. "Liberalism," observed Whitney M. Young, "seems to be related to the distance people are from the [Negro] problem." Apparently Northern well-wishers who had been willing to go South to stir up the rednecks were reluctant to confront conditions in their home cities. Youth, generally, is disaffected: The National Student Association is now confronted by Students for a Democratic Society. These dissidents believe that "the liberal program of NSA is inadequate to bring about the meaningful social change that is necessary to create a truly democratic society in America." In other words, liberalism and true democracy are incompatible. Even that traditionally arrière-garde institution the American theater has taken note of the disrepute into which liberalism has fallen. In the words of Clive Barnes, the new play *The Niggerlovers* "seems to be making the point that white liberalism is merely the mirror image of white racism, and that one could not exist without the other." While the protagonist of the comedy *Scuba Duba* is, according to Mr. Barnes, "a good white Partisan Review liberal reader whose wife has gone off with a Negro, and he finds himself — quite sincerely — spilling out the most obscene racist hatred." On the other hand, the bold and tactless Dr. William Shockley believes that scientific attempts to determine intelligence differences between Negroes and whites are systematically thwarted by "inverted liberals." With equal disdain, both Left and Right dismiss today's liberal as an ineffective, guilt-ridden, hypocritical masochist, resembling nothing so much as one of Jules Feiffer's cartoon characters whose inner frustrations and confusions can be read at inordinate length on one of those huge balloons to which the shakily drawn head seems diminutive afterthought.

Words like "liberal" and "conservative" are of course notoriously difficult to define. More to the point, they are impossible to apply accurately to individuals who tend to vacillate from issue to issue, depending upon health, age, weather, and the stock market. It should be noted, however, that there has never been much liberal sentiment in our middle-class society. Americans are about evenly divided between conservatives and reactionaries. The late President Kennedy was a conservative; former President Eisenhower was a reactionary. Neither was radical, if only because each was a shrewd politician who had learned the famous paradox of our system: to do anything one must obtain power but to obtain power one must do nothing. Unlike nature, the American voter adores a vacuum.

In any case, major politicians dislike political labels. An exception was Barry Goldwater, who took pleasure in the word "conservative" and all that he thought it stood for. But even he used to say in private that it was a shame, really, they couldn't come up with some other word to describe man's best instincts, since the word "conservative" had been hopelessly traduced by sinister liberals. Now the word "liberal" has also become anathema to those militant social reformers who are presently converging upon the center stage of our national life.

Two events have caused this change: the President's war in Asia and the Negro minority's struggle for economic parity with the white majority. The war in Asia became active at the end of the Kennedy administration, and though many liberals like to place the full blame upon Lyndon Johnson and his

Texas reactionaryism ("There's an old saying down in Texas, if you know you are right, just keep on coming and no gun can stop you"), from the beginning the war has been prosecuted and escalated by such liberal officials as Rusk, Bundy, and Rostow, with considerable assistance, at least in the early stages, from all sorts of liberal outriders, most of whom can now be found on quiet campuses, writing memoirs and waiting for the Kennedy restoration. But their early complicity in a war which today's young activists find not only ugly but irrelevant to American interests made many people suspect, perhaps unjustly, that these particular liberals prefer the pompous show of power to truth or right action. Recently, the stern Andrew Kopkind dismissed *all* liberals as "a sorry lot; they spent the late forties and early fifties feeding Communists and radicals to the McCarthyites (the *other* McCarthy), came briefly to glory in the days of the New Frontier, and suddenly were deposed by the onrush of history and the whim of President Johnson." Even those liberals who have remained outside the bright circle of power appear dim to the young and restless, who grow each day more frustrated by a war that they can find no moral basis for, a war in which many of them have refused to serve, a war that should go away but does not. As a result, there is now a strong movement to mount the barricades and bring the whole structure down—hypocritical liberals, paranoid Texans, greedy salesmen, gobbling consumers . . . smash the whole works and begin again. The war has split the country like no other issue in modern times, except that of the Negro revolution.

For more than a generation, conservatives have tended to blame white liberals for artificially creating discontent among the Negroes. In the thirties and early forties it was an article of faith that the Negroes only began to get uppity when Eleanor Roosevelt started giving them ideas (the Eleanor Clubs met regularly in order for maids to compare notes on how best to burn dinner, overstarch shirts, and generally behave in a sassy manner). It would be nice if this were true. Actually Mrs. Roosevelt and her fellow travelers tended to follow events, not lead them. It was not the liberals but the Second World War which gave ideas to the illiterate sharecropper and the pool-hall hustler, to the janitor and the day laborer, to all of those who were suddenly wrenched from what seemed to be their immutable humble condition and allowed to taste new pleasures and dignities they not unnaturally liked. What war began, the television commercial continued in the postwar world. Not to have the money to buy the gadgets a whole nation worshiped was too cruel a deprivation to be borne. And so, in response to the growing discontent of the poor, liberal whites and militant Negroes forged a series of alliances which led to various postwar reforms, culminating in the apotheosis of Martin Luther King during the dreamy golden Eisenhower years.

But though liberals saw to it that, on paper at least, Negroes were finally able to enjoy most of their Constitutional rights, the expectations of the Negroes as a whole were simply not met by society. Despite much talk of justice and fair deals, the liberals could neither shatter the walls of prejudice nor make effective programs to ensure for the Negro his share of consumer goods. To date every Federal aid program has been a bust. The fault is not the liberals' nor even that of those entrenched reactionaries who control so many Congressional committees and prefer the expensive slaughter of Asians to the less ambitious task of bettering conditions at home. The fault is more one of effective organization than of deficient will. Federal agencies begin with great energy and excitement, then metamorphose into vast existential organisms entirely oblivious to the purpose for which they were founded. According to Daniel P. Moynihan, "The Federal government is good at collecting revenues, and rather bad at disbursing services." He has even gone so far as to propose Federal financing of programs that would be *entirely* administered at the local level. This positively Manichean heresy is gaining considerable support among disturbed social meliorists.

Meanwhile, those liberals who raised such hopes a decade ago are now being blamed by the Negroes for everything from the failure of the Head Start educational program to the proliferation of rats in the slums. Essentially moderate Negro leaders like Floyd McKissick of CORE are now forced by the rising passions of their constituency to lash out at all whites, with particularly bitter emphasis on the failure of the reformers.

Last Labor Day's confrontation between white liberals and Negro activists at Chicago was a splendidly comic and highly dangerous affair. The National Conference for the New Politics began hopefully with talk of running the Doctors King and Spock for President and Vice President. But this project was torpedoed by a Negro minority called the Black Caucus. Headed by James Forman of SNCC, the Caucus took charge of the conference and rammed through a thirteen-point program calculated to distress all but the dizziest of Black Muslims. Nevertheless, in an ecstasy of masochism, the white majority allowed the black minority to have its will and, as one observer remarked, "the walls of the Palmer House dripped with guilt." Mr. Forman and his brightly costumed goons brought a nice touch of African democracy to Mayor Daley's Chicago. Tactically, Mr. Forman and the Mayor could learn quite a lot from each other but, unfortunately, they may soon have no common language since Mr. Forman's group now urges blacks to learn Swahili even though a speaking knowledge of English might be more helpful. In any event, it was made plain that should the liberals wish to start a third party in order to end the war in Vietnam and make a decent society for both black and white, they would have to proceed without the most active of the Negro groups. Strained relations between the races are now developing into non-relations which, some believe, are prelude to what Rap Brown happily refers to as a "guerrilla war against the honkie white man."

If nothing else, the troubles last year have convinced even the most indifferent of the white majority that one tenth of a nation is seriously disaffected. The problem now is what to do. Certain Negro leaders equate the current situation with that of Africa in the last years of the colonial empires, and they believe that the white imperialist warlords can be overthrown by Mau Mau tactics. But the colonial analogy is a false one. Whites outnumber blacks in the United States; they control the country's wealth; they are not about to be driven into the sea. As a result, the rhetoric of the day grows more and more violent while the "solutions" proposed become less and less realistic. CORE currently favors an optional society. Those Negroes who find too demoralizing the white devil's company can take refuge in all-black communities; those Negroes who can tolerate a mixed environment will be allowed to live wherever they like among the whites, who, needless to say, will *not* have the right to segregate themselves.

The threat of nuclear catastrophe abroad and race war at home has convinced many of the need for a drastic change not only in American policy but in the institutions which make and execute that policy. The New Left is on record as wanting not to "capture the present power structure but to parallel it." The tactics of parallelization are often beautifully weird but by no means ineffective. For instance, between a liberal (conservative) candidate like Pat Brown and a conservative (reactionary) candidate like Ronald Reagan, the rule is to support the reactionary since he is bound to be repressive in his methods and so bring the day of revolution that much closer (it should be glumly noted that the policy of supporting the worst man was much employed during the declining years of the last French Republic but one). To the radical, the real enemy is the liberal who delays the revolution by limiting the excesses of the unenlightened.

Needless to say, the tactics of the radicals may prove to be more successful than their aims. Human institutions are fragile affairs at best, and easily smashed. But what is to take the place of those we now possess? It is not enough to be against unjust wars and in favor of the good life for all citizens. Almost everyone shares those simple liberal sentiments; in fact, they are Constitutional. The trick is how to stay out of unjust wars if one's country is, no matter how innocently, a world empire? Or how best to ameliorate the lot of millions of citizens against whom there are innumerable irrational prejudices not susceptible to legislation? These are problems not easily handled in a quasi-democracy where a majority probably approve of unjust wars (do you favor the overthrow of Godless Communism by force?), and keeping their dusky brothers away from switchblade knives, white girls, and the competitive labor market.

Yet in a society of conflicting interests the only democratic way in which matters can be improved is through politics, and politics means the compromising of extremes in order to achieve that notorious half loaf which the passionate and the outraged never find sufficient. Though Americans are not, usually, passionate and outraged in everyday life, at heart we are still instinctively puritan with exaggerated notions of good and evil, and a theoretic dislike of compromise. As a result, we have always regarded with a certain contempt the working politician who wheels, who deals, who does not truly believe. Fortunately, through sloth and indifference, we have evolved a system of government which is often inadequate, sometimes corrupt, always hypocritical, yet enormously successful at ensuring for most of its citizens political stability and a wide prosperity quite unknown to the majority of nations. But now our great Affluency is threatened from within as well as from without and, as always, crisis provokes the irrational response and makes attractive the extreme gesture. Summon a new Constitutional Convention, cries the Right Wing, and sanctify once and for all the holy rights of private property, while putting the shiftless in their place. Undermine the system so that it will collapse, whispers the Left, and then reassemble the pieces, making something altogether new and pure, with justice for all but the unjust, even though the unjust are the majority.

In sharp contrast to those who would move and shake the society to its foundation are the men and women who have opted out. Whether known as hippies or Diggers or just plain "beautiful," they are not merely a current fad, to be succeeded by goldfish eaters or flagpole sitters. Their defection is important, and if the present society does not change, their numbers will grow. Unable to find work worth doing, or a community in which human connections can be made, thousands of men and women have withdrawn from the consumer society and formed groups where worldly possessions are shared, and where individuals can attempt to give to human life a value which the society around them quite obviously does not. For it is hardly a secret that in our vast megalopolises man's traditional relationships have broken down. The family is not, to say the least, what it was, while grotesque overpopulation has smashed the old human scale of community and substituted for it a frightening world of frightened strangers with nothing in common save a dread of the anonymous others. It is not surprising that the delinquent youth as well as the professional criminal finds it easier than ever to kill. Since there are so many people, born to no purpose and put to no use, what can it matter? There are plenty more where the victim came from. The young are peculiarly victimized by city life. Unable to find values worth emulating, they become bored, listless, hostile. Those who join gangs are at least making the effort to be human, even in joint destructiveness. At every level agoraphobia is prevalent. To this general malaise, the hippies have responded gently, the gangs violently, the conservatives with irrelevant platitudes, the radicals with threats of murder in the streets and the smashing of the society as it is presently organized.

At the center of all these passions is that odd man out, the liberal whose temporizing influence is dismissed as mere sinister (or dextrous, depending upon the adjective-giver) shilly-shallying. It is enough to make the ADA weep. Yet the boredom with liberal values is understandable, for we are moving into strange territory, and it does not take an unusually inspired prophet to note that once again the wheel of man's history has begun to turn and the human race is about to experience one of its periodic smashups. After all, nearly half of those born since the race began are now alive, and there is not enough food for them to eat.

Since 1959, the so-called Third World's population has been increasing at the rate of twenty-six per thousand per annum, while increased food production can feed only fifteen of those twenty-six. According to agronomists, at some point between 1974 and 1980 world famine will occur, and there is now no way of avoiding it despite talk (but of course no large-scale action) of extracting food from the sea, etc. It is even too late for enforced birth control if such a thing were possible, which of course it is not since every human being has the God-given right to add as many new people to the world as he wants though the whole race starves as a result. Recently the fearless Dr. Shockley proposed *total* birth control, with the Bureau of the Census determining which couples might be allowed to add new citizens to the tax rolls. Something on this order will doubtless come to pass in time, but it will be too late for the present generations. Only disease, famine, and war can reduce our doubling billions to manageable size. Disease we have nearly eliminated; famine we are beginning to suffer and will continue to suffer on the largest scale; war may finally prove to be nature's way of restoring the balance between us and an environment we have poisoned and used up.

It is no accident that in this falling time, anthropology should be the most looked-to of the sciences. From Claude Lévi-Strauss to Konrad Lorenz, the latest texts are studied eagerly, almost desperately, as we attempt to understand precisely what sort of animal man is, and what his ecological fate may be. We are told that our aggressiveness is innate (as most parents discover, the will of the permissively brought-up child is quite as fierce as that of his overdisciplined brother): nature's way of assuring the survival of the fittest. Aggression is a characteristic of our species, and the secret of our success. But under certain stresses, our healthy aggressiveness (origin of love and music, architecture and the Olympic Games) becomes irrational and violent. On a large scale the result is war, an activity which many used to regard (the liberal Theodore Roosevelt for one) as an enormous stimulus for good. And it is true that in the wake of war, great economic and social advances are often made: the West German industrial comeback, the American Negro's new sense of himself. Even in the slow lazy times of peace, human societies (like certain human paranoids) need the idea of the Enemy to keep them alert and inventive. What earthly government would now be in space were it not for fear of Them?

Since a ritual hostility to members of other tribes is the normal condition of our race, one cannot view the future with much optimism. Significantly, we are one of the few mammalian species that have no inhibition about killing their own kind. Also, unlike the sensible rat, we do not respond to overcrowding by automatically ceasing to breed. Therefore, able to kill one another with ease yet not able to control the making of babies, it would appear that a kindly and ever-resourceful nature has programmed us for war. In which case the grand collision that so excites the radical temperament may be at hand, and we are launched upon necessary nightmare: the elimination of half the race in order that the rest may survive and begin again.

It is a tribute (though a small one) to the liberal temperament that it tends to be unnatural. Trying to make things better, trying to compromise extremes, trying to keep what we have from falling apart, the liberal goes about his dogged task; and in times of relative stability he can occasionally succeed in making improvements. Certainly he knows that, as Hegel put it, "Nothing happens unless individuals seek their satisfaction in the issues of their society." But when the cry of "blood" begins, as it seems to do at least once a generation, the liberal's voice is no longer heard and he himself looks altogether absurd, the maverick lemming who tries to climb the hill rather than join his excited peers in their long deadly swim. Yet each acts as he must, and if those structure-minded anthropologists are correct, our behavior is entirely predetermined. In which case, by acting as though man's condition can be improved, the liberal simply demonstrates his predictability, his constant variation to the common theme, and does what he must since there is nothing else for him to do and no world elsewhere.

Gore Vidal: Subject

In *The Secret Miracle*, Borges remarks of his author-protagonist, "Like every writer, he measured the virtues of other writers by their performances, and asked that they measure him by what he conjectured or planned." This seems to me a sad truth. Even André Gide, when young, used to wonder why it was that strangers could not tell simply by looking into his eyes what a master he would one day be. The artist lives not only with his performances (which he tends to forget), but with his own private view of what he *thinks* he has done, and most important, what he still plans to do. To the writer of a given book, what exists in print is only a small, perhaps misleading, fraction of the great thing to be accomplished; to the critic, however, it is the thing itself entire. Consequently critic and writer are seldom on the same wavelength.

As it must to all American writers who stay the course, and do not have the luck (sometimes good) to die after a first success, I am now confronted with a volume called *Gore Vidal*. It is the work of Ray Lewis White, a young professor at the University of North Carolina. For two years he has written me probing letters (sensibly, he never proposed a meeting), examined my papers at the University of Wisconsin, and immersed himself in what is probably, in plain bulk, the largest *oeuvre* of any contemporary American writer. At all times he has had my sympathy, even awe, as he worked his way through a career that has endured for a quarter century. The result is now at hand, one hundred fifty-seven dense pages, describing and judging ten novels (stopping short of the apocalyptic *Myra Breckinridge*), four plays and seven short stories. Omitted are the politics, most of the essays, the political journalism, the television writing and performing, and the movie hack work. Omitted, too, is the personal element. There are no revelations. Unlike Mary McCarthy, the Subject (as I shall now be known for modesty's sake) does not extend confidences to biographers nor, to Mr. White's credit, were they solicited. He has addressed himself entirely to the work, only bringing in the life as a means to show when and where — if not why — something was written. From this point of view, his book is meticulous and, I would suspect, accurate. Suspect because the Subject has no memory for dates or chronology. As a result, the story of his life unfolds for him like that of a stranger. Even so, the effect is disquieting: what a lot of time the Subject mis-used or simply wasted. And of all that he wrote, how little now seems to him remotely close to what he originally planned and conjectured (but still plans and conjectures!).

Mr. White's detailed plot outlines of the novels and plays will doubtless not encourage many people to read the original works; worse, in an age of non-readers, those who like to know about writing without actually reading books will be quite satisfied to skim Mr. White's study and feel that their duty to the Subject has been more than discharged since it is well known that in any year there is only One Important Novelist worth reading (there is some evidence that the Subject's year occurred at the end of the Forties). Yet perhaps it is best to be known only in outline: part of the genius of Borges is the lovely way he evades making books by writing reviews of novels that he has not written, demonstrating not only what he might so perfectly have done but inviting our respect for then not doing it.

Mr. White divides the Subject's career as novelist into three parts. The first phase was both precocious and prolific. Between the ages of nineteen and twenty-four (1945-1949), the Subject wrote and published six novels. The first was the war novel *Williwaw*, still regarded by certain romantics as a peak he was never again to scale. Among the other five novels, only *The City and the Pillar*, and perhaps *A Search for the King*, have much interest for anyone today except as paradigms of what was then the national manner: colorless, careful prose, deliberately confined to the surface of things. Then, according to Mr. White, came the second phase and the flowering.

Between 1950 and 1953 the Subject published *The Judgment of Paris, Messiah* and the short stories in *A Thirsty Evil*. These works resembled hardly at all the books that had gone before. But unfortunately the Subject was by then so entirely out of fashion that they were ignored. Only gradually did they find an audience. For some years now the paperback edition of *Messiah* has been much read, particularly on the campuses, and now *The Judgment of Paris* ("Vidal's Peacock-like novel-as-dialogue") is being discovered. But the original failure of these books made it necessary for the Subject to earn a living and so from 1954 to 1961, he wrote plays for television, Broadway, films, as well as criticism and political journalism; concluding his head-on encounter with the world by running for Congress in 1960 — all in all, an interesting and profitable decade. But looking over Mr. White's neat chronology at the beginning of the book, what a waste it now seems. Yet the Subject was having his life if not art; and Strether would have approved. Then, world exhausted, the Subject resumed an interrupted novel about the apostate emperor Julian, and so became a novelist once more, embarked upon his third (and terminal?) phase.

What does Mr. White make of all this? He is cautious, as well he might be; in many quarters his author is still regarded with profound suspicion. He is adroit at demonstrating the recurring themes from book to book. He makes, however, inadequate use of the essays, relying too heavily upon newspaper interviews — usually wrong — or on taped answers to questions in which the Subject has a tendency to sound like General Eisenhower with a hangover. He also betrays his youth when he tries to reconstruct the literary atmosphere in which the books were published. He places *In a Yellow Wood* (1949) in the company of books by Busch, Heyliger, Burnett and Mayo, who also dealt with the problems of a returned veteran. It may be that these novels were most worthy but they were quite unknown at the time. *Lucifer with a Book, That Winter, Barbary Shore* were the relevant books everyone read. But then no one has yet captured the sense of excitement of the literary scene in the Forties. Between VJ day and the beginning of the Korean war, it looked as if we were going to have a most marvelous time in all the arts; and the novel was very much alive, not yet displaced at the vulgar level by movies, at the highest by film. Each year was the year of someone new. 1944 Saul Bellow. 1946 the Subject. 1947 Calder Willingham and John Horne Burns. 1948 Norman Mailer and Truman Capote. 1949 Paul Bowles. 1950 Louis Auchincloss. 1951 William Styron, and so on — for a short while.

These complaints registered, Mr. White has written — how for me to put it? — a most interesting book, astonishingly exact in detail and often shrewd in judgment. The series to which it belongs is aimed at a university audience and Mr. White has kept within the bounds prescribed. Here and there one sees the beginning of something extra-academic, but he shows his tact, as one must in dealing with a living author little prone to autobiography. The inner life will come later — inevitably, since all that is apt to be remembered of any mid-20th century author is his life. Novels command neither interest nor affection but writers do, particularly the colorful ones who have made powerful legends of themselves, like Hemingway and Mailer. Eventually novels will be read only to provide clues to the author's personality; and once each of his characters has been satisfactorily identified, each of his obsessions duly noted, each key turned in its giving lock, the books may then be put aside for good, leaving us with what most concerns this artless time: the story of the author as monster most sacred, the detritus of his life enriched by our fascinated gaze, the gossip of his day our day's gospel. Of such is the declining kingdom of literature in which Mr. White has staked out with some nicety the wild marches of a border lord.

[*New York Times Book Review*, September 1, 1968]

The Twenty-ninth Republican Convention, Miami Beach, Florida, August 5-8, 1968

THE dark blue curtains part. As delegates cheer, the nominee walks toward the lectern, arms loose, shoulders somewhat rigid like a man who. . . . No, as Henry James once said in quite a different but no less dramatic context, it cannot be done. What is there to say about Richard M. Nixon that was not said eight years ago? What is there to say that he himself did not say at that memorable "last" press conference in Los Angeles six years ago? For some time he has ceased to figure in the conscious regions of the mind, a permanent resident, one had thought, of that limbo where reside the Stassens and the Deweys and all those other ambitious men whose failures seemed so entirely deserved. But now, thanks to two murders in five years, Richard Nixon is again a presidential candidate. No second acts to American careers? Nonsense. What is lacking are decent codas. At Miami Beach, we were reminded that no politician can ever be written off this side of Arlington.

The week before the convention began, various Republican leaders met at the Fontainebleau Hotel to write a platform, knowing that no matter what wisdom this document might contain it would be ignored by the candidate. Nevertheless, to the extent issues ever intrude upon the making of Presidents, the platform hearings do give publicity to different points of view, and that is why Ronald Reagan took time from his busy schedule as Governor of California to fly to Miami Beach in order to warn the platform committee of the dangers of crime in the streets. The Governor also made himself available to the flower of the national and international press who sat restively in a windowless low-ceilinged dining room of the Fontainebleau from two o'clock to two-thirty to "just a short wait, please, the Governor is on his way," interviewing one another and trying to look alert as the television cameras, for want of a candidate, panned from face to face. At last, His Excellency, as Ivy Baker Priest would say, entered the room, flanked by six secret servicemen. As they spread out on either side of him, they cased us narrowly and I knew that simply by looking into my face they could see the imaginary gun in my pocket.

Ronald Reagan is a well-preserved not young man. Close-to, the painted face is webbed with delicate lines while the dyed hair, eyebrows, and eyelashes contrast oddly with the sagging muscle beneath the as yet unlifted chin, soft earnest of wattle-to-be. The effect, in repose, suggests the work of a skillful embalmer. Animated, the face is quite attractive and at a distance youthful; particularly engaging is the crooked smile full of large porcelain-capped teeth. The eyes are interesting: small, narrow, apparently dark, they glitter in the hot light, alert to every move, for this is enemy country — the liberal Eastern press who are so notoriously immune to that warm and folksy performance which Reagan quite deliberately projects over their heads to some legendary constituency at the far end of the tube, some shining Carverville where good Lewis Stone forever lectures Andy Hardy on the virtues of thrift and the wisdom of the contract system at Metro-Goldwyn-Mayer.

The questions begin. Why don't you announce your candidacy? Are you a candidate? Why do people feel you will take votes away from George Wallace? Having answered these questions a hundred times before, the actor does not pause to consider his responses. He picks up each cue promptly, neatly, increasing the general frustration. Only once does the answer-machine jam. "Do you *want* to be President?" The room goes silent. The smile suddenly looks to have been drawn in clay, fit for baking in a Laguna kiln. Then the candidate finds the right button. He pushes it. We are told what an honor it is for any citizen to be considered for the highest office on earth. . . . We stop listening; he stops listening to himself.

"Governor, even though you're not a candidate, you must know that there is a good deal of support for you. . . ." The questioner's irony is suitably heavy. Reagan's lips purse — according to one biographer this is a sign he is displeased; there was a good deal of lip-pursing during the conference not to mention the days to come. "Well," he speaks through pursed lips, "I'd have to be unconscious not to know what was going on but. . . ." As he continues the performance, his speech interlarded with "my lands" (for some reason Right Wingers invariably talk like Little Orphan Annie), I recalled my last glimpse of him, at the Cow Palace in San Francisco four years ago. The Reagans were seated in a box, listening to Eisenhower. While Mrs. Reagan darted angry looks about the hall (displeased at the press?), the star of Death Valley Days was staring intently at the speaker on the platform. Thus an actor prepares, I thought, and I suspected even then that Reagan would some day find himself up there on the plat-form. If only because as the age of television progresses, the Reagans will be the rule, not the exception. "Thank you, Governor," said a journalist, and everyone withdrew, leaving Ronald Reagan with his six secret servicemen — one black, a ratio considerably better than that of the convention itself where only two percent could claim Africa as motherland.

Seventy-second Street beach is a gathering place for hustlers of all sexes. With some bewilderment, they watch one of their masters, the Chase Manhattan Bank made flesh — sweating flesh — display his wounds to the sandy and the dull, a Coriolanus but in reverse, one besotted with the vulgar. In shirtsleeves but firmly knotted tie, Nelson Aldrich Rockefeller stands on a platform crowded with officials and aides (most seriously crowded by the Governor of Florida, Claude Kirk, who wears a bright orange sports jacket and a constant smile for his people, who regard him, the few who know who he is, with bright loathing). Ordinarily Rockefeller's face is veal-white, as though no blood courses beneath that thick skin. But now, responding to the lowering day, he has turned a delicate conch pink. What is he saying? "Well, let's face it, there's been some disagreement among the pollsters." The upper class tough boy accent (most beautifully achieved by Montgomery Clift in *The Heiress*) proves effective even down here where consonants are disdained and vowels long. Laughter from the audience in clothes, bewildered looks from the hustlers in their bathing suits. "Like, man, who *is* it?"

"But now Harris and Gallup have agreed that I can beat. . . ." Rockefeller quotes at length from those polls which are the oracles of our day, no, the very gods who speak to us of things to come. Over and over again, he says, "Let's face it," a phrase popular twenty years ago, particularly among girls inclined to alcoholism ("the Governor drinks an occasional Dubonnet on the rocks before dinner," where did I read that?). Beside him stands his handsome wife, holding a large straw hat and looking as if she would like to be somewhere else, no loving Nancy Reagan or loyal Pat Nixon she. The convention is full of talk that there has been trouble between them. Apparently . . . one of the pleasures of American political life is that, finally, only personalities matter. Is he a nice man? Is she happy with him? What else should concern a sovereign people?

Rockefeller puts down the polls, takes off his glasses, and starts to attack the Administration. "Look at what they're doing," he says with a fine vehemence. "They're *exhilarating* the war!" But although Rockefeller now sounds like a peace candidate, reprising Bobby Kennedy and Eugene McCarthy, he has always been devoted to the war in Vietnam and to the principle underlying it: American military intervention wherever "freedom is endangered." Consequently — and consistently — he has never found any defense budget adequate. Two years ago at a dinner in New York, he was more hawk than Johnson as he told us how the Viet Cong were coldbloodedly "shooting little mayors" (the phrase conjured up dead ponies); mournfully, he shook his head, "Why can't they learn to fight fair?" Nevertheless, compared to Nixon and Reagan, Rockefeller is positively Lincolnesque. All of us on 72nd Street Beach liked him, except perhaps the hustlers wanting to score, and we wished him well, knowing that he had absolutely no chance of being nominated.

By adding the third character to tragedy, Sophocles changed the nature of drama. By exalting the chorus and diminishing the actors, television has changed entirely the nature of our continuing history. Watching things as they happen, the viewer is a part of events in a way new to man. And never is he so much a part of the whole as when things do not happen, for, as Andy Warhol so wisely observed, people will always prefer to look at something rather than nothing; between plain wall and flickering commercial, the eyes will have the second. As hearth and fire were once center to the home or lair so now the television set is the center of modern man's being, all points of the room converge upon its presence and the eye watches even as the mind dozes, much as our ancestors narcotized themselves with fire.

At Miami Beach television was everywhere: in the air, on the streets, in hotel lobbies, on the convention floor. "From gavel to gavel" the networks spared us nothing in the way of empty speeches and mindless interviews, but dull and uninformative as the events themselves were, something rather than nothing was being shown and the eye was diverted while the objects photographed (delegates et al.) reveled in the exposure even though it might be no more than a random shot of a nose being picked or a crotch rearranged. No matter: for that instant the one observed existed for all his countrymen. As a result the delegates were docile beyond belief, stepping this way and that as required by men with wired helmets and handmikes which, like magic wands, could confer for an instant total recognition.

The fact that television personalities so notoriously took precedence over the politicians at Miami Beach was noted with sour wonder by journalists who have begun to fear that their rendering of events that all can see into lines of linear type may prove to be as irrelevant an exercise as turning contemporary literature into Greek. The fact that in a hotel lobby it was Eric Sevareid not John Tower who collected a crowd was thought to be a sign of the essential light-mindedness of the electorate. Yet Sevareid belongs to the country in a way few politicians ever do. Certainly most people see more of David Brinkley than they do of their own relatives and it is no wonder that they are eager to observe him in the flesh. Only Ronald Reagan among the politicians at Miami exerted the same spell, and for the same reason: he is a bona fide star of the Late Show, equally ubiquitous, equally mythic.

Miami Beach is a rich sandbar with a drawbridge, and in no sense part of the main. The televised convention made it even more remote than it is. So locked were we all in what we were doing that Miami's Negro riots on Wednesday went almost unnoticed. There are those who thought that the Republicans deliberately played down the riots, but that is too Machiavellian. The fact is no one was interested. For those involved in creating that formidable work of television art, the 29th Republican convention, there was only one important task, creating suspense where none was. Everyone pretended that Reagan and Rockefeller could stop Nixon on the first ballot and so persuasive is the medium that by continually acting as if there might be a surprise, all involved came to believe that there would be one.

Even Nixon who should have known better fell victim to the collective delusion. On Tuesday he made his deal with Thurmond: no candidate for Vice-President displeasing to the South. Yet there was never, we now know, any danger of the Southern delegations switching to Reagan, despite the actor's enormous appeal to them. After all, how could they not love a man who had campaigned for a segregationist Southern politician (Charlton Lyons of Louisiana), who had denounced the income tax as "Marxist," and federal aid to education as "a tool of tyranny," and welfare as an "encouragement to divorce and immorality," and who generally sounded as if he wouldn't mind nuking North Vietnam and maybe China, too? He was their man but Nixon was their leader.

By the time the balloting began on Wednesday night, it was all over. There were of course idle pleasures. Everett Dirksen prowling from camera to camera, playing the part of a Senator with outrageous pleasure. Strom Thurmond, High Constable of the South, staring coldly at the delegates with stone catfish face. John Lindsay of New York, slyly separating his elegant persona from any words that he might be called upon to say. The public liked Lindsay but the delegates did not. They regarded him with the same distaste that they regard the city of which he is mayor, that hellhole of niggers and kikes and commies, of dope and vice and smut. . . . So they talk among themselves, until an outsider approaches; then they shift gears swiftly and speak gravely of law and order and how this is a republic not a democracy.

A lady from Vermont read the roll of the States as though each state had somehow grievously offended her. Alabama was plainly a thorn to be plucked, while Alaska was a blot upon the Union. She did achieve a moment of ribald good humor when she asked one state chairman *which* Rockefeller his state was voting for. But long before the Yankee virago had got to Wisconsin it was plain that Nixon was indeed "the one" as the signs had proclaimed, and immediately the Medium began to look in on the hotel suites, to confront the losers, hoping for tears, and reveal the winner, hoping for . . . well, *what* do you hope for with Nixon?

The technician. Once nominated Nixon gravely explained how he had pulled it off. He talked about the logistics of campaigning. He took us backstage. It was a nice background briefing, but nothing more. No plans for the ghettos, no policy for Asia, just political maneuvering. He did assure us that he would select "a candidate for Vice President who does not divide this country." Apparently he would have a free hand because "I won the nomination without paying any price or making any deals." The next day of course he revealed the nature of his deal with the Southerners and the price he must now pay for their support: Spiro Agnew of Maryland. Despite the howls of the party liberals and the total defection of the blacks. Nixon had probably done the wise thing. He could now give Wallace a run for his money not only in the necessary South but also among the lower white orders in the North who this year are more than ready to give their dusky cousins what the candidate once referred to, in angrier days, as "the shaft."

Thursday was the big day. Agnew was proposed, opposed, nominated. A lumbering man who looks like a cross between Lyndon Johnson and Juan Perón, his acceptance speech was thin and ungrammatical; not surprisingly, he favored law and order. Adequate on civil rights when he became governor, Agnew behaved boorishly to the black establishment of Baltimore in the wake of riots last spring. This made him acceptable to Thurmond. Even so, all but the most benighted conservatives are somewhat concerned at Agnew's lack of experience. Should Nixon be elected and die, a man with only one year's experience as governor of a backward border state would become Emperor of the West. Though firm with niggers, how would he be on other issues? No one knows, including the candidate himself whose great virtue, in his own eyes, "is that I try to be credible — I want to be believed. That's one of the most priceless assets." So it is. So it is.

Nixon is now on stage, ready to accept for a second time his party's nomination. He is leaner than in the past. In a thickly made-up face, the smile is not unappealing, upper lip slightly hooked over teeth in the Kennedy manner. With his jawline collapsing in a comforting way, the middle-aged Nixon resembles the average voter who, we are told, is forty-seven years old. The candidate swings neatly to left, hands raised, two forefingers of each hand making the victory salute. Arms drop. Slide step to right. Arms again extended above head as hands make salute. Then back to center stage and the lectern. The television camera zooms in on the speech: one can see lines crossed out, words added; the type is large, the speech mercifully short.

Nixon begins. The voice is deep and slightly toneless, without regional accent, like a radio announcer's. We have been told that he wrote his own script. It is possible. Certainly every line was redolent of that strange uncharm characteristic of the man. He spoke of Eisenhower ("one of the greatest Americans of our time — or of any time") who was watching them from his hospital bed. "His heart is with us!" the candidate exclaimed, reminding us inadvertently that that poor organ was hardly the General's strongest contribution to the moral crusade the times require. No matter, "let's win this one for Ike!" (A rousing echo of *Knute Rockne*, a film in which the youthful Ronald Reagan had been most affecting.) Nixon next paid careful tribute to his Republican competitors, to the platform and, finally, to Spiro Agnew "a statesman of the first rank who will be a great campaigner." He then drew a dark picture of today's America, ending with "did we come all this way for this?" Despite the many hours of literary labor, Nixon's style was seldom felicitous; he was particularly afflicted by "thisness": "This I say is the real voice of America. And in this year 1968 this is. . . ." The real voice of America, needless to say, is Republican; "the forgotten Americans — the nonshouters, the nondemonstrators"; in short, the nonprotesting white Protestants, who must, he enjoined, commit themselves to the truth, "to see it like it is, and to tell it like it is," argot just slightly wrong for now but to Nixon "tell it like it is" must sound positively raunchy, the sort of thing had he been classy Jack Kennedy he might have heard at Vegas, sitting around with the Clan and their back-scratchers.

Solemnly Nixon addressed himself to Vietnam. His Administration would "bring to an honorable end the war." How? Well, "after an era of confrontation, the time has come for an era of negotiation." But in case that sounded like dangerous accommodation he quickly reminded us that since the American flag is spit on almost daily around the world, it is now "time we started to act like a great nation." But he did not tell us how a great nation should act. Last January, he said that the war will end only when the Communists are convinced that the U.S. "will use its immense power and is not going to back down." In March he said, "There is no alternative to the continuation of the war in Vietnam." It is of course never easy to determine what if anything Nixon means. When it was revealed that his recent support of public housing was not sincere but simply expedient (his secret remarks to a Southern caucus had been taped), no one was surprised. "He just had to say that," murmur his supporters whenever he contradicts himself, and they admire him for it. After all, his form of hypocrisy is deeply American: if you can't be good, be careful. Significantly, he was most loudly applauded when he struck this year's favorite Republican note: *Remember the*

Pueblo. "The United States has fallen so low that a fourth rate military power like North Korea [can] hijack a United States naval vessel. . . ." Quite forgotten were his conciliatory words of last spring: "If the captured American Intelligence spy ship violated North Korean waters, the United States has no choice but to admit it."

Nixon next praised the courts but then allowed that some of them have gone "too far in weakening the peace forces as against the criminal forces." Attacks on the judiciary are sure-fire with Republicans. Witness the old Nixon five years after the Supreme Court's 1954 decision on the integration of schools: "the Administration's position has not been, is not now, and should not be immediate total integration." Like Barry Goldwater he tends to the radical belief that the Supreme Court's decisions "are not, necessarily, the law of the land." Happily, once the present Attorney General is replaced, it will be possible to "open a new front against the filth peddlers and the narcotics peddlers who are corrupting the lives of our children." As for the forty million poor, they can take heart from the example of past generations of Americans who were aided not by government "but because of what people did for themselves." Those small inequities that now exist in the American system can be easily taken care of by "the greatest engine of progress ever developed in the history of man — American private enterprise." The poor man who wants "a piece of the action" (Vegas again) is very apt to get it if the streets are orderly and enough tax cuts are given big business to encourage it to be helpful.

If Nixon's reputation as the litmus-paper man of American politics is deserved, his turning mauve instead of pink makes it plain that the affluent majority intend to do nothing at all in regard to the black and the poor and the aged, except repress with force their demonstrations, subscribing finally not so much to the bland hortatory generalities of the platform and the acceptance speech but to the past statements of the real

Nixon who has said (1) "If the conviction rate was doubled in this country, it would do more to eliminate crime in the future than a quadrupling of the funds for any governmental war on poverty." (2) "I am opposed to pensions in any form, as it makes loafing more attractive to [sic] working." (3) To tie health care to social security "would set up a great state program which would inevitably head in the direction of herding the ill and elderly into institutions whether they desire this or not." Echo of those Republicans in 1935 who declared that once Social Security was law "you won't have a name any longer, only a number." Most ominous of all, the candidate of the military-industrial complex has no wish to decrease the military budget. Quite the contrary. As recently as last June he was warning us that "the United States has steadily fallen behind the Soviet Union in the leveling of its spending on research and development of advance systems to safeguard the nation." In short, there is no new Nixon, only the old Nixon experimenting with new campaigning techniques in response, as the Stalinists used to say, to new necessities. Nixon concluded his speech on a note of self-love. Most viewers thought it inappropriate: since no one loves him, why should he? To his credit, he sounded slightly embarrassed as he spoke of the boy from Whittier — a mis-fire but worth a try.

Friday. On the plane to New York. A leading Republican liberal remarks, "Awful as it was, he made a vote-getting speech." He is probably right. Nixon has said in the past that no Republican can hope to get the Negro vote, so why try for it? Particularly when the principal danger to Nixon's candidacy is George Wallace, in the North as well as South. Nixon is also perfectly aware of a little-known statistic: the entire black vote plus the entire vote of whites under twenty-five is slightly less than one-fourth of the total electorate. Since Nixon has no chance of attracting either category, he has, by selecting Agnew, served notice that he is the candidate of that average forty-seven-year-old voter who tends to dislike and fear the young and the black and the liberal; in fact, the more open Nixon is in his disdain of this one-fourth of a nation, the more pleasing he will seem to the remaining three-fourths who want a change, any change, from Johnson-Humphrey as well as some assurance that the dissident forces at work in American life will be contained. The great technician has worked out a winning combination and, barring the (obligatory?) unexpected, it is quite likely that it will pay off and Richard Milhous Nixon will become the 37th President of the United States.

[*New York Review of Books*, September 12, 1968]

A Manifesto

TEN percent of the human beings ever born are now alive and breeding like bacteria under optimum conditions. As a result, millions live at famine level. Yet even with the fullest exploitation of the planet's arable land — and a fair system of distribution — it will not be possible to feed the descendants of those now alive. Meanwhile, man-made waste is poisoning rivers and lakes, air and soil; the megalopolis continues to engulf the earth, as unplanned as a melanoma and ultimately as fatal to the host organism. Overcrowding in the cities is producing a collective madness in which irrational violence flourishes because man needs more space in which to *be* than the modern city allows.

But because the West's economy depends upon more and more consumers in need of more and more goods and services, nothing will be done to curb population or to restore in man's favor the ecological balance. Present political and economic institutions are at best incapable of making changes; at worst, they are prime contributors to the spoiling of the planet and the blighting of human life. It could be said that, with almost the best will in the world, we have created a hell and called it The American Way of Life.

To preserve the human race, it is now necessary to reorganize society. To this end, an Authority must be created with the power to control human population, to redistribute food, to purify air, water, soil, to re-pattern the cities. Specifically:

The Authority must have the power to limit births by law. All the usual means of exhortation will be used to convince the citizenry that it is not a good thing to create at random replicas of themselves when the present supply of human beings is already too great a burden for the earth's resources. Put bluntly: to bring into the world an unwanted human being is as antisocial an act as murder. The endlessly delicate problem of who should be allowed to have children might be entirely eliminated by the anonymous matching in laboratories of sperm and ova. If this were done, the raising of children could then be entrusted to those who show some talent for it, on the order of certain of the Israeli kibbutzim.

The Authority must have the power to exploit the food resources of the nation in order to feed not only the 10,000,000 Americans currently at famine level but to use surplus food to assist the feeding of other countries, on condition that they, too, reduce population.

The Authority must have the power to divert waste from air and water, even though this will mean the sad banishment of the combustion engine from the automobile, and the placing of many factories underground.

The Authority must have the power to begin the systematic breaking up of the cities into smaller units. To avoid a re-creation of the present ghettos, living areas should be limited not only in size but, to avoid that deterioration which is due to poverty, each family entrusted with the raising of children should be given a minimum living allowance.

The Authority may *not* have the power or right to regulate the private lives of citizens.

It is a paradox of the acquisitive society in which we now live that although private morals are regulated by law, the entrepreneur is allowed considerable freedom to use — and abuse — the public in order to make money. The American pursuit of happiness might be less desperate if the situation were reversed.

Since planned (and perhaps anonymous) breeding will eliminate the family as we now know it, those not engaged in bringing up the young would then be free to form whatever alliances they want, of long or short duration, in any mutually consenting arrangement with either sex, on the principle that each man has the right to do as he likes with his own body, including kill it with alcohol, cigarettes, drugs or a bullet. By drawing a line between what is private and of concern only to the individual and what is public and of concern to all, the Authority could begin to realize something of the spirit of this nation's early charters.

Finally, the Authority may not limit free speech in any form, including criticism of itself. In fact, the Authority's affairs should be under constant surveillance by watchful committees as well as by the press, though it might be advisable to deny the employees of the Authority any sort of personal public notice since love of glory has wrecked more human societies than all of history's plagues combined. Unsung managers constantly scrutinized by the wise: that is the ideal, partially achieved in another time (and for quite a different purpose) by the Venetian Republic.

These then are the things which must now be done if the race is to continue. Needless to say, every political and economic interest will oppose the setting up of such an Authority. Worse, those elements which delight in destroying human institutions will be morbidly drawn to a movement as radical as this one. But it cannot be helped. The alternative to a planned society is no society. If we do not act now, we shall perish through sheer numbers, like laboratory rats confined to too small a cage. The human race is plainly nothing in eternity but to us, in time, it is everything and ought not to die.

A Brief Dialogue

Each of us contains a Private Self and a Public Self. When the two have not met, their host tends to be an average American, amiable, self-deluding and given to sudden attacks of melancholy whose origin he does not suspect. When the two selves openly disdain each other, the host is apt to be a strong-minded opportunist, equally at home in politics or advertising. When the selves wrangle and neither is for long dominant, the host is more a man of conscience than of action. When the two are in fierce and total conflict, the host is lunatic — or saint.

My own two selves wrangle endlessly. Hedonistic and solipsistic, my Private Self believes the making of literature is the whole self's only proper task. The Public Self, on the other hand, sees world's end plainly and wants to avoid it, sacrificing, if necessary, art and private pleasure in order to be of use. A Manifesto has given the two selves a good deal to quarrel about, and in their endless dialogue some of the many questions A Manifesto is bound to raise are posed, if not always answered.

Private Self: It is typical of you to state what needs to be done and then not tell us how it should be done — whether it ought to be done I'll get to in a moment.

Public Self: And typical of you to dislike any kind of general statement (not to mention political action). One must first draw attention — in the broadest way imaginable — to the nature of the crisis. If the race is not to die of overpopulation, we must . . . .

Private Self: You've made your point. But first, do you

really think anyone can change our present course? And, second, why not let the thing die? I find beautiful the vision of an empty planet, made glass by atomic fission, forever circling a cooling sun . . . .

Public Self: And you enjoy accusing *me* of rhetoric! I ignore your second question. The thing must not die. As for the first: it is possible to reduce population drastically in one generation. In two generations a viable balance could be arrived at . . . .

Private Self: Could. Yes. But will it come to pass? Remember when we were in Egypt and Hassanein Heikal explained to us that even under Nasser — with all his power — the fellahin could not be persuaded to practice birth control . . . .

Public Self: When persuasion fails, other means will be used.

Private Self: Yes! Force. That Authority of yours gives me the creeps . . . .

Public Self: I don't like it much myself but without it nothing will be done. The Authority must be absolute in certain areas.

Private Self: How does this square with your lofty guarantee of private freedom to everyone?

Public Self: There is only one limit to private freedom: no new citizen can be created without permission.

Private Self: And who will grant permission?

Public Self: Geneticists, biologists, anthropologists, politicians, poets, philosophers . . . in a year one could get some kind of general agreement as to *how* to proceed. Later, decisions would be made as to which types should be perpetuated and which allowed to die out. . . .

Private Self: I must say, not even the Nazis. . . .

Public Self: None of that! No demagoguery. The Authority's aim is to preserve and strengthen human types through planned breeding. Eugenically, we have had enormous success with everything from cattle to hybrid corn. So why not people? A family in which the members are prone to die of cancer at an early age should probably not be allowed to continue. . . .

Private Self: That means that John Keats would not be reproduced because he had a weak chest which his descendants might inherit, along with his genius. . . .

Public Self: What strains are best worth preserving I'm willing to leave to science . . . with a good deal of overseeing from other disciplines. Anyway, since we descend from common ancestors, no seed can ever die: all men are cousins.

Private Self: Save that for television. Incidentally, it will be decades — if ever — before sperm and ova can be matched outside the human body. . . .

Public Self: One must think in terms of decades as well as of today. In any case, the early stages should be simple. A moratorium on births for a year. Then an inquiry into who would *like* to have children . . . a smaller group than you might think, particularly if the tribe no longer exalts the idea of reproducing oneself. After the last war the Japanese realized that if they were to survive they would have to reduce population. They did so by making it, literally, unfashionable to have large families; overnight they reversed the trend of centuries. It can be done.

Private Self: But only in a disciplined society like Japan. It would be impossible in our country. The United Statesman is conditioned from birth to think only of himself. To think of any larger unit is to fall victim to the international menace of communism.

Public Self: I suspect we shall probably have to write off the generations now alive. They cannot be changed. But the newborn can be instilled with a sense of urgency.

Private Self: Oh, yes. The newborn! How do you plan to bring up the children?

Public Self: At first in the usual way through the family . . .

even though the family as we have known it is ending due to the pressures of urban life. Incidentally, contrary to current tribal superstition, the family is not a biological unit. It is an economic one whose deterioration began the day it became possible for women to work and bring up their children without men.

Private Self: With men or without, in the family or in a commune, someone is going to have to look after those few children that you will allow us. Who is that someone?

Public Self: Those best suited.

Private Self: Their parents

Public Self: Probably not. Very few people are good parents, a fact most are willing to admit — too late.

Private Self: But aren't children psychologically damaged by being brought up communally. . . .

Public Self: Not necessarily. The recent confrontation between a number of American psychiatrists and the products of an Israeli kibbutz was revelatory. The men and women who had been raised communally were alarmingly "healthy."

Private Self: I daresay the end of the family will benefit humanity, but it will destroy the novel. . . .

Public Self: Don't worry. Mythmaking is endemic to our race. Neurosis will simply take new forms.

Private Self: To get back to the Authority. Just who and what is it? And in the United States is it to be achieved through constitutional means?

Public Self: Ideally, the Authority and the Constitutional establishment should exist side by side, each complementing the other. Shabby as our democracy is, I think it a good idea to retain it.

Private Self: But the world is not ideal. President and Congress will not suffer the existence of an Authority over which they have no control.

Public Self: What about the C.I.A., the F.B.I. . . .

Private Self: Flip liberal cant. Congress and President would want control. And once they had it, nothing would be accomplished. Can you imagine those Senators who are in the pay of the oilmen allowing the combustion engine to be superseded?

Public Self: Ultimate power must reside in the Authority.

Private Self: Dictatorship?

Public Self: Yes. But involving only those things that affect the public at large: environment, food, population. . . .

Private Self: Do you really think it possible to order totally the economic and biological life of a country and yet not interfere in the private lives of its citizens?

Public Self: Why not?

Private Self: Because no dictatorship has ever confined itself to the public sector. Sooner or later the dictator. . . .

Public Self: The Authority is not a dictator but a changing group of men, representing the widest and most divergent interests. . . .

Private Self: Too wide and too divergent and it won't function. . . .

Public Self: All interests will be subordinate to the stated aims of the Authority. Those aims will not be open to dispute.

Private Self: Like "Marxism" in one-party states? I would think that whoever or whatever controls the public life of a society will automatically control the private sector.

Public Self: Obviously there will be a constant tension between public and private necessities. And it is possible that the private will lose. It usually does in authoritarian societies. But then it does not do very well in libertarian ones either. Witness the small-town American's terror of his neighbors' opinion. However, the one novelty I offer is a clear demarcation between public and private. The state may not intrude upon private lives as it does now. And private lives may not intrude upon the public welfare as they do now. And what is "good" and "bad" for the society's welfare will be set down with a minimum of ambiguity.

Private Self: I find your Authority a potential nightmare. The world is already shrinking. Soon there will be no escape from the managers with their Telexes and computers. No border to cross. No place to hide.

Public Self: I am as alarmed as you by a world in which it is altogether too easy for the managers to have their way. And not only through instant communications but through mind-altering drugs and genetic rearrangements of the unborn. . . .

Private Self: Genetic rearrangement! That ought to appeal to you: men bred to be gods, but *whose* gods?

Public Self: Something to brood on. Anyway, I do see the end of the *laissez-faire* society. Quasi-democracies like England and the United States are already moving toward totalitarianism — of Left or Right makes no difference. The result is the same: the control of the individual. Wanting to bolster currency, the British curtail travel and thus limit freedom. Our poor, needless to say, are quite as enslaved as they were when their ancestors built the Pyramids. In fact, they are worse off because technical means now exist for the state to control all its citizens simultaneously. The true nightmare is not the Authority. It is the popular television performer who will subvert the state simply for something to do. . . .

Private Self: That's you. Don't deny it!

Public Self: I confess that if it weren't for you, I might give it a try.

Private Self: I'll bet you would! And we'd both be shot down, probably on *The Tonight Show*.

Public Self: Since an authoritarian society is inevitable, I am for accepting it but only in order to achieve certain goals. Once they are achieved. . . .

Private Self: The Authority will wither away?

Public Self: Hopefully. But of course it will not. Something else will take its place. But that is far in the future.

Private Self: Exactly how is the Authority to come into existence?

Public Self: A Party for Human Survival must be formed in the United States, and elsewhere. Naturally — again ideally — it would be best if the Authority were voted into power by a majority. With proper education, through television, it could happen. . . .

Private Self: But if not?

Public Self: Then the Party will seize power and establish the Authority by force.

Private Self: You see yourself as Lenin?

Public Self: With you on my back, I am a natural victim. Anyway, if it does not happen, a *mindless* authority will come into being, one dedicated not to human survival but simply to its own aggrandizement, and we shall perish.

Private Self: What is wrong with that? It is not written in stars that we endure for all eternity. So why not let it end? The way it does for each of us. I have known from birth that when I die the world ends, too.

Public Self: For us it ends. But there are others.

[*Esquire*, October 1968]